JENKS

A passion for motor sport

JENKS

A passion for motor sport

Foreword by
STIRLING MOSS OBE

Published in collaboration with the British Racing Drivers' Club by
MOTOR RACING PUBLICATIONS LTD
Unit 6, The Pilton Estate, 46 Pitlake, Croydon CR0 3RY, England

First published 1997
Reprinted 1997

British Library Cataloguing in Publication Data

Jenks : a passion for motor sport
    1. Jenkinson, Denis, 1920-1996 2. Motorsports 3. Sports journalism
    I. Blunsden, John
    070.4'49'7967'092

ISBN 1-899870-22-9

Printed in Great Britain by
The Amadeus Press Ltd, Huddersfield, West Yorkshire

Acknowledgements
On behalf of Denis Jenkinson, the publishers wish to thank all the contributors of words and pictures for this book. A particular debt of gratitude is owed to John Fitzpatrick and the Board of the BRDC for the inspiration for the book in its original form, to Stirling Moss OBE for agreeing to furnish the Foreword, to Haymarket Magazines Ltd for permission to reproduce material from *Motor Sport*, to Brenda Vernor for photographic research in Italy, and especially to Doug Nye and Geoffrey Goddard for researching and making available material from the Denis Jenkinson Archive.

CONTENTS

FOREWORD
by STIRLING MOSS OBE

Mention the name Denis Jenkinson, or preferably Jenks, and my mind immediately goes back to two occasions which will remain vividly in my memory for as long as I live. The first was that wonderful moment in the late afternoon of May 1, 1955, when we realized that our work for the day was over and we had achieved just about everything we had set out to do more than 10 hours earlier.

Not only had we won the Mille Miglia, but in doing so we had managed to shatter just about every existing record and, because for once the entire event had been staged on dry roads – a rare occurrence in Italy at that time of year – our average speed of only a little under 100mph was unlikely ever to be beaten.....and so it proved.

Although it had been my privilege that day to be the man behind the wheel of the meticulously prepared Mercedes-Benz 300SLR, this had been in every sense a two-man achievement, for there is no way I could have fulfilled so emphatically one of the greatest ambitions of my motor racing career without that extra special ingredient – the navigational input, incredible stamina and implicit trust of the little chap with the big red beard who sat so stoically and fearlessly beside me all the way from Brescia to Rome and back again.

Long before we agreed to join forces for our combined-op to break the Italian grip on this famous classic event I knew Jenks to be a man of unusual qualities. In particular I admired his ability – which I found to be rare amongst motoring writers of the time – to ask all the right questions, because they were based on an acute and highly knowledgeable observation of everything that was going on around him.

His views on racing drivers were invariably interesting, often pungent and at times unflattering, but they were always worth listening to and they deserved respect, for Jenks had an unusually perceptive eye and could spot a phoney at a thousand paces. He tended to be quite sparing with his praise for drivers, but I found this to be refreshing, because it meant that whenever he sauntered up and said, "You did a good job, there", it really meant a lot, and you knew instinctively that you had done something rather special and that it hadn't passed unnoticed.

For my other lasting memory of Jenks I have to travel forward 40 years from the first – to that day when we came together again for what turned out to be his last public appearance, at the 1995 Goodwood Festival of Speed. When we climbed aboard that very same 300SLR for a series of demonstration climbs up the hill in the grounds of Goodwood House it was an emotional moment for both of us. It was as though the clock had been turned back, except that sadly, Jenks was now very frail, having been far from well for some time. But his mind and his wit were still as sharp as ever.

He was clutching the famous 'roller box' with the Perspex window through which he read his pace-notes, and when the time came to climb aboard, Susie, my wife, offered to hold the box while he got himself comfortable, but he would have none of it. "No thank you," he said, then added: "It's not that I don't trust you, my Dear, but I know who trained you!" Nothing – nothing at all – would have parted him from his famous 'secret weapon' that day.

When we got to the top of the hill after our first run, we parked up and began reminiscing while we waited for the others to complete their climbs. The trip had done him a power of good, and clearly he had enjoyed every second of it, because suddenly he was bubbling with all his old enthusiasm as we engaged each other in a rash of "Do you remembers...?".

He reminded me of the moment when, as we left Florence on the big day, he saw me glance at my wrist-watch as we headed towards the testing Futa and Raticosa passes on the next leg to Bologna. "I knew you were keen to do Florence-to-Bologna in the hour," he chuckled, "so when I saw you look at your watch I rubbed my hands together in eager anticipation because I knew I was about to witness something really exciting. "God almighty, Jenks," I said, "I'd been working myself ragged, driving flat-out all day long, and then you wanted me to go even harder?". He just sat there and laughed... Fear? He didn't even understand the word!

When you spend as much time with someone as we did in the months preceding our first Mille Miglia together, you get to learn a lot about each other, and long before we were on that starting ramp at Brescia I knew that I would have the right man beside me; here was one person who, come what may, would not let me down, and I sensed that he felt the same way about me.

Our bond of mutual trust ran very deep and became the foundation of a close friendship which was to persist ever after. Over the years Jenks became one of our most popular house guests, and Susie in particular would be delighted when she heard he was coming because she knew that he was sure to have her in stitches with all his tales and repartee, because of course he was a magnificent story teller.

Inevitably, quite a lot of our chat would be about the days before my main racing career was brought to a premature halt in 1962, and although Jenks was to remain close to the racing scene right through to the Nineties, and admired much of the technical development which helped to transform it into what it is today, he retained a fondness for the less commercially dominated old days which, for all their imperfections, were enshrined in a friendliness long gone from Formula One.

It is no coincidence, I believe, that a considerable amount of his writing for the *BRDC Bulletin* in recent years was devoted to nostalgic matters, and for many of us they reawakened happy memories, while for the younger generations his pieces should have been classified as essential reading, if only to help them view the current scene from a much broader perspective.

I am glad that through this book Jenks' words are now being made available to a much wider audience, also that a selection of his writings in *Motor Sport*, which we all read so avidly at the time, have also been brought back into print again. The unbridled enthusiasm which flavoured his words inspired many others to follow in his footsteps and become motor racing journalists in their own right. Several of them became his close friends, and within the covers of this book they write movingly of what this has meant to them.

As for myself, I feel privileged to have known and enjoyed the friendship of a quite remarkable character. He certainly enriched my life in many ways, and like so many others who have been similarly blessed, the world will never seem quite the same without him. We all miss him deeply, but we can at least be thankful that his words will survive indefinitely as a reminder of his unquenchable enthusiasm and resolute spirit.

'Chez Jenks' – deep in the Hampshire woods; the centre evidence of one man's passion for old cars, fast cars and motorcycles and even faster cars; an archive treasure trove of motor sporting memorabilia; and amongst the surrounding trees, a resting place for the remains of a bewildering variety of vehicles which had served their purpose until they could serve no more.

INTRODUCTION

This is a book written in part by – and in part about – a quite remarkable man. A man whose passion for motor sport in all its forms was of such intensity that it gave him a lifestyle of sublime contentment in surroundings so spartan and devoid of the basic comforts of 20th century living that all but the most fanatically motivated would have found them unbearable. But eccentrics do tend to tear up life's conventional rule book, and Denis Jenkinson, regardless of his many other attributes, was most certainly an eccentric.

Better known as DSJ, the initials with which he would sign off to the many thousands of devoted readers of his magnetically attractive words in *Motor Sport* – for approximately 40 years he entertained and informed them in his role as the magazine's Continental Correspondent – and simply as Jenks to his friends, colleagues and many close contacts throughout the sport and industry, he devoted his life to the pursuit of speed and excitement, and through an inquisitive and perceptive eye, an audacious outspokenness and a capacity for fearless comment, he would remain an observer and commentator of considerable influence for much of his life.

He was never trained as a journalist, and indeed never considered himself to be one; he preferred to be thought of as a storyteller, someone whose function in life was to let others – less privileged than he had become – know just what it was really like out there. For this, his credentials were unsurpassed. In his early motorcycling days (two wheels were cheaper than four!), how better to experience the thrill of racing at top level than from the 'chair' of the Sidecar World Champion, Eric Oliver?

But his greatest sporting achievement – and for which he rightly earned enduring fame – was as Stirling Moss' passenger, navigating the maestro and his Mercedes-Benz 300SLR to their record-shattering victory in the 1955 Mille Miglia road race, an experience which a few days later would form the background for Jenks' most famous piece of writing, which is reproduced in full within this book.

A great personal bond between Stirling and Jenks was formed in the aftermath of their huge success, and they were to remain close friends thereafter. It was sad, and yet entirely appropriate, that Jenks' last public appearance, subsequent to a mild stroke, but prior to the massive one which ultimately led to his death in November 1996, should bring these two team-mates together again in that very same car, for a demonstration drive at the 1995 Goodwood Festival of Speed. It is most gratifying, too, that Stirling should have agreed to write a Foreword to this book, echoing some of the words he delivered so movingly at Jenks' funeral.

For the book's conception we have to travel back to 1994. It all began with a telephone call from John Fitzpatrick in his role of Secretary of the British Racing Drivers' Club. Would Motor Racing Publications be interested in publishing a book by Jenks, built around the contributions he had written over a number of years for the *BRDC Bulletin*?

We had been trying for years to entice Jenks to do a book with MRP, but though he had been happy enough in principle, he never raised much hope of it happening quickly. "These days, books strike me as being too much like hard work," he would joke down the telephone, "and I can always look around me and find something else I'd rather be doing." Clearly, it was only likely to happen if he ran out of things to do today, which seemed highly unlikely.

So the BRDC project seemed to be an excellent idea, especially if the book could be timed to coincide with and celebrate Jenks' 75th birthday, which was part of the plan. Jenks, for his part, became equally enthusiastic, and soon he was invading his meticulously kept files for material from which he was to add relevant 'sidebars' to some of his main stories, whilst simultaneously producing five or six more of the latter well ahead of schedule, so as to bring his total for the book up to 50 within the agreed time schedule.

It was shortly after completing his 50th piece that he suffered a relatively minor stroke which, although it did not completely incapacitate him, slowed him considerably as he continued with characteristic determination to work on his additional material. Then came that massive stroke in January 1996 and its devastating after-effects, culminating in his death 10 months later at Lynwood, the Berkshire home of the motor industry charity known colloquially as BEN, where he had been looked after with such infinite care and compassion during his final days.

In the meantime, production of Jenks' book had been deferred in the slim hope that perhaps this tough little character would yet again make a miraculous recovery, possibly not a complete one this time, but one which would be sufficient for him to be able to contribute – perhaps with the assistance of others – a few more eloquent and passionate words of recollection. Tragically, it was not to be. But such was his enthusiasm for this project, which had grown by the week, that it was inconceivable that Jenks' book should not still be published, even though circumstances had dictated that it would now have a somewhat different structure.

The nucleus of his BRDC writings remain, along with such additional material as he had produced before he was laid low. But there is now much more, for this is no longer a book to celebrate a 75th birthday, but one which celebrates a complete and quite extraordinary life, one driven by an extreme passion for motor sport in all its forms.

It was important, we felt, that some of his closest friends and colleagues, people with whom he had shared so many of his enthusiasms and spent so many enjoyable hours in 'motor sport chat' should have the opportunity to explain what Jenks' company has meant to them and how, even before they came to know him, they had been influenced by his words and his achievements. Although he had written widely elsewhere – in books as well as magazines – his fame, and his following, grew principally through the pages of *Motor Sport*, and so it was important that certain of his writings from within the magazine should also be selected for reproduction.

It was no easy task, the choice being so vast, but four pieces, which vary greatly in length, seem most appropriate. In one of his Continental Notes, he provides a scene-setter during the weeks of practice for what was to prove Stirling's and his epic drive in 1955; then comes that year's famous Mille Miglia race report; it is followed by his report on the 1956 event, which ended in disaster and provided the framework for more dramatic writing of a different kind; and finally, one of the last pieces he produced for the magazine, where he writes of the pyramid of opportunity for motoring and motor sport enthusiasts in Britain as he watches a convoy of owners setting off in their cars in pursuit of some simple harmless fun. It is a fitting reminder that, though his career had taken him to the most exalted heights of the sport, with all the attendant commercialism which he tolerated with considerable difficulty, he remained at heart what he had always been, someone who simply loved the world of cars and speed.

His enthusiastic writing over many years has inspired countless thousands in their own pursuit of pleasure through a love of cars and motor sport, and we feel sure that Jenks, had he been able to see the final pages through to press, would have wished 'his' book to be dedicated to all these fellow-enthusiasts, with whom he felt such a strong bond. This, on his behalf, we happily do, coupled with our earnest hope that Jenks himself would have approved of the book in its final form. It would have been comforting to hear him say "Mmm.....[long pause].....like that", which in 'Jenks-speak' would have been praise indeed.

John Blunsden

1

ALTERNATIVE RACING

1953 Naples Grand Prix

In the early days of the development of the Silverstone circuit by the British Racing Drivers' Club I didn't attend many meetings. I was living in Europe, racing motorcycles and covering various Grand Prix and circuit races for *Motor Sport*, so it was an ideal life with little call to return to the homeland. At places like Berne, Pau, Bordeaux, Nurburgring, Solitude and many others there would be motorcycle races on the Saturday and car races on the Sunday. Eventually I gave up the motorcycle racing part as a profession and became a full-time motor racing journalist.

There was so much happening in Europe that I had little desire to return to the UK to watch motor racing, and in consequence I later realized that I missed out on some classic occasions. I didn't complain, for what I had seen in Europe was every bit as classic, but it would have been nice to have been able to divide myself into two.

One such occasion was the weekend of May 9/10 in 1953, when the BRDC held the International Trophy meeting at Silverstone on the Saturday and the Naples Grand Prix was due on the Sunday. With today's high-flying jets one could attend both meetings, but in those days it was out of the question. I was already in Italy at the time, so there was no problem; I just motored south to Naples, in itself a long journey as there was no *autostrada* south of Milan.

Our own Mike Hawthorn had just joined the *Scuderia Ferrari* and they sent him to England with a four-cylinder Formula Two car as well as a 4.1-litre V12 sports Ferrari, and a huge crowd turned out to watch. I would have liked to have been there to see Mike, for he won his heat of the International Trophy, then won the final, and for good measure he also won the 17-lap Production Sports Car race. The British crowd loved it, and the day was completed by Stirling Moss winning the Production Touring Car race in a Jaguar Mk VII and Don Parker winning the 500cc race in his Kieft.

For those who were there it was a day to remember; for those of us who were not there it was a day to regret, except that I had rather an exciting day in Naples. It was the occasion of the 10th Grand Prix of Naples, held on the street circuit in the hills of Posillipo, just outside the city and overlooking the Bay of Naples. The circuit was a figure of eight, and where the two loops met there was a crossroads, where in each direction you turned right, there being a line of straw bales diagonally across the intersection. There were 20 corners of varying radii in a distance of 4.1 kilometres, so it was something of a scratcher's delight, and most of the roads were surprisingly wide, so overtaking was not a problem.

When I got to Naples and looked at the entry list I knew I was going to see something special, for unlike Silverstone, which had gathered together something like 80 competitors, the Naples race had attracted eight! Now I had heard the saying 'Quality rather than quantity', but this seemed ridiculous until I read that the *Scuderia Ferrari* had entered three cars, to be driven by Alberto Ascari, Giuseppe Farina and Luigi Villoresi, and the Maserati factory had entered two cars to be driven by Juan-Manuel Fangio and Froilan

Gonzalez. The remaining three entries comprised local lads, one with a sports Maserati and the other two with Fiat-based specials.

The race was held over 60 laps, a distance of 152 miles, the weather was very hot, and there was no love lost between the rival Italian teams. This was not a World Championship event, so there were no points to be gathered, but the honour of the *Scuderia Ferrari* and the *Casa Maserati* was at stake. You may think that a field of five serious cars could not make a Grand Prix, but believe me, when they were driven by Ascari, Farina, Villoresi, Fangio and Gonzalez the pace became as hot as the weather.

Ascari was a master at starts, and the uphill start at Naples saw him away into the lead. Behind him Farina and Fangio had a real 'ding-dong', with Gonzales and Villoresi behind them. The local Maserati driver went out after five laps and one of the Fiat specials at 23 laps, so the giants had a nice clear run.

When Ascari's accelerator pedal came adrift and he stopped at the pits, the Farina/Fangio battle became even more serious as it was now for the lead. Ascari rejoined after losing four laps and proceeded to set new lap records with regularity, knocking it down from 2min 15sec to an eventual 2min 7sec.

The best way to describe the Farina/Fangio battle is to quote a paragraph from my report in *Motor Sport* at the time: 'This meant that Fangio was leading (Ascari's pit-stop), but not for long, for Farina tried really hard and eventually got on the inside of a right-hand bend, both cars sliding wildly all over the road as they accelerated away on the wrong lines and the wrong locks. In the scuffle to get the lead, which Farina got on lap 25, Fangio's Maserati received a dent in the tail that was clearly caused by a protruding Ferrari nose. Farina was now well away and the crowd loved it.'

This epic race lasted 2hr 12min 17.1sec, and the average speed was just short of 70mph, the final order being Farina (Ferrari), Fangio (Maserati), Gonzalez (Maserati), Villoresi (Ferrari) and Ascari (Ferrari).

To anyone who never saw any of these giants in action, it would put it into perspective if, today, Nigel Mansell was to compete at Silverstone with a lone Williams, while Alain Prost (McLaren), Ayrton Senna (McLaren), Michele Alboreto (Ferrari), Gerhard Berger (Ferrari) and Nelson Piquet (Lotus) were taking part in a small Grand Prix in southern Italy. I still think I did the right thing in 1953 when I went to Naples, and I would do the same thing today.

I think I was probably the only Englishman at that Naples race, and certainly the only English journalist. That evening the Naples club gave a splendid

This was one of the sights of Silverstone I missed by being in Italy that day. Hawthorn on full-noise with the 4.1-litre V12 Ferrari sports car must have been well worth watching!

banquet to honour the victors, Farina being the winner and Ascari the moral victor. It was a very happy evening and everyone made impromptu speeches, including myself, though I can't imagine what I said, but it was in my best (worst!) Italian, which was very limited. With lots of "*Grazia, Ferrari e Maserati, Napoli, bello circuito*" and a few rounds of "*Nuvolari, Borzacchini e Campari*" thrown in for luck, I seemed to get by, and I received a rousing cheer, especially from Ascari, who had known me in previous years when I was leaning out of a racing sidecar at places like Berne, Pau, Monza and so on.

Happy days indeed, and they were to continue for another 35 years!

2

A MOMENT TO REMEMBER

Rosberg's 160mph lap

There are some things in motor racing which are memorable to me, even though they do not figure strongly in the overall history of motor racing. One of these was the end of the qualifying for the 1985 British Grand Prix at Silverstone.

The lap record at Silverstone had always been of interest, particularly because the trace of the circuit had remained almost unchanged for many years. When Gonzalez put in a lap at 100.65mph during practice for the 1951 Grand Prix, and Farina recorded the fastest race lap and official lap record at 99.99mph, history was in the making, for an average of 100mph round the airfield perimeter track caught the imagination.

It was not until 1953 that the official lap record was set at over 100mph, when Farina went round at 100.16mph in the Ferrari Thinwall Special during a *Formule Libre* race. At the time Grand Prix racing had been relegated to Division Two and none of the cars could approach a 100mph lap.

Keke Rosberg could always be relied upon to get the best out of a Formula One car over one lap, but even by his high standards his qualifying lap in the Williams-Honda FW10, which broke the 160mph barrier, was something exceptional.

Once the new Formula One for 2½-litre cars began in 1954 speeds rose steadily until Graham Hill left the record at 111.62mph in 1960 with the rear-engined BRM. The 1½-litre Formula One cars took five years to reach full development, and once again it was Graham Hill with a BRM who pushed it up to 114.29mph. All this was normal development progress that was taken for granted, and there was none of the excitement that had accompanied Farina's 100mph lap in 1953.

With the return of serious horsepower in 1966, when the 3-litre formula was introduced, the lap record went up by leaps and bounds and passed the 120mph and then the 130mph marks almost unnoticed. By the time the Woodcote chicane was introduced in 1975 in a vain attempt to slow things down a bit, James Hunt had put the lap record up to 134.06mph with a McLaren-Cosworth DFV.

The chicane slowed things up a little bit, but not for long, and the 140mph and 145mph barriers were passed almost without comment, for the increase in speeds of the 3-litre cars was continuous and relentless. The advent of turbocharging, and the dramatic increase in power once the technology had been mastered, saw a lap at 150mph almost as a matter of course. When Rene Arnoux recorded 151.969mph to gain pole position for the 1983 British Grand

Prix I am sure we would have all been very disappointed if it had been at *under* 150mph.

In 1985, pre-race testing had shown that 155mph laps were going to be commonplace, but nobody expected the phenomenal pace of Formula One development to make such a big leap forward once the serious business of qualifying for the Grand Prix began. The first afternoon of qualifying saw the estimated 155mph lap surpassed so easily that everyone set their sights on a 160mph lap. At the beginning of the year such speeds never entered anyone's mind, but before the first qualifying was halfway through 157mph had been passed, then 158mph, and Prost (McLaren-Porsche) and Rosberg (Williams-Honda) were both over 159mph.

These were the days when qualifying was a 'no holds barred' exercise and Friday and Saturday afternoons were much more exciting than race day. In the dying minutes of the Friday qualifying hour Rosberg held pole position with 159.668mph. Nobody missed returning for Saturday's qualifying.

With only two sets of qualifying tyres allowed to each driver and turbochargers screwed down for maximum boost, and with weight pared to the legal minimum, qualifying laps were a 'one-shot' business. The drivers had to be wound up tight from the word go, with but one lap to get settled, one all-out flying lap and one to cool off; if you weren't paying attention you could easily miss a driver's heroic effort.

The timekeepers and commentators were co-operating nicely and circuit radio was keeping everyone informed of the progress. With the instant Longines-Olivetti timing apparatus a driver's performance could be read out as he crossed the timing line.

As always, there was only a handful of drivers vying for pole position, but they were giants of the art of high-speed driving. On their first set of tyres it was clear that the front-runners were Rosberg (Williams-Honda), Prost (McLaren-Porsche), Piquet (Brabham-BMW), Senna (Lotus-Renault), Mansell (Williams-Honda) and Alboreto (Ferrari). Rosberg's run came as near to 160mph as made no odds, but there was more to come on the second runs.

Rosberg was having a purple patch with his Williams-Honda in the summer of 1985. A month before his terrific qualifying lap at Silverstone he won the US East Grand Prix here on the streets of Detroit (despite the partly blocked radiator), and in between came pole position followed by a hard-fought second place between Piquet and Prost in the French GP at Le Castellet.

14

Then a small shower of rain fell and that looked like being the end of serious qualifying.

But then the sun shone brightly and the track literally dried before our eyes. With only a few minutes of the qualifying hour left there was a mad rush by the top drivers; they had all been psyched-up for high-speed motoring when the shower of rain came, and they were reluctant to cry off. Most of the drivers of the slower cars had finished their qualifying, so the track was virtually empty as, one at a time, the real chargers had their final fling; as soon as one came in another one went off.

For anyone who enjoys seeing Grand Prix drivers on the absolute limit, with everything the car can give, there hasn't been another occasion like it. Senna did 159.146mph, then Prost did 159.184mph and Piquet did 159.326mph: others, like Mansell, de Angelis, Alboreto and Fabi, were in the 'slow' bracket at 158mph.

Almost as the qualifying hour was ending Rosberg went out and, driving way over the limit all the way round, he stopped the timers at 160.925mph. Qualifying finished and you could feel the tension all round the circuit collapse like a deflated balloon. It wasn't until it was all over that you realized just how tightly you had been wound up, and you were only spectating. It was a moment not to have missed, and had you gone to the bar for another pint you would have missed it.

I have a nasty feeling that we shall never witness another landmark like it, but I suppose those people who saw the first 100mph lap of Silverstone probably thought the same thing 35 years ago.

That 160mph lap took Rosberg 1min 5.591sec to cover the 3 miles, and among his many comments afterwards was the fact that Silverstone seemed very small! At that speed there were no straights; by the time you were under control from one corner you were starting to position the car for the next one. Even Hangar Straight became a long, fast S-bend from Chapel to Stowe! From leaving the Woodcote chicane, as it then was, at 125mph the Williams-Honda crossed the timing line at 161mph, reached 185mph by the end of the pits and entered the braking area for Copse at nearly 190mph. That is the sort of performance that would make your eyes water. Even the fiery Finn was a little breathless afterwards and needed a cigarette to regain his equilibrium.

3

A MEMORABLE EVENT

1955 Syracuse Grand Prix

It was the end of the 1955 season and the last big race was the Targa Florio in Sicily. It had been quite a year for British drivers, for Moss had won the Mille Miglia, then he had won the British Grand Prix at Aintree, and now he and Peter Collins had won the Targa Florio, all for the German Mercedes-Benz team.

There was one more event, of minor international importance, and that was the Syracuse Grand Prix, in the far corner of Sicily. It was not a World Championship event and was not even sufficiently important in the Italian calendar for the *Scuderia Ferrari* to send their cars. However, the Maserati factory took it very seriously and sent four team cars, as well as supplying factory support to numerous customers. It was run to the existing Formula One rules, and the works Maserati team cars were the 250F models with which they had chased the Mercedes-Benz team in vain in the big events. Luigi Musso, Luigi Villoresi and Harry Schell were driving regular team cars, and a fourth was taken along for Carroll Shelby to try his hand at Grand Prix racing.

There were four private owners of 250F Maseratis – Horace Gould, Roy Salvadori with Sid Greene's car, Louis Rosier and Luigi Piotti – while Volonterio had an older car and Vidille and Scarlatti had old four-cylinder Ferraris.

As I was in Sicily for the Targa Florio it was no great strain to drive over to Syracuse for the race the following weekend. Having spent most of the Targa Florio time with Carroll Shelby I thought it would be interesting to see how Old Shel' got on with his first Grand Prix drive.

There were two English cars entered for the race, from Connaught Engineering. They were the 1955 B-Type cars, with 2½-litre four-cylinder Connaught/Alta engines, one with a fully streamlined bodyshell and the other with the open-wheel orthodox single-seater bodywork.

When practice began the Connaughts had not arrived, though the drivers were there. One was Les Leston, a well-known fellow, who was due to drive the streamlined Connaught when it arrived, and the other was C A S Brooks, a dental student from Manchester, who was virtually unheard of in Europe, though anyone who had been watching British club racing would have known him. I had seen him once at a Goodwood club meeting, driving a Le Mans Replica Frazer Nash, and could not fail to see an inborn talent and sense of balance and artistry that made most people look like amateurs; he took Woodcote Corner in one long controlled slide and beautifully placed for the chicane which followed, then nicked it through the chicane and made it all look very easy. The driving of Brooks was so smooth and effortless, very fast

They couldn't understand what that odd looking car with the 'unknown' English driver was doing on the front row of the grid for what should have been an all-Italian affair, but Tony Brooks and his Connaught were soon giving them a grandstand view of history in the making. Luigi Musso, with Luigi Villoresi alongside him, led away from pole position in his Maserati 250F, but Brooks, after a slow start, was leading the Syracuse Grand Prix by lap 15 and the four works Maserati drivers could do nothing about it. But the Italians would soon know all about Tony - within four years he would be winning Grands Prix for Ferrari!

and flowing, with the car balanced beautifully at the edge of adhesion.

When I saw that he was entered to drive the works GP Connaught I was intrigued, but when the Maserati team asked me about the English entry that so far had not appeared, I could not give them a clear answer. They were not worried about them, just interested that the Connaught team should journey

TONY BROOKS REMEMBERS

Jenks and Stirling Moss were not the only ones for whom the 1995 Goodwood Festival of Speed evoked strong 40-year memories, as the first driver for 32 years to win a Grand Prix in a British car recalls:

For the first time in 40 years I eased myself into the cockpit of a 1955 B-type 2½-litre Formula One Connaught at the Goodwood Festival of Speed and suddenly I felt terribly old!

Could it really be 40 years since I first sat in a Formula One car in the paddock at Syracuse, Sicily, which had seemed to a young dental student at the time to be at the other end of the world?

Rodney Clark of Connaught had invited me to drive a Formula One car in the Syracuse Grand Prix, presumably on the strength of half a dozen national events in a four-year-old 2-litre Connaught, which constituted my only single-seater experience. I suspect he was desperate because nobody wanted to travel so far in late October to drive a car noted for its under-powered and fragile engine. It might not even survive practice in order to qualify for the starting money!

It was fortunate that at the time I was more preoccupied with my imminent dental surgery exams than with what I had agreed to do on the race track, and I studied on the long flight via Rome to Catania and then shared a taxi to Syracuse.

The cost of a hire car was out of the question, so the only way to learn the circuit was to hire a Vespa. Almost the entire length of the course was lined on both sides with stone walls, and its surface was little better than an average Sicilian main road, but as I had always raced with the attitude that the road itself was all that was available to me, whether marked by grass, tubs or whatever, I did not feel inhibited by its character.

The Connaught team arrived on the morning of the last day of practice, exhausted by their 2,000-mile drive to Sicily. Practice was very limited, in order to conserve the cars, and I don't believe I did more than 15 practice laps, while my team-mate, Les Leston, fared even worse with mechanical problems, but I started on the front row of the grid and completed my practising in the race!

Once in the lead I was very conscious of the fragility of the Alta engine, so I reduced my maximum rev limit by 500rpm. However, the unit had good torque and the Connaught chassis was excellent, so I was able to maintain my lead to the finish, becoming part of the first British car-and-driver combination to win a Grand Prix for 32 years.

Only those familiar with international motor racing at the time can appreciate how impossible it was considered to be to beat the foreign cars, and to some people Syracuse seemed like motor racing's equivalent to Roger Bannister's first four-minute mile, which broke down the athletes' psychological barrier.

With a better engine, Connaught would have been a regular Grand Prix winner, but it fell to Vanwall to fly the flag, and British supremacy was finally established when the Vanwall team won the first World Manufacturers' Championship for Britain in 1958, after Stirling Moss and I had won three Grands Prix each.

all the way to Sicily, such a long way by road in those days.

After the first day of practice it was just a question of in which order the works Maserati team were going to finish the race. None of the private owners could match the speed of the factory cars, so it was more or less decided that Musso would win as he had done so well against the Mercedes-Benz team, Villoresi would be second, Harry Schell would be third, driving the experimental streamlined 250F, and 'new boy' Carroll Shelby would be fourth.

Old Shel' accepted this, as he was the factory guest, but he told me quietly that he was out to beat Harry Schell until it came to the last lap, because he reckoned if he couldn't out-drive Harry he might as well give up trying to get into Grand Prix racing.

When we arrived at the circuit next day, on closed roads on the edge of the town, the Maserati works team more or less decided there was little point in wearing out their cars. In the paddock were the two Connaughts in their British Racing Green, contrasting strongly with all the red cars. The streamliner for Les Leston aroused a certain amount of interest as it was much sleeker than Maserati's idea of a fully-enclosing streamlined shell, but no-one took much notice of the chunky open-wheeled Connaught, with the quiet young man sitting in it waiting to go out and practice.

Musso and Villoresi had set the best time at 2 minutes 9 seconds and they could see no point in going any faster as there was no opposition for the factory Maserati cars. Brooks did three laps and then had a spin, which nobody took much notice of, but when the times for those three laps were seen there was a panic in the Maserati pits. His first flying lap was 2.13, his second was 2.10 and his third was 2.07. He spun on his fourth lap.

After stopping at the pits to apologize to Mike Oliver, who was running the Connaught pit, he went out again and did 2.06 and then 2.05.4. Meanwhile, the Maserati team were galvanized into action and after a lot of hard driving and 'press-on' tactics Villoresi scratched a lap in 2.04.7 and Musso got one in at 2.03.6. Schell and Shelby were nowhere near.

The grid line-up was three-two-three, which meant that the front row was Musso, Villoresi and Brooks, and everyone was looking very puzzled, unable to believe it was true. Everyone, that is, apart from about a dozen English people comprised of the Connaught team and Gould and Salvadori with their helpers. I seemed to be the only English journalist/reporter present, and my Italian colleagues were looking very disbelievingly at the green car on the front row.

The 70-lap race was unbelievable for everyone. Brooks made a poor start and the four works Maseratis went off ahead, to the cheers of the crowd. But at the end of the first lap Brooks had passed Shelby, on lap 4 he passed Schell, on lap 8 he passed Villoresi and on lap 15 he passed Musso. Apart from the handful of people who knew about Tony Brooks and about Connaught there was total disbelief. An unknown English driver in an unknown English car was leading the entire Maserati factory team, to say nothing of the private 250F Maseratis.

This was Tony's first Grand Prix race in Europe, so he was being very careful. After letting Musso back into the lead, he settled down and retook the lead with no effort and reduced the lap record to 2.00.2, at which point Musso went by the Maserati pit shaking his head in disbelief and making signs of despair. With a 50-seconds lead, Brooks eased off in the closing laps and won the race at an average speed of nearly 100mph. He looked almost embarrassed when he had to face the plaudits of the organizers and the crowd, for they appreciated a winner, no matter what he drove or where he came from.

Then the fun started. The Italian press had been all set to telephone their stories to *Gazetta dello Sport* in Milan, *Stadio* in Bologna, *Resto di Carlino* in Rome and all the other important Italian newspapers, eulogizing on the total victory of the magnificent Maserati team. Now they had to explain that the Maserati team had been beaten, not by Moss or Hawthorn or Collins, but by an unknown driver, and worse still he was driving an unknown car.

Long-distance telephones in 1955 were not the most efficient things in Italy and the noise in the press room was really more fun than the race. Italians shouting into a phone trying to pronounce Connaught was a riot. "No, Musso did not win, he was second. The winner was Brooooookes in a Connuft. Yes, Brooooookes, Eenglish. No, not in Maserati, in a Conauft, yes, English car. Villoresi? He was third. No, Musso did not win, no, he did not have trouble, yes, an Englishman won in an English car. The other factory Maserati cars were 5th and 6th. Oh yes, a Maserati was fourth, Horacchi Goooold, yes another *inglesi*. Yes, Brooooookes, Tonino, a dental student, yes, it is true." That sort of dialogue was going out all over Italy, and to France, Switzerland and Germany as well; and of course to England.

Meanwhile, darkness had fallen outside, and in one of the pitlane garages the scrutineers had demanded that the Connaught cylinder head be removed. They measured the bore and stroke of the Alta engine. The works Maserati team gathered round: "93.5 by 90mm" announced the scrutineer. A pause, and then: "2,470cc capacity". Formula One rules stated a maximum of 2,500cc.

There was an uneasy silence and everyone drifted away, except the Connaught team members and the handful of English people, who all smiled happily and went off for a wash and brush up before the prize-giving. It was quite a party for that handful of people from Great Britain.

4

CHEATING? HEAVENS NO!

1952 Reims Grand Prix

Back in 1952, Grand Prix racing in the Grand Manner had subsided due to the withdrawal of the Alfa Romeo 159 team and the inability of BRM ever to be race-worthy. Almost overnight, the *Grandes Epreuves* were run to the existing Formula Two, for unsupercharged 2-litre cars, of which there was a good variety. The *Scuderia Ferrari* 4½-litre V12 cars had been the only serious entry in the Valentino GP held in Turin, run to the existing Formula One, and when all the races went Formula Two, Ferrari was still the major force. The works team of Alberto Ascari, Luigi Villoresi and Giuseppe Farina drove the four-cylinder Tipo 500 Ferrari 2-litres and there was nothing to match them.

Just occasionally, the six-cylinder 2-litre Gordinis, or Cooper-Bristols, or HWMs would cause a slight flurry by making a momentary challenge, but such flurries never amounted to much.   .

With the *Grandes Epreuves* counting towards the Drivers' World Championship, the French confused the issue by running a series of races to the Formula Two called *Les Grands Prix de France*, of which one was nominated to be the *Grand Prix de l'Automobile Club de France* and to be their *Grande Epreuve*.

These *Grands Prix de France* were all run to a format of a three-hour race, and while it was a foregone conclusion that the Ferrari team would win all the *Grandes Epreuves* and the World Championship, it was hoped that they would not enter all the French events. With any luck, one of the Gordini team members could win this French Championship, and each event was called A Grand Prix of France, not The French Grand Prix. It seemed like a good national idea, but the *Scuderia Ferrari* spoilt it by entering for all the events and invariably winning, so not only was Ascari going to be World Champion, he was also going to be Champion of France!

The French World Championship event was held at Rouen-les-Essarts and The Grand Prix of France at Reims, on the very fast triangular circuit of Reims-Gueux, was run by the *Automobile Club de Champagne*, whose ebullent Secretary was Raymond Roche, who had thought up the idea of the French Championship within the World Championship.

The race meeting at Reims was always an event run in the Grand Manner, and regardless of Rouen-les-Essarts having the World Championship title, the Reims event seemed much more important. The Ferrari trio of Ascari, Villoresi and Farina prepared for the race confident of a 1-2-3 finish, their only possible opposition coming from the Gordini team of Robert Manzon, Jean Behra and Prince Bira, whose hope of lasting three hours flat-out was pretty thin.

From the second row of the starting grid Jean Behra tucked in behind the Ferraris of Ascari and Farina, a gallant challenge clearly doomed once the Ferraris got into their stride on the long Thillois straight. Imagine the

Jean Behra, seen here on opposite-lock leaving the Nouveau Monde hairpin at Rouen during the 1952 French Grand Prix, was often entertaining to watch aboard the 2-litre Gordini, but he never had one going quite as well as in that year's Reims Grand Prix, when he outpaced all the Ferraris.

excitement in the grandstands when Jean Behra led the field round the Thillois hairpin way down at the beginning of the long straight running up past the pits. The excitement was even greater when the blue Gordini was still ahead as they finished the opening lap. It was still leading on the next lap, and the next, and the next. Ascari was clearly rattled by having the ex-motorcycle champion of France leading him in the blue Gordini.

The two cars passed and repassed, going as if in a 10-minute sprint, not a three-hour race, and most of the time the Gordini was ahead. Ascari was having to keep the Ferrari in the slipstream of the Gordini just to hang on to second place, and he had the nose of the Ferrari almost touching the tail of the Gordini, but Behra wasn't worried. This dice went on for 14 laps, with the Ferrari getting hotter all the time due to very little air getting to the radiator because Ascari was running so close to the Gordini. At the end of lap 14 the Ferrari's plugs cried 'enough' and the red car slithered into the pits for a new set, leaving Behra way out on his own.

There had been 22 cars at the start, but there had only been two cars in the race as far as the crowd were concerned, and now there was only one. Farina had taken over second place, but he was 16 seconds behind and struggling to keep up. Villoresi's Ferrari had expired, and after a new set of plugs were put in Ascari's car Luigi took it over, but too far behind to be of much consequence.

There were still two hours to go, and the crowds settled down holding their thumbs (French equivalent of crossed fingers). Unbelievably, the six-cylinder Gordini never missed a beat and Behra never put a wheel wrong, the little French car just went on and on.

As the race moved into the closing laps the French commentator began to eulogize over this magnificent performance by the French racing car. At the time there was a national collection going on to support French racing cars, and he was imploring the patriotic crowds to support this fund now that they could see for themselves that France had a 'Ferrari-beater'. As the clock ticked towards the three-hours and Behra set off on his last lap the commentator really gave forth, applauding this magnificent victory by a French racing car, driven by a great French driver, and so on and so forth. At this the crowds screamed and yelled for him to shut up, he was tempting fate; there was still 2½ minutes to run. (There is nothing new in Murray Walker tempting fate in his TV commentaries!)

The whistles and shouts from the crowd were so vociferous that the commentator *did* shut up, and everyone looked towards the Thillois hairpin holding their breath. Eventually, the blue car, driven by the rugged little Frenchman with the chequer band round his crash helmet, came into view. As he crossed the finishing line the crowd went wild with excitement. The *Marseillaise* rang out and Jean Behra was carried shoulder high. It was a great day for French motor racing.

Some weeks later, Maurice Trintignant was visiting the Gordini works and wandering through the racing department when he saw a row of pistons on the bench that he hadn't seen before. When recounting this story many years later he said he had been very conscious of the size and shape of a 2-litre Gordini piston, and these were visibly bigger. When he picked one up and asked what they were for he was quickly ushered away to look at something much more interesting!

It was a year later that a six-cylinder 2½-litre Gordini appeared in a *Formule Libre* event in preparation for the 1954 Formula One of 2½ litres! Jean Behra never again made a 2-litre Gordini go like that one at Reims on that memorable day...

5

BEHIND THE WHEEL

Driving the Renault turbo

I often say to my colleagues in journalism who, like me, stand on the sidelines and watch people race: "You must take part or you will never really know what it is all about." I am not saying that they must become professional racers and aim for Formula One, but that they must compete in some form of motorized sport, even a humble driving test. There are a lot of them who write quite well on racing matters until something untoward happens, and then they are lost. A driver is blamed for doing something stupid or dangerous or unnecessary, and they are quick to support the popular view. Had they done any competition themselves they might have had a better appreciation of the situation.

Some of them have never even sat in a racing car, let alone driven one, and as for having been on a starting grid with 10 or 20 other cars all round, and then jostled down to the first corner... they have about as much conception of what it is like as I have of flying at Mach 1.

Occasionally, the more adventurous journalists get the opportunity to drive a racing car in a test session, and that can be revealing. When the Regie Renault were racing their turbocharged Formula One cars they kindly allowed selected racing journalists to drive one of their Grand Prix cars. It was all nice and safe, on a wide open airfield runway, with the car mounted on treaded tyres and the turbos screwed down to give around 600bhp. Even so, it was an experience that few of us had tasted before, and the first thing that was noticeable was the number who stalled the engine on their first start! This prompted the suggestion that the next time they saw a driver stall at the start of a Grand Prix perhaps they would be a bit more sympathetic.

There was one chap who was going up and down the runway in fine style

It's my turn to sample a spot of real Formula One power, though with the turbo screwed down to give a maximum of 600bhp regular Renault drivers Prost and Cheever would have found it pretty tame. Even though you know you can't do the car justice, it is important if you write about motor racing that you have at least some first-hand experience of what it is like.

until, on one lap, he booted it out of the hairpin turn a bit too soon and spun. He was complete master of the situation, provoking the spin into a full 360-degree turn without stalling the engine and carrying on as if nothing had happened. Talking to him afterwards and commenting on his competence I suggested that it wasn't the first time he had driven a Formula One car. He admitted that this was true, for he had tested a number of F1 cars for his Italian magazine, and added that he had also done quite a bit of saloon car racing at a national level. It did not surprise me, for he looked at home the moment he put his helmet on.

The next one to spin the Renault looked the complete opposite, even to being unused to donning overalls in a paddock; he walked nearly half a mile to a secluded toilet to take his trousers off (and it was an all-male party)! When he spun out of one of the hairpins he went way off into the shrubbery, stalled the engine and had to be pulled out, returning to the paddock mumbling about "hitting a wet patch". I told him not to worry, for at least his spin meant that he had the throttle well open, unlike some of our colleagues, who went so slowly that they wouldn't have spun had the car been on 'slicks' and it had been raining.

That exciting day ended with yours truly getting over-confident and giving the Renault a full-throttle change from second to third at about 120mph and keeping up with it as it got away into a 360-degree spin, but stalling the engine as it passed the point-of-no-return. That meant sitting helplessly in the middle of the runway until the long-suffering Renault mechanics came and plugged in the slave battery.

Chatting about it afterwards, we all had a very different view of a Grand Prix start. We tried to visualize what it must be like to be in the middle of a Formula One grid with 25 similar cars all round you. Quite honestly, none of us could contemplate it, and when someone said "...and all trying to get to the first corner first, on a track about a quarter of the width of our runway", everyone agreed that a journalist's life wasn't a bad one.

Driving a racing car is one thing, but to actually be on a start-line, even in a standard Metro or a Formula Ford car, is a different world altogether. You can

only really learn about racing by racing. Keke Rosberg used to say, when asked how he kept fit, that the best way was to race. He reckoned that the best way to train for driving a Formula One car was to drive a Formula One car. I think Nelson Piquet and Ayrton Senna would have agreed with that.

I have never done any serious racing at Silverstone, but occasionally I have a dabble in a vintage-car event, but even then there is much to learn which you would not think about if you stood on the sidelines. In one practice session, approaching Becketts hairpin, I couldn't think why a marshal was waving a BLACK FLAG. A moment later an ERA came by my slow old Lagonda and I realized that I was wearing a tinted visor that had made BLUE look like BLACK!

Hauling that big Lagonda round the hairpin was hard work, as it didn't have enough power to break traction and slide the tail round, even though I kept trying. It always ended up in a big tyre-bending understeer, losing speed all the time, until one glorious lap I got it right and sailed around the hairpin in a lovely controlled tail-slide. It was the last lap, but at least I returned to the paddock happy in the knowledge that I had taken Becketts 'about right' on

My deep interest in all things Frazer Nash brought me many enjoyable moments, including this sunny day at the 1955 Rushmoor sprint meeting, when I 'borrowed' Le Mans replica VMF 701 and managed to make FTD over the quarter-mile.

THE HAIRIEST MOMENTS IN THE RACE

As Jenks pondered on what it must be like to take part in the opening seconds of a Grand Prix, he could think of no-one better qualified to tell him than **Mark Blundell,** *a driver he had long admired as "a real racer with a refreshing lack of bullshit". This is what Mark had to say to Alan Henry, who asked him on Jenks' behalf:*

The more experience you have, the better you can accommodate and handle the pressure. When I first started in F1 I would be getting wound-up at 8.30am on race morning, but the more experienced you get it's possible to calm down and control it, then when you're in the car and you come round on the parade lap you're totally focused. All systems go!

You're focused on the red light, then you see the green light, and suddenly you're involved in the hairiest moments in the race; when you're surrounded by 25 other guys at somewhere like Estoril and the track's narrow; you're wheel-to-wheel, already up to fourth/fifth gear, 140/150mph – I mean, we're all jockeying for position – the dust, people banging wheels, the sheer noise. Then you get through the first corner – wow! – and within a lap or two you settle down.

But it's just as if you've had an injection! Then you may have the red flag and another restart. No! I don't want to go through that again! But then you think – it's another start, another opportunity. It's addictive. It's an acceleration of adrenalin, heart-rate – like with an athlete – you need to harness it and focus it to your benefit. But you have to control it – control it and then stabilize it. If you can learn to do that, you're OK. You get this from experience.

Sometimes you can even feel stressed-out and tired after the initial exertion – even scared, slightly, when someone jumps out from behind you. I also think your mind works on two planes when you are really concentrating hard in a Grand Prix car. It's difficult to explain, to be honest. It's almost as if your mind is wandering, but it isn't. It's as though there is a complete boundary of concentration, but also a second part of you that is absorbing other information. And I can't say that happens to me anywhere else but when I am in a racing car.

You come in for a pit-stop, really pumped-up, and within that six or seven seconds there will be one single moment when you think 'I didn't know he had green eyes'. It's almost like a 'reality check'. It's a bit funny and I don't pretend to understand it...

The hairiest moments of any race are during the opening few seconds. Even on a track as wide as Monza everyone is so preoccupied with getting to the first corner first, or at least overtaking as many cars as possible on the way there, that wheels can become tangled and cars can be eliminated almost before the rear wheels have stopped spinning. This time, all was well at the start of the 1970 Italian Grand Prix as Ickx's Ferrari out-accelerated Rodriguez's BRM, Stewart's March and winner Regazzoni's Ferrari.

one lap. Then a friend who had been ahead of me said: "Did you get caught out by the oil on Becketts on the last lap?". My reply was "Oil? What oil?" After he had gone away the penny dropped. If I had seen the oil flag I would have panicked and crashed.

[It occurred to me after writing all the foregoing that I must have been preaching to the converted as all the readers of my column were presumably qualified British Racing Drivers. But I was sure they would have agreed that you won't learn much about racing by standing on the sidelines, and if the adrenalin hasn't flowed when you've been behind the wheel, you haven't raced.]

I did once meet a chap who said: "Adrenalin? What's adrenalin?" His hobby was pressing wild flowers.

6

MY FAVOURITE TROPHY

Gran Premio Nuvolari

I suppose if you dabble in competition motoring long enough you are bound to acquire the odd trophy or medal. Some people keep them beautifully polished and displayed in ornate cabinets for their friends to admire; others keep them up in the loft or stuffed in a cupboard, like Innes Ireland used to do. I don't have very many, and I conform to the Ireland method of keeping cups and trophies, but there is one that I keep in my workshop, a place where I spend most of my time, and I have been known to give it a clean, not for the benefit of my friends, but for my own pleasure and satisfaction.

This ornate cup is about 15 inches tall and the inscription reads as follows: *Gran Premio Tazio Nuvolari della Mille Miglia Mantova, 1° Maggio 1955.* I didn't win this trophy myself, Stirling Moss won it, but I was with him when he did so. The occasion was his memorable drive in the 1955 Mille Miglia with a 300SLR Mercedes-Benz, covering the 1,000 miles (actually 1,597 kilometres) in 10hr 7min 48sec, an average of 157.65km/h (97.95mph). This included one stop of 18 seconds at Pescara for some fuel, a 60-second stop at Rome for new rear tyres and more fuel, and the two mandatory stops, at Rome and Bologna, to have the fibre disc wired to the steering column punched by an official.

The eight other controls were dealt with on the move, thanks to our own signalling system and the enthusiasm of the officials with the rubber stamps who ran alongside the car and stamped our route card, which I held firmly on the side of the cockpit. We had calculated that we could lose a second at each of the controls by actually coming to rest to have the card stamped, and eight controls meant eight seconds; the previous year, second place overall had been lost by nine seconds!

Tazio Nuvolari had died in August 1953, and in memory of the greatest of all Italian racing drivers the 1954 Mille Miglia race was diverted from its normal route on the last leg of the 1,000 miles, from Cremona to Brescia, and made a dogleg to pass through Mantova. This was Nuvolari's home town and the Automobile Club of Mantova inaugurated the *Gran Premio Tazio Nuvolari* to

You should never value a trophy by its size, but rather by what it stands for, which is why this one always meant so much to me, even though the man who really won it was Stirling Moss. At least I was able to share in his supreme effort on the Cremona-Mantova-Brescia final leg of the 1955 Mille Miglia because I was sitting right alongside watching him sweat!

be awarded to whoever made the fastest time on the 134-kilometre leg, Cremona-Mantova-Brescia.

As Peter Miller has stressed so lucidly in his book *Conte Maggi's Mille Miglia*, the whole concept of the event was speed. Aymo Maggi always said: "The one who runs fastest must win", and so it was from 1927 to 1957. There were no handicaps, no compromises, no adjustments. To win the Mille Miglia you had to travel from Brescia to Rome and back in a shorter time than anyone else, the actual time being immaterial. Stirling's time in 1955 was an all-time record.

It was only fitting that Nuvolari should be remembered in the form of the annual trophy for the fastest competitor on the final leg of the course, through his home town. The 134 kilometres (83¼ miles) were mostly flat and straight, but did include passing though the town of Mantova, where there was a route-card stamping control, and through a number of small villages and the outskirts of Brescia, leading up to the finish on the *Viale Rebuffone*.

When we started this last leg in the 1955 race we were convinced that we were holding a strong second place, for we had accounted for everyone except Fangio, who had started ahead of us. We had no idea we were in the lead, for we had not seen Fangio's Mercedes-Benz at the depot in Sienna, having an injection pipe replaced. There was no question of letting-up and settling for second place; Stirling was never like that in his racing career, it was flat-out right to the flag.

As we left the town of Cremona we passed a group of English people, members of the BRDC and BARC, who waved enthusiastically, probably knowing from the radio that we were in the lead. Our maximum speed in the SLR was our cruising speed, just over 170mph, and we sat at that speed for most of the way to Mantova. Through the town and into the control it was as fast as Stirling could go. The card was stamped 'on the trot' and as I saw the rubber stamp descending I gave Stirling the signal to take off, which he did as always on full-noise. Some seven kilometres before Brescia we crested a rise at our full 170mph, my hand signal indicating a blind brow to be taken 'flat', being faithfully interpreted by Mr Moss.

At this point we grinned at each other, knowing exactly why. There was too much noise from the engine and exhaust for us to talk to each other, but three months of practice had perfected a sort of deaf-and-dumb sign language with which we conversed during the race. In practice we had decided that this particular brow was our make-or-break point for finishing the race. We calculated that if the engine blew up as we breasted that brow at 170mph-plus we could coast for 5 kilometres, and had agreed between us that we were prepared to push the car the remaining 2 kilometres to the finishing line.

As things turned out we didn't have to put our strength to the test, for the Mercedes-Benz never missed a beat all day. Stirling took the last corner in a full-blooded opposite-lock power-slide, and we crossed the finishing line at a good 100mph. We were overjoyed at finishing and well content with the thought that we were second. Imagine our joy and disbelief when we stopped and were told we had won. We did not really believe it until we saw Fangio arrive after us. Then we just fell about.

The tradition of the Mille Miglia was such that you did not collect your trophies until the following year, at a big gathering before the next Mille Miglia. There was a standard cup, the *Coppa Franco Mazzotti*, that was given to everyone who finished, whether first or last. It is a very simple cup that carries no date or inscription, and the only way you could get one of these was to complete the course. The fancy cups with their inscriptions and details covered almost every aspect of the event – class victories, leaders at the various controls, leaders on category and awards from almost every town that you passed through. Whether you drove a Fiat 500 or a 4.9 Ferrari, these were cups to win (and the money, of course) and Stirling gathered up arms full of awards, as you would expect.

The day after the 1955 race I had been invited to a lunch with the organizers and the Automobile Club of Mantova, and had learnt that Stirling had made the fastest time on the leg Cremona-Mantova-Brescia, thus winning the *Gran Premio Tazio Nuvolari*. The Mantova club officials had been a little disappointed that we hadn't come to a complete stop at their control point because they had known that Stirling was leading and wanted to slap him on the back as he sped off on the last section to Brescia. Our 'non-stop' system of getting the card stamped had caught them out. The President of the club told me how they had all been at the control point when the buzz went round: "Here comes the leader, Sterleeny Moss", and before they could focus on the silver Mercedes-Benz we were gone! I explained how our whole race strategy had been built up on not wasting seconds, never mind minutes.

We had covered the 134 kilometres of the *Gran Premio Tazio Nuvolari* in 39 minutes 54 seconds, an average speed of 198.464km/h (123.319mph), and that at the end of nearly 1,000 miles of racing on public roads. For me, as passenger and navigator, that last leg was the end of a perfect day, and when we went to the prize-giving before the 1956 event and Stirling said: "Do you want any of these cups?" I chose the Tazio Nuvolari trophy. It was, and still is, a cup full of meaning.

Count Aymo Maggi was so right. "The one who runs fastest must win"; we had not only run fastest for the whole event, but right through to the finish. When his race was banned in 1957 and the Brescia club turned the event into a mountain rally, Maggi wanted nothing to do with it. The present social event that is supposed to commemorate the never-to-be-forgotten Mille Miglia must make poor Aymo turn in his grave.

7

TEAM SPIRIT

Team Lotus 1978

Running any sort of team calls for a lot of strength of character in the team manager, whether he is trying to control a darts team or a Formula One team. In some sports the team members simply have to work together or there never will be any results, while in others a certain amount of individualism can be allowed.

In these days with motor racing of the 'sprint' variety rather than long-distance, the accent is more on the individual, especially in Formula One, where the obsession is to attain the status of World Champion. It is equally individual in the attainment of becoming Formula First Champion.

From the driver who is in the car winning the race, right down through the team to the girl who has to sit all day at the telephone switchboard, teamwork is all-important. If everyone is giving of their best for the team, success will come. It is when a 'team' consists of more than one car and more than one driver that things change.

Many years ago, a well-known team manager told me that he couldn't see the point of operating a team of three cars and three drivers. He pointed out that his object was to win the Grand Prix, not finish second or third, and if he could be 100 per cent certain of having the best car, the best driver and the best back-up team of engineers and mechanics he would be quite happy to enter just one car. The only justification he could see for having three cars and drivers was that he did not have total faith in his number-one driver, or in the car. "It's an admission of failure before we start", he used to say.

It can be done, and has been done, in quite recent times, but it is rare for a team to consist of one man and one car. In 1989 FISA insisted that all entrants for the Formula One World Championship must field a team of two cars and two drivers, but like so many FISA dictates, this rule was not rigidly adhered to. The majority of entrants do have the problem of controlling two drivers, and it can be a problem. You may have the two best drivers in the world on your strength, but if they do not get along with one another you have problems. A team with two lesser drivers who are much more compatible could well give you better overall results. While everyone's aim is to win the Grand Prix, and only one driver can do that, it can be of moral assistance to have a strong second driver. If he is in the second place on the grid then it prevents any of your rivals being there, which can't be a bad thing.

At the end of the race, to have your two cars in first and second place is not only good for team morale, it is depressing for the other teams, and important for winning the Manufacturer's Championship, as both cars count points. Unfortunately, the media world give scant coverage of the Manufacturer's Championship, being obsessed with pop stars and human stories and dramas.

Over the years, there have been some classic examples of poor team control,

Ronnie Peterson dutifully running in the wheeltracks of his Lotus team-mate Mario Andretti during the 1978 Dutch Grand Prix, having just lapped Arturo Merzario. Ronnie played it strictly by the rulebook, which said that that year Mario should have precedence in the all-conquering Lotus team.

some serious, some amusing and some potentially damaging. In one race, two cars from the same team were on the front row of the grid and on only the third corner of the opening lap the drivers ran into each other and spun off into retirement. It was all a bit of a joke as it was happening, and nobody was hurt and the cars were not very damaged, but the team manager was not amused. Two weeks later, at the next race for which the team were entered, the two drivers in question were withdrawn and reserve drivers took their places. They were back in the team for the following event, but the point had been made and taken. On another occasion, a well-known driver behaved in a rather uncouth manner to his team and was politely told that his entry for the next race had been withdrawn. That not only got his total attention, but evoked a sincere apology. These were examples of a strong team manager commanding the respect that was due to him.

Too many times there have been examples of undisciplined action by drivers that have brought forth no hard rebuke, simply because the team manager (or team owner) has been too weak. We had a classic example some years ago of a team finding themselves in complete control of a race, the two drivers running first and second. They could have toured round on the last lap side-by-side in a derisory fashion to illustrate their total annihilation of all the opposition and could have staged a dead-heat if necessary. Such a demonstration of strength would have destroyed any hopes that the opposition might have nurtured of beating them in the future. But weak team management did not make this happen; instead, the two drivers raced against each other on the last lap as if they were in rival teams and came so close to hitting each other and crashing that it would have been a dicey moment even if they had been in rival teams. By sheer luck, not judgment, they survived the incident and the number-two driver stole the race from the team number-one. The media and the spectators loved it, but I thought it was stupid and illustrated very poor team management, which could have backfired on the whole organization. On reflection I think it did, but noboby realized it until much later.

In 1978, Team Lotus had a model set-up which to this day reflects well on the drivers concerned and the strength of Colin Chapman as the leader of the team. The Lotus Formula One car was as good as they come, and Chapman had signed up Mario Andretti as his number-one driver. The number-two was Ronnie Peterson, the enthusiastic young Swede who was as fast as anybody. Right from the start Colin made it clear that Mario was No 1 and Ronnie was No 2, and you didn't argue with Colin Chapman. The two drivers got on very well together, Mario the Italian-born naturalized American and 100 per cent professional racing driver, and Ronnie the quiet, uncomplicated and affable Swede, a motor racing enthusiast from his childhood and an amazing driver who knew only one way to go, and that was flat-out.

Their whole driving strategy was based on the knowledge that the team was capable of dominating races, so Mario asked Ronnie to agree to staying comfortably behind in second place. Not too close, but equally not too far back to allow anyone to entertain thoughts of getting between them. If anything intruded on Mario's race strategy and he knew he could do nothing about it, but equally knew that Ronnie could, then he would flick on his red rear foglight as the signal for the young Swede to go by and 'get stuck into it'.

Such a situation could have arisen if someone in third place began to challenge seriously, and Mario couldn't go faster for some reason or another. It was a very simple bit of team discipline, which you knew Mario would observe scrupulously and he hoped Ronnie would. "No red light, stay behind", or alternatively, "Red for go."

Colin Chapman, a man of many parts – a brilliant ideas man, a talented racing driver during the formative years of Lotus, a tough taskmaster, and above all a leader who inspired intense loyalty.

This was illustrated to perfection in the South African Grand Prix at Kyalami in 1978. Patrick Depailler had a surprisingly strong lead, with Lotus second and third, when with 15 laps to go the Tyrrell began to emit puffs of smoke from a gearbox oil leak on to the exhaust pipes. The Lotus pair began to close up, Ronnie Peterson sitting dutifully behind Andretti. With only three laps to go there was every likelihood of Andretti catching the ailing Tyrrell, but suddenly Andretti's engine popped and banged as he was nearly out of petrol. Quick as a flash, a red light came on at the back of his Lotus and, equally quickly, Ronnie flashed by. While Mario shot into the pits for a quick refill, Ronnie was giving it all he had got.

As he started the last lap he had the blue Tyrrell in his sights and it was one of the most exciting last laps I have ever seen. Halfway round that lap Peterson had the Lotus alongside the Tyrrell, and the two cars took a fast right-hander side by side. Wheel-to-wheel they raced for the next corner, with Ronnie now on the inside, and with only three more corners before the finish the Lotus nosed in front. They finished half a second apart, with the black and gold John Player Lotus in the lead. Poor Mario could only claim seventh place, but it was a race to remember.

That season ended with Lotus winning the Manufacturer's Championship, Mario Andretti winning six races and Ronnie Peterson winning two races, with Mario claiming, justifiably, the crown of World Champion.

Team spirit at its best; and to me it still seems like it was only yesterday...

8

CHRISTMAS DAY MOTORING

On the road with a racing car

It is always gratifying to receive letters commenting on my reminiscences, and they seem to come from far and wide. For example, a column I had written provoked a letter from the far reaches of Canada, in which Merv Therriault recalled an occasion when he was working for Team Lotus, which brought back happy memories to me, too.

1957 had been a very good year for Britain in Grand Prix racing, for after years of people floundering around at the back, Mr Vandervell's Vanwall team had shown that Britain could take on anybody in Grand Prix racing. Tony Brooks and Stirling Moss had won the British Grand Prix at Aintree, then Stirling had won the Grand Prix of Pescara, and finally the Vanwalls had annihilated the Ferraris and Maseratis at Monza in the Italian Grand Prix.

I began to think about doing something appropriate to wind up the year at Christmas time. Other magazines were doing Christmas road tests of unlikely vehicles, with esoteric things like measuring the acceleration of a pogo stick, or the maximum speed of a steamroller. For *Motor Sport* my thoughts were totally on Grand Prix racing, though I occasionally helped the editor by road-testing the more exciting vehicles. For this purpose I plotted out a figure-of-eight route that covered pretty well the whole of the county of Hampshire, where I lived, and did timed runs in the faster road-test cars. There were no motorways in those days and, more to the point, there were no speed limits on the open roads and traffic was pretty sparse at night. I used to start on the Surrey/Hampshire border at 2am and cover my 180-mile route while the world was asleep. Most memorable was a Mercedes-Benz 300SL Gullwing, which averaged 78mph on the opening stretch Camberley-Salisbury, cruising across Salisbury Plain at 130-135mph (oh, happy days!).

However, to return to my Christmas road test. I thought it would be fun to drive a Grand Prix car on the public roads, and what better time to do it than lunchtime on December 25. With everyone sitting down to Christmas dinner between 12 noon and 3pm I reckoned the roads would be pretty clear. I also bargained on the police having Christmas dinner at the station, because I was intending to bend some of the rules just a tiny bit. The plan was to cover my figure-of-eight route on the open roads of Hampshire in a full-blooded Grand Prix car in full racing trim!

The big question was what car to use. I approached David Yorke, the Vanwall team manager, and he warmed to the idea. A Vanwall was going to be worth 'going inside' for if I got caught. Plans progressed favourably, and it was decided to move the start to the rear of a friendly public house, rather than the cafe in the High Street, as it would attract less attention and I could zoom out onto the main road and be gone before anyone realized what was happening.

But as the time drew near David had second thoughts, and duty-bound he had to mention it to Mr Vandervell. Tony thought it was a riotous idea at first, but then he thought about the consequences if I got stopped by the police and the reflections it would have on his VP Products firm and the Vanwall team. So the idea was called off.

I then approached Bruce Halford to see if he would lend me his 250F Maserati. He was all for co-operating, but the snag was that the Maserati was at the factory in Modena having a winter overhaul. He reluctantly had to turn the idea down as there was no way the 250F could be finished and brought to England in time for Christmas Day.

I could see the whole thing fizzling out, so I rang Colin Chapman of Lotus. I had known Colin for many years, and he was always one for 'a bit of a lark', and while he did not have a Grand Prix Lotus he was quite prepared to lend

This was the piece of paper I hoped would keep me out of trouble if I was stopped while driving a Formula Two Lotus on the road on trade plates, though I doubt if it would have done so! Unfortunately (or was it fortunately?) it wasn't put to the test.

ROAD VEHICLES (REGISTRATION & LICENSING) REGULATIONS, 1953.	L 3	Nº 637443

EXTRACT FROM REGISTER RECORDING THE
USE OF LIMITED TRADE LICENCES.

Plate No. *OO7 MH* Date of use *25 DEC* Time of Departure *1.0 pm*

Description of Vehicle *LOTUS*

Registration Mark or Chassis No. *F2/2*

Purpose of use (as defined in the Regulations) and destination or route. *Test Hampshire*

Name of Driver *Jenkinson*

Descriptions of Persons carried (if any)

Name and Address of Licensee *Lotus*

Signature of Licensee or his Agent

NOTE: This slip must be produced by the Driver of the vehicle upon request of a Police Officer or Local Taxation Officer

This murky and badly exposed snapshot is the only photographic evidence of my Christmas Day transport as delivered for road test – the result of light getting into the camera. But at least it proves it actually happened.

me a Type 12 Formula Two single-seater and agreed to bring it down to the pub on a trailer on Christmas morning.

Christmas Day was fine and dry, though a bit chilly, and during the morning I did a rapid run round the course in an Austin 105 that *Motor Sport* had on test, to check the route, weigh up the traffic density, note down any patrolling police cars and generally 'spy out the land'. True to his word, Colin arrived in a Ford Anglia with the F2 car on a trailer behind. It was in full racing trim, straight-through exhaust, no road equipment of any sort, a full-race Coventry Climax four-cylinder engine and the famous Lotus progressive-change gearbox, 'wobbly-web' alloy wheels and disc brakes.

With Colin was Merv Therriault, who wrote me that letter from Vancouver. While he 'fitted' me into the narrow cockpit, Colin said: "You'd better borrow our Trade Plates, they might soften the blow if you get stopped"; a kindly thought that had not occurred to me when negotiating for the Vanwall or the 250F Maserati. There was no way to fix the front plate on the Lotus, so we abandoned it and slung the rear one across the tail as a gesture. They were what are known as Limited plates, which meant that the law demanded that my journey was specified on an official form.

Colin cautiously filled in the form: Plate No 007MH. Date of use: 25th December. Time of Departure: 1.00pm. Registration Mark or Chassis No: F2/2. Description of vehicle: Lotus. Purpose of use: Test Hampshire. Name of driver: Jenkinson. Name and address of licensee: Lotus Engineering. Signature of licensee or his agent: ACBC.

It was all very official (well, sort of) and if I was stopped I had to say: "Oh dear, the front plate must have fallen off." The question of an open exhaust, no mudguards, no audible warning of approach, a racing car on the road, undue speed, and anything else the law could think up, we reckoned would tot up to a pretty hefty fine, but with a bit of Christmas spirit would not involve a gaol sentence.

While Merv warmed up the Climax engine I donned crash helmet and goggles and told various friends to stay by their telephones in case I needed help. Colin said: "I'm not stopping, good luck and goodbye", and he motored off back to London.

The little Lotus was a revelation on the open road and hummed along at 80-90mph on the first section of the route which involved a bypass and some roundabouts. Out beyond Basingstoke, heading for the open plains, I wound the Lotus up to about 120mph in fourth gear, snicked into top and was just getting ready to reach its terminal speed when the revs shot up and there was no drive to the wheels. As I began to slow I made various checks and it was obvious that something had broken in the transmission.

On this deserted stretch of road there were a couple of houses and, with great presence of mind (not wishing to be found by the side of the road), I turned sharp right into a gateway, still freewheeling at about 50mph, and coasted up the long drive, well away from the road. Wishing to telephone for help, I knocked at the front door of the big house and politely asked if I might use the telephone as my car had broken down.

The household was in a complete flap; Christmas dinner was ready and the guests hadn't arrived. The lady of the house was on the verge of a fainting fit, the gentleman was trying to calm things, and in the middle of it all there was this chap telephoning for help. They kept rushing to the door and peering down the drive, looking in vain for their guests, and I am sure that the single-seater racing Lotus standing on the gravel did not register with them. They were totally obsessed with their own problem of Christmas dinner being ready and no guests.

I got through to a friend and told him where I was and he said he would come out with a towrope. As I was leaving, the guests arrived and there was pandemonium on all sides. The lady of the house was gasping: "They're here, they're here", the gentleman was wishing everyone a "Happy Christmas", children were shouting and yelling, dogs were barking...it was all too much. I quietly left and pushed the Lotus out through the mass of cars and wheeled it down to the gate.

My friend arrived, we hitched up the towrope and set off back to base, happy to arrive safely without encountering the law. My Christmas dinner? I didn't have one, but I remember having quite a few beers to drown my sorrows. When Lotus got the car back they found that a driveshaft had sheared, luckily inside the universal joint, so it all stayed together. They also found that the driveshafts had been put on the wrong way round from that to which they had been used, and the reversal loading was too much for the splines.

Among my souvenirs I still have that brown slip of official paper with the date 25th December on it. Thanks, Merv, for jogging my memory.

The Formula Two Lotus-Climax in its more natural environment, on a race track, with Colin Chapman himself testing the prototype car.

9

A LONG JOURNEY

'Auntie' Rover to Africa

At the end of the 1957 season a Grand Prix was organized on a circuit just outside Casablanca, in French Morocco, and in those days most of us only knew Casablanca as the name of a film. With air transport still being a bit primitive, expensive and relatively scarce, the natural thing to do was to plan to drive to Morocco.

It so happened that my friend Edward Eves, who worked for *The Autocar* in those days and was known as 'Midland Ed Fred', was also thinking of driving to Morocco, as was another chum, Jesse Alexander, who was based in Europe representing *Road & Track*. So naturally we got together and formed a 'crew' for a journey into the unknown; we had all motored extensively throughout Europe and Scandinavia, as well as the Iberian Peninsula, but none of us had ever ventured across the Mediterranean sea to the African continent.

In those days Jesse and I were doing all our motoring in Porsche 356 Coupes, while Ted was more inclined towards cars from the British Midlands motor industry, and we smiled indulgently when Ted said he could borrow a Rover for the trip. The P4 series of Rovers were always known as 'Aunties' in a friendly and respectful manner, for they were pretty austere, dignified and not at all sporting, like everyone's maiden aunt. In addition, the instrument panel was like a good quality mantlepiece, and what's more it had a clock in the centre. Also, the Rover's bodywork came well down, all round, like Auntie's skirts, so that you did not see any of the underpinnings, like springs, axles, exhaust systems and so on, as with many of the more 'flighty' saloon cars of the day. Auntie's interior was warm and comfortable, like a Victorian drawing room.

On Sunday, October 20, the trip started for me with a lift in a VW Beetle to Goodwood for the Motor Show Test Day, where I met Jesse and his wife in their Borgward and joined them for a long cross-country run to Dover, where we met up with Ted and the Rover 90, which he had driven down from the Midlands. On the night ferry to Dunkerque we hatched our plan.

Jesse's wife would continue on in the Borgward to their home in Switzerland. and the 'three men in the Rover' would head off south-west to the far corner of France, cross into Spain, hopefully being able to get visas at the frontier, and then travel due south through Madrid and on to Gibraltar, where we would cross on the ferry to Tangier. Then it would be a simple run through Spanish Morocco, into French Morocco and down the coast to Casablanca, a distance of 1,696 miles. There were no motorways in those days, and we did not intend to drive through the night, or forego the luxuries of

'Auntie' Rovers may have had a reputation for being staid and sedate transport, but 'our' Rover 90 cruised happily all day long at 80-85mph with three of us on board and covered 5,000 miles to Morocco and back without trouble. One of the locals eyed 'Auntie' enviously, contemplating a part-exchange perhaps?

food and drink; but it was obvious that Auntie Rover was going to have to lift up her skirts and get on with it.

A 'plan of travel' was drawn up. We would take turns at driving, navigating or resting, in strict rotation, and to avoid any friction among the crew, duties were agreed upon. The driver would drive and concentrate on that alone, the passenger would read the maps and navigate, and as a luxury was permitted to play with the radio to his own choice. The third member sat in the back and shut up. Stints of 200 miles were agreed upon, and 200 it would be, not 201, 205, 210, or "...just to the next village..." Regardless of where we were it was agreed that as the odometer moved from 199 we would slow to a stop for a crew change. This was a rapid move round, the passenger/navigator would get out and slide into the back of the car, the driver would move across to the front passenger seat and the backseat passenger would slip into the driving seat.

We found the Rover was very happy cruising at an honest 80mph in silence and comfort, and at the first 200 miles the change round went smoothly and we were on our way again. As the second 200-mile mark arrived we were on a long deserted *Route Nationale* and it occurred to us that it ought to be possible to change round on the move. As 199 came up on the trip we slowed to around 40-50mph, the passenger climbed over into the back, the driver slid across the bench seat, keeping his foot on the accelerator pedal and one hand on the steering wheel, and the chap in the back climbed forward over and into the driving seat, catching the accelerator pedal as the new navigator let it go. It worked like a charm, and from then on this became the normal routine and we were soon changing formation at a comfortable 60mph.

In Spain we decided to reduce the stints to 100 miles now that we had perfected our crew changes, and in addition it meant that two of us had to suffer less if we did not like the navigator's choice of music! We were fortunate in that our driving styles were very similar so that it was a happy ship no matter who was at the wheel. The only slight discord would be if the driver overdid things a bit and Auntie squealed her tyres inadvertently round a tightening bend, or put a wheel off onto the loose. If that happened the other two members of the crew would sing in unison "a touch of the Fangios?" and the back of the driver's neck would turn a bit red. Today we would say "a touch of the Sennas?"

We just missed the Spanish boat to Tangier and had to take a British boat from Gibraltar, which meant spending a night on 'the Rock', which after France and Spain came as a bit of a cultural shock, but the next day in Morocco put things into perspective.

Arriving in Casablanca on Thursday evening, we patted Auntie on the rump, for she had done well, spending most of her travelling time at between 80 and 85mph and never missing a beat. After the weekend of the race it wasn't a simple case of retracing our steps back to Dunkerque; with 'Midland Ed Fred' nothing was simple. By doing some more protracted motoring we could make Turin in time for the Press Day of the annual Italian Motor Show, so Monday saw an early start and another '100-mile stage' trip back to Tangier, across to Gib and hot-foot up through Spain. In those days the frontiers of Spain closed at 9pm and we made it into France with a minute to spare. As Auntie Rover's brakes were beginning to show signs of wilting it was agreed that a more leisurely pace across the south of France would be a good thing, so we settled for one-hour stints rather than 100 miles, and went back to the more leisurely change-round of actually stopping as the hour ticked up.

We visited the Turin Motor Show, then set off into Switzerland to deliver Jesse Alexander to his home, and Ted and I did the last leg of our long journey, arriving in England from the night ferry in pouring rain. I stepped off in London and caught a train back home to Hampshire and Ted returned the Rover to Solihull, with nearly 5,000 miles added to the 12,000 it had already covered as a 'demonstrator' and we all had a very healthy respect for 'Auntie' Rover.

10

A DIFFICULT QUESTION

The most memorable race

The 1957 Italian Grand Prix at Monza was a truly memorable race, for that was the day when Britain's supremacy in Grand Prix racing, through the Vanwall team, was put beyond question. The Vanwalls of Stuart Lewis-Evans (in pole position), Stirling Moss and Tony Brooks were joined on the front row of the grid by Fangio's Maserati, but it was to be Moss' day; Stirling was over 41 seconds ahead of Fangio at the flag.

Some time ago, someone asked me which was the most memorable race I had seen, and I was at a total loss to give them an answer. I must have watched over 500 major races through the years since I saw my first motor race in 1937, and it is an impossible task to pick out one that was the most memorable.

Many of the races I have completely forgotten, but not surprisingly, many are remembered as if they were yesterday, and indeed some were only yesterday, because I am still adding to my total.

Mike Hawthorn winning the French Grand Prix in 1953 will always stay in my memory, not just for the wonderful wheel-to-wheel dice he had with Fangio, but the fact that we had a young English driver who could take on the world's best in Grand Prix racing.

Stirling Moss winning the Italian Grand Prix in 1957 with the Vanwall is another memorable race, with Fangio once more relegated to second place behind an English driver. This time the memorable part was not so much the driver as the car, for Tony Vandervell's Vanwall team had finally set the seal on their supremacy. Vanwall first, Maserati second, Ferrari third, and there were no 'ifs' or 'buts', it was total domination of the opposition.

Vanwall had already won the British Grand Prix and the Pescara Grand Prix, but these paled into insignificance against the Monza victory, at the very heart of Italian Grand Prix racing; it was all the more memorable because the Italians had ruled the roost since 1946, with only the brief period of defeat by Daimler-Benz in 1954 and 1955. That was the day for me that Great Britain took a strangle-hold on Grand Prix racing and it has never really let go since.

Going back to my early days, when my following of motor racing was limited to English events, I will always remember the Imperial Trophy race at the Crystal Palace circuit in 1938. Grand Prix cars like Mercedes-Benz, Auto Union, Maserati and Alfa Romeo were purely academic to me, known only through reading Rodney Walkerley in *The Motor*. Reality, in as much as being able to see and hear and smell racing cars, was the world of ERA, MG, Riley and Alta, and from the time I saw my first photograph of an Alta racing car in 1935 I was an Alta enthusiast. Don't ask me why, it was just one of those love-at-first-sight things. Even now, at vintage race meetings at Silverstone, I can stand by an Alta and feel bathed in a rosy warmth of satisfaction. I stand by an ERA and think, "yes, it's alright, but..." I have a similar differentiation of feeling between Maserati and Ferrari, and today I get that feeling beside a Formula One Honda engine, but not alongside a Renault Formula One engine. Don't ask me why.

However, to get back to 1938. October 8 was the day that George Abecassis won the Imperial Trophy with his silver and red Alta. In second place was Bira

When Gilles Villeneuve won the 1981 Monaco Grand Prix with the Ferrari turbo, I knew that the normally aspirated Formula One engines had effectively had their day, at least until the regulations were changed again. Villeneuve's was a wonderfully controlled drive, which made me highly emotional as he took the chequered flag.

in an ERA and third was Eugenio Minetti in a Maserati. There were five other ERAs further down the results. It was indeed a joy-day for Alta enthusiasts. By today's standards it was not exactly a wild spectacle, for the winning average speed was only 52.08mph and the race had lasted a mere 38 minutes, but to a schoolboy satiated with motor racing it was the real world. Having gone to the meeting on a push-bike, a 52mph average was a world apart.

Of more recent memorable races, the 1988 Belgian Grand Prix at Spa-Francorchamps will remain memorable in my mind, for it was the day when Ayrton Senna drove one of his most perfect races, demonstrating the pure art of Grand Prix driving on one of my favourite Grand Prix circuits. His average speed was 126.416mph, and when I met him in the paddock afterwards, albeit very briefly, just to shake his hand and say with all sincerity: "Well done," I could not help noticing the fatigue in his dark brown eyes.

A couple of weeks later I was able to get him to tell me about the race in detail and the amount of hard thinking he had had to do when he started to lap the tail-enders, then the midfield runners and finally some quite respectable front runners. The mental planning and sighting of cars that he was going to catch and the calculating and anticipation of where he was going to pass them and how he was going to pass them was quite remarkable. I commented on the fact that he looked tired after the race, and he said: "Physically, no problem; but mentally it was a very hard race". Senna went through traffic with such an ease that you might think the traffic was not there. Until I had that opportunity to listen to him it was difficult to realize that his traffic driving was not as easy as it looked.

For as long as I can remember the name of the *Scuderia Ferrari* is one that continually leaves memorable occasions in the mind. In the 1930s the *Scuderia Ferrari* name was synonymous with Alfa Romeo racing, and over the years the official title of the team has changed from things like *Ferrari SpA*, to *SEFAC Ferrari*, and now it is Fiat-Ferrari; but to me it will always be the *Scuderia Ferrari*.

The Monaco Grand Prix of 1981 was one of my memorable races to watch. It was the first victory by a Ferrari turbocharged 1½-litre and we knew on that day that the death-knell had been sounded for the normally-aspirated 3-litre engines. Renault had shown the possibilities, but I was not completely convinced of the future of Formula One until Ferrari produced a turbocharged 1½-litre. That victory in 1981 was a memorable day. I actually threw my cap in the air and shouted for joy as Villeneuve got the chequered flag, for the spirited young Canadian was one of my heroes and I felt he had set Grand Prix on the way to a new and exciting technical era, which was to turn out to be true.

Another Ferrari landmark which was memorable for me was the Austrian Grand Prix of 1970 on the majestic Osterreichring. It was here that the *Scuderia Ferrari* got themselves out of a doldrum and back on the winner's rostrum. There were something like 30,000 Italian racing enthusiasts at that race, having poured across the frontier in the Dolomites. Jacky Ickx and Clay Regazzoni finished first and second, and at 11pm that Sunday evening Italian-registered cars were still streaming through the little town in which I was staying, the drivers and their friends singing, shouting and waving flags as they headed for home.

To pick one memorable race that I have seen is completely impossible. Perhaps my trouble is that I have seen too many races, but I have no intention of putting an end to my score. In reality, if you love motor racing like I do then any race is memorable, but some are more memorable than others! Perhaps one day I will tell you about some that I would rather forget...

11

BOOKS

Some good reading

The winter months are a good time to catch up on some serious reading, not of glossy magazines, but good solid books with stiff covers. Back at the end of 1989 I wrote that it would be nice to read a book about the 1990 Grand Prix season, and how Senna and Honda were going to win all the races, but that sort of book was not on the bookshelves yet, though no doubt Honda R&D were working on a HiTech way of doing it. But on second thoughts, a complete book on the forthcoming season would rather spoil the pleasure of watching Grand Prix racing!

I felt that there was little point in reading a book on the season just ended for that was still fresh in the memory, and for most people the season of 1989 was best forgotten. So I turned to *Cars are my Life*, by Ferry Porsche, or to give him his full title, Professor Dr Ing H C Ferry Porsche. You do not have to be a Porsche fanatic to enjoy this book, though it does help, but you do need to have an engineering view of cars to really appreciate a lot of the things in it. For anyone who thinks that road cars are just assembled and sold to the customer, the Porsche story is very revealing as to just how much work goes into a prototype before production begins.

One paragraph stopped me in my tracks, for it was about a racing driver, of whom Dr Porsche had this to say: "(He) was an amazing phenomenon, a daredevil and an exceptional driver who right from the start drove very quickly indeed. Part of the reason for this may have been that he had never driven a racing car before and this was the first Grand Prix car he had ever raced. As a result he was able to attune himself to the new design since he was totally unfamiliar with conventional designs. He was a very talented driver,

At a time when everyone else's hero was Tazio Nuvolari, mine was Bernd Rosemeyer, who graduated to car racing from a successful career on two wheels – an excellent apprenticeship. Typically, Rosemeyer had his tricky-to-handle Auto Union (No 5) up amongst the Mercedes-Benz opposition from the start of the 1937 Donington Grand Prix, which tragically was to give him his last victory; a few weeks later he was killed whilst attempting a new speed record on a German autobahn.

but was also prepared to take great risks and was continually striving to achieve a better lap time simply because he enjoyed driving. Incidentally, his daredevil character and his desire to go ever quicker aroused the anger of the older and more established drivers who grumbled 'why does he always have to keep going faster and faster? We're already driving fast enough!'"

You may think, like I did, that Ferry Porsche was talking about Ayrton Senna, or Gilles Villeneuve, or Jim Clark, or Stirling Moss, but in fact he was talking about Bernd Rosemeyer driving for Auto Union in 1935 to 1937. To me the description was of a 'racer', and 'racers' have never changed, and I really do not see why they should; that is as long as Japanese or German HiTech allows a driver to sit in the Grand Prix car and touch things. When the day arrives when a Grand Prix car is fully automated, to win at record speed, it will be a fascinating period of racing, but I shall miss seeing the 'racers' rising to a challenge.

This idea of the fully automated racing car may sound far-fetched, but I was long past my youth when I heard that TriStars were making fully automatic landings, even though the passengers were not told about it. After some years the captains were allowed to announce over the cabin intercom that "we have just made an automatic landing", and though some passengers were a bit startled to hear the announcement, the TriStars had been doing it for quite a while.

I imagine no-one will be told about the first fully-automated Grand Prix car in case the FIA 'throw a wobbly', and the last person to be told will be the driver as he would instantly tell his cronies in the press corps, and then everyone would know.

It will be like car-to-pit telemetry, which had been going on for some time before the people next door found out, and like ELF announcing that turbocharged engines had been running on lead-free fuel some years after they had started doing so. Even more apposite was the admission by AGIP, ELF, Mobil, Shell and Wintershell that the fuel they were supplying for the works turbocharged engines was not petrol, as the general public knew petrol, but specially blended mixes schemed up in their laboratories which complied with all the FISA rules as regards specification. This was not announced by the fuel companies until the end of the season, when officialdom found out that the BMW engines in the winning Brabhams were running on synthetic fuel. There was about to be a big technical fuss when the other companies quietly said: "Ahem! We are using similar fuels."

Back in the Sixties Goodyear happened to mention that their racing tyres were tubeless, and FISA became all excited on one of their 'safety' aspects. Certain people were about to call for 'an investigation' when Goodyear added: "Don't panic, all our racing tyres have been tubeless for more than a season already.

A fully automated Grand Prix car may sound fanciful, but next time you land at Heathrow, think of the days of a 707 lumbering clumsily onto the runway. It wasn't that long ago.

Which leaves us a long way from Dr Porsche and his autobiography. Another autobiography that anyone interested in racing will enjoy is that of Juan-Manuel Fangio, published by PSL, who also published the Porsche book. Naturally, Fangio's original book was written in Spanish, but this is a first-class translation, which I had the honour of editing in this English edition. I have probably read it three, or even four times during the production, and it never ceases to fascinate me, for much of it is about Fangio's life and friends in Argentina, of which so little is really known.

I was fortunate enough to be reporting on European racing at the time of his

10 years of racing in works teams, but even so I learnt so much from this book that I never knew at the time. I watched that greatest of all his races, the 1957 German Grand Prix, and drove round the circuit next day to look at the marks on the earth banks where he had deliberately let the Maserati tyres touch, to stop it sliding. And the corner where he had passed Mike Hawthorn, as Mike so graphically described to me after the race, and the places where Fangio had brushed the banks at very high speed while Mike was trying all he knew to keep up, but freely admitted that there was no way he was going to drive to such fine limits, even had he been capable.

What I did not know was that Fangio was wound up so tight during that race that it took him two or three days to unwind, and for a couple of nights he just could not sleep.

On another occasion, when racing a 4CLT/48 Maserati in France, everything seemed to be in order, but I never knew Fangio had been up half the night working on the engine, repairing practice damage, which his Italian mechanic had said was unrepairable.

But best of all are the philosophical remarks that he makes all through the book, as a matter of course, to explain why he did what he did, and they apply to any real racing driver, from years before Fangio's time right through to 1990 and certainly on to the year 2000. He won the Driver's World Championship five times, four of them in succession, so all our current World Champions have still got a long way to go. He never became a 'European' like some international racing drivers, he always remained an Argentine, and Argentina was always 'home'. Like England was to Graham Hill, Australia to Alan Jones and Brazil to Ayrton Senna.

12

BEAD COUNTING

Serious road-testing

Over the years of my involvement with journalism and writing about motor cars and motor racing I have occasionally been involved in the practised art of road-test activity. Road-testing for a magazine or newspaper is something of a profession in itself, but it is one in which I never had much interest. I never objected to trying a car, especially new ones when they first appeared on the market, but the business of analyzing them, gathering masses of statistics and then writing about them was not really my world.

In my early days, when I was already up to the eyes in racing, with little time for anything else, I went for a ride with a friend who was involved in road tests for the weekly 'Bloater'. We were in the latest saloon product of a famous British manufacturer, and that in itself was not exactly my scene, sports and GT cars being my real interest. This friend was a very neat, smooth and fast driver and it was always pleasant to travel with him in his own sports car.

But putting on his 'road-tester's hat' he became impossible and I was glad when the trip finished. He took the poor little engine up to valve-bounce in the gears, was brutal with the clutch and the brakes, and to cap it all he deliberately bounced one front wheel up a kerb to 'test' the suspension. I was

Just popping down to the bank! Somebody suggested that I must have been applying for a loan in order to fill the tank, but if anything I was demonstrating just how tractable these cars were if you treated the right pedal with respect.

horrified by the whole business and decided that if that was the way professional road-testers drove I didn't want to know about it. When I suggested that he wouldn't drive his own car in that manner, he laughed and said: "You must test these things to the limits". My feeling was that the manufacturer's R&D department would surely have done all these things before the car went into production.

Some while later I was asked to "do a road test" of another family saloon to help out a staff shortage. I drove off in this pride of the British motor industry and was appalled. It was a dreadful car, even driving it quietly. These were the days of the great new discovery, the 'steering column gear change' (whatever happened to that awful idea?). Viewing the car as a family saloon, I could not find anything nice to say about it, and in the report I said so. That was not very popular, to say the least, and resulted in a great fuss between the manufacturer and the proprietor of the magazine, which got very bitter and twisted before it died. Once again I felt that road-testing was not my scene.

I have always been fairly straight-forward in my writings, and if I don't like something I say so. Equally, if I praise something then it means I like it. It all seems quite simple to me, but the world of professional road-testing is not like that. It seems that if something is awful you must say it "could do with improving". If something is pathetic you must say it is "adequate".

One road test that I really enjoyed, although it was not meant to be a road test in the professional sense, was 10 days spent with a Ford GT40 in road-going trim. It was memorable; a highlight in 50 years of motoring. When it was suggested that we should "take figures" with it, fooling around with stopwatches, measuring tapes, fifth-wheels, accelerometers and other gadgets, I said: "No thank you, this car is for driving and motoring with a capital M". I really enjoyed writing about that car, but comment was made by a colleague as to why I hadn't done a proper road test!

There was one fairly happy period of my life when the magazine decided it would not try and do professional road tests, but instead we would go off on an interesting 'jolly' (or Boondogle, as they say in California), using a manufacturer's latest product, and write it up more objectively, rather than filling the pages with facts and figures and technocratic analysis, which was more interesting to me. Even better was the idea that an enthusiastic new member of the staff, one Alan Henry, writing under the initials A.H., would write the story, I would plan the trip and provide the background, and our enthusiastic production manager, Michael Tee, would arrange the car and do most of the driving.

These 'jollies' worked well, and one excellent one was a trip to Scotland in a Jaguar XJ12 saloon, allowing us to sample 'grace, space and pace' in the best possible manner. It wafted us up the motorways from London to Carlisle in a very impressive manner, so that we arrived in comfortable time for dinner with no effort at all. The following days we 'toured' Scotland, visiting various motor racing venues like Bo'ness and Rest-and-be-Thankful hill-climbs, old racing circuits like Charterhall and Turnberry, and new ones like Ingliston and Knockhill. It was all very splendid and enjoyable, the normal situation being that Michael would be driving, I would be in the passenger seat reading the maps and navigating, and Alan would be resting comfortably in the back. His work was yet to come, writing about the car when we got back.

We were using the V12 Jaguar as it was intended, for fast, easy, comfortable travel about the place, not trying to find out if it oversteered or understeered, or turned-in properly, or suffered rear-end breakaway and so on. It had wafted up to 115 to 120mph on the odd occasion, with no drama at all.

Coming south on the A82 from Glencoe, Michael inquired as to when we intended to "take figures" of the car's performance. We said we had no intention of "taking figures" because it was not that sort of car. He then asked about the maximum speed of the XJ12, to which we replied that it was academic, but it could be in the region of 135-140mph. There was a silence for a few miles and then we came to a magnificent long straight, whereupon Michael changed down and floored the accelerator! That great saloon really did gather itself up and get going, and the fact that the driver's head had sunk into his shoulders and little horns had appeared in front of his ears suggested to Alan and me that we were about to find out what the maximum speed of a Jaguar was.

The speed crept up relentlessly, and the road seemed to be getting narrower; 110mph came up, then 115, then 120, and I looked at Michael, who had his eyes rivetted to the road a long way ahead. I vaguely recall seeing the speedometer needle registering 132mph, but then I am not sure where I was looking. It seemed to go on forever, and I just hoped that no car would come the other way, for the Jaguar seemed to be filling the width of the road.

Eventually Michael lifted off and we dropped down to 60-70mph. "What was the highest reading we got on the speedo?", demanded Michael. "I have no idea", I replied, adding: "I had my eyes shut." Our 'tester' was furious. "I couldn't look at the instruments, I was far too busy", he said.

Then he turned to Alan, sitting benignly in the luxurious rear compartment, and said: "Alan, did you see what speed we reached?" "No", came the voice from the back, "I was counting my beads".

Serious road-testing is a very challenging business.

13

THE DAY THE POPE CAME

Down this street?

As I wrote this column in 1990 a lot of people were getting ready to 'do the Mille Miglia' and have a lot of fun and excitement. Afterwards, tales were to be told of fantastic 100mph dices in Alfa Romeos, Jaguars, Aston Martins, even Maseratis, going flat-out for 80 or 100 miles. When I listen to tales like this I can't help thinking that in the original open-road event it was a 1,000-mile RACE, not a time-trial.

When you left Brescia it was 1,000 miles, or 1,600 kilometres, without let-up apart from refuelling stops, providing your car would stand it. Stirling Moss and yours truly were lucky; our Mercedes-Benz 300SLR was 100 per cent reliable and we were able to cover the 1,000 miles in 10hr 7min 48sec to win the 1955 event at an average of 97.96mph.

Stirling had driven flat-out all day, leaving at 7.22am and getting back to Brescia a few seconds before 5.30 in the afternoon. A full day's motoring by any standards, but equally heroic were all those drivers who won their class, for they also drove flat-out all day. In the 2-litre sports class Francesco Giardini drove the whole way on his own in an A6G Maserati to win the class and finish fourth overall. He took 11hr 15min 32sec. In 11th place overall was our own George Abecassis, who drove alone in an Austin-Healey for 12hr 21min 43sec.

That year, 279 cars finished within the 24 hours allowed to qualify for a Franco Mazzotti Cup, and the last man was Marzani in a tuned Fiat 1100 saloon. He won an identical cup to the ones Stirling and I had won for finishing first overall. The Mille Miglia was basically a simple affair in which you merely had to start and finish at Brescia. If you finished within 24 hours you won a cup and membership of the Club Mille Miglia; if you did not finish you got neither. Naturally, there were enormous fringe benefits, with prizes for class wins, class leadership at various towns throughout the day, and so on. The dice of the day must surely have been that of a driver named Cipolla, who drove an ISO Isetta bubblecar on his own for 20hr 8min 0sec, finishing 267th at an average speed of 49.28mph. He must have really been flat-out.

In 1975, my friend Alan Henry and I decided it would be fun to do a retro-run over the 1955 Mille Miglia route, and I took along my roll of pace-notes to make sure we did not get lost. On the mountainous run north through Siena to Florence and on to Bologna we went through one village in the mountains where the street was cobbled and only just wide enough for our big touring Mercedes-Benz, though in truth a couple of Fiat 500s could squeeze past each other. Alan had never been around Italy before and had only read about the Mille Miglia. "Hold on," he said, "are you telling me that the race came down this street?" I insisted that it did, for I remember the shattering noise the 300SLR made with its side exhausts blasting against the walls of the houses. "How fast were you going through here?" – "about 130mph..." – "I don't believe it, you're having me on," he said. We had come to a stop just before the narrowest part and I could see he thought I was romancing. Then I noticed an elderly lady approaching, so I lowered the window and in my best Italian I said: "Excuse me, madam, have you lived here long?" "All my life," she said, so I went on: "You will no doubt remember the days when racing cars used to come through your village in the famous Mille Miglia motor race?"

"Oh yes, of course," she said, "every year the racing cars used to come..."

"And they came down this street, going in that direction?"

"Of course, it's the only way through the village, there is no other road."

"They must have been exciting days for you, living here?"

"Oh, they came every year, but did you hear about the day the Pope came? Now that was a day to remember."

She then proceeded to recount in great detail the wonderful day when the Pope visited their village. "He came right down the actual street where we are. That was a day to remember. He came without any warning, and the whole village was simply going about its business, when he came. And he blessed everyone and spoke to many people. That was a day to remember."

I tried my best to explain that I remembered passing through her village 20 years before, when "*Stirleeny Moss, il corridore inglesi ha vinto il Mille Miglia*," but she merely said: "Oh yes, the racing drivers came every year. But you should have been here the day the Pope came, there never has been such a day."

As we drove on down the cobbled street at a circumspect 15mph between the houses and front doors that opened out directly onto the street, Alan was looking very bewildered and was murmuring "130mph!" He then said: "But supposing someone had stepped out of their front door?" I said: "They would have got the chop, and we would probably have wrecked a perfectly good Mercedes-Benz 300SLR."

"Yes, but..." he said. I told him that if 'buts' came into your thoughts you didn't do the Mille Miglia, it was a MOTOR RACE, not a 'jolly' or 'picnic parade'.

As we left the village and carried on along the route, I laughed and said: "...but we should have been there the day the Pope came". Alan still looked a little disbelieving, but said: "I bet the Pope didn't do 130mph through that narrow street".

14

THE NEW SILVERSTONE

End of an era

For nostalgic readers, and those who do not realize that racing cars have their engines at the back, I must point out that I am writing here not about an ERA, but about an era, a period, or a passage of time. The era in question is the 42 years of the use of Silverstone's airfield as a racing circuit, up to the point in 1990 when racing on the Grand Prix circuit round the perimeter of Silverstone's fields came to an end and work started to transform the old layout into a very interesting and exciting new one.

The first Grand Prix circuit to be laid out on the disused airfield was rather complex and 'fiddly', and someone looked at it and decided that this was not real motor racing, so it was completely rethought to produce a fast and challenging layout, rather than a lot of stop-and-go, and thus the real essence of Silverstone was established. Motor racing should be fast and exacting, and to this day the Silverstone circuit has been precisely that, with speed and high-speed corners providing the essence of the circuit.

For 40 years there had been an ongoing battle between racing drivers and the circuit, and the drivers had continually come out on top. The whole essence of a racing driver is surely to strive to go faster than anyone has gone before under given conditions. Nobody has ever set a lap record and stood back completely contented, though there may be a moment of intense satisfaction at setting a new record, but the urge is always there to do better; if that urge is not there then I don't reckon you are a proper racing driver, and it has been like that since motor racing began. It was there in the human being long before the motor vehicle was invented, and there are some wonderful tales of skill and bravery about men with the competitive spirit taking a coach-and-four flat-out down a hill or round a dicey corner.

From the circuit owners' and race promoters' points of view this is the whole essence of racing, but a modicum of caution has to be introduced if you are using this to entertain a paying public. If motor racing was purely a research and development project, carried out in private, then you could let your racing driver reach out for the unattainable until he either reaches his objective or destroys himself in the attempt. But when motor racing is a spectacle for the public to enjoy, you must take certain precautions, and it is these considerations that have evolved at Silverstone over more than 40 years. This long and continual battle between the racing driver and the circuit owners has seen Silverstone change from a disused airfield to a circuit that brings forth few complaints from anyone involved in motor racing, especially at the Grand Prix or Formula One pinnacle.

On what is basically the same circuit, we have seen lap speeds climb from 90mph to 160mph, and this impressive increase in speed and performance has gradually changed Silverstone from a circuit with 'long straights' to one with 'no straights at all'. Yet the basic layout has not changed, but it does emphasize the change in all-out performance of the Grand Prix car in 40 years. Hangar Straight has not changed in length, but it is no longer the

The new series of curves at Becketts was an inspired piece of circuit modification, replacing the tight right-hander which had upset the rhythm of an otherwise fast circuit with a really testing challenge for top drivers – something that has become all too rare these days.

straight where you could relax and perhaps look at the instruments. On a 160mph lap, by the time the g-forces have diminished after Chapel Curve they are beginning again as you line up for Stowe Corner.

Over the years the circuit 'responsibles' have been forced to make small alterations, particularly at the popular Woodcote area, because they have become conscious of the fact that the spectator in the grandstand does not really want a racing car in his lap if something goes wrong, but he still wants to be close enough to the action to really 'experience' the speed and excitement.

This development at the circuit has been continuous and not always popular with some people, but the overall controlling body of motor racing has always had to keep a fairly firm eye on things. Things like Armco barriers, earth

48

banks, run-off areas, wire-netting debris fences and tyre walls have all been introduced to keep pace with the ever-increasing speeds produced by the racing car designers and their top drivers.

If we had been content to continue racing at an average speed of 85-90mph round the Silverstone circuit, we could have continued with spectators sitting on the grass with a length of rope between them and the cars, and old oil-drums full of concrete could still be used to mark the corners (and we could join a mile-long queue to go to the solitary toilet!), but nobody whose heart is in racing would have been satisfied; we must keep going faster and faster, or else what is the point of it all?

The world governing body of motor racing, the FIA, change the rules to try and keep things under control, but still we go faster and faster, so every now and then they come up with rules to curb speeds, some of them reasonable, some of them very peculiar, but everyone has to conform if worldwide motor racing is to survive and not disappear in a storm of confusion that gets stamped out by Government order.

Lap speeds at Silverstone around the 160mph mark stretched the minds of some officials in the International Federation, and behind the scenes there were some 'clucking noises' about things like chicanes where cars were reaching nearly 200mph, but before any of this could gell the BRDC and Silverstone Circuit management took the bull by the horns and decided to remodel the circuit in a fairly drastic fashion, not necessarily to slow it down, but to make it more interesting and officially acceptable and, above all, to maintain the real spirit of Silverstone, which has always been racing of the highest order at high speed. The phrase 'dauntingly fast' is often applied to Formula One cars on fast laps round Silverstone, and with the new layout that phrase is still very apt.

Some circuits have been lucky to be built on land with sharply varying contours, but a circuit that grew up on an airfield has a distinct handicap, so Silverstone Circuits took the plunge and decided to change the contours themselves. As a result, some parts of the circuit are slower than before, such as Stowe Corner, but others are faster, such as Becketts. Holes and valleys created by bulldozers are destined to provide some interesting 'vertical changes of direction', but fast, challenging corners are still the keynote. Anyone who regrets the passing of Stowe Corner should transfer their attention to the replacement for the old slow Becketts Corner; the new layout has some exacting swerves entered at close on 190mph.

Stowe itself, being entirely new, should see a lot of 'experimentation' by drivers before they get it correct, and if anyone does not appreciate the meaning of understeer they will after a few goes at the new Stowe Corner as it curves more and more round to the right, dropping down into the man-made depression as it does so.

Woodcote and Copse were to remain unchanged (for the time being), so those people who never leave the pit and paddock area would not notice any real difference; the cars would still cross the start-line at over 170mph and touch 190mph under the pits-straight bridge, but a whole new and interesting world would await drivers when they got into top gear on the way to Maggotts Curve.

[Little did I know when I prepared this piece in 1990, before the bulldozers got to work to reshape the circuit and the land surrounding it, that the new configuration would have such a short life, and that Silverstone would be the subject of even more fundamental changes within the next four years. But my final words seem equally appropriate today. They were: Silverstone is dead, long live Silverstone.]

15

MONZA

The home of Italian speed

I will not suggest that we compare Monza with Silverstone, even though they are both high-speed Formula One circuits, but whereas Silverstone can host a Grand Prix and a Garden Party at the same time, Monza can only really put on a Grand Prix. The whole layout and ambience of Monza is about speed, noise, excitement and racing, and since I first went there in 1948 it has never lost that ambience, even though it has undergone enormous changes over the years, as any circuit has to if it is going to keep pace with the developments of the Grand Prix car.

I haven't missed an Italian Grand Prix at Monza for more than 40 years, yet I still get a tingle of excitement when I see the road signs indicating the town of MONZA. As I drive alongside the stone wall that encircles the Monza Park in which the circuit is situated the excitement begins to build up. That wall is very old, covered in creeper in places, crumbling here and there, but it was clearly built in the days when it encircled The Royal Park of Monza, long before motor racing was thought of.

If practice or testing for a Grand Prix has begun you can hear the scream of racing engines coming through the trees, and always that sound is of racing engines on full throttle, seemingly continuously, and there is no more

Monza back in Italy's glory days. One of my favourite Formula One cars, the Alfa Romeo Tipo 158, being wheeled to the grid for the 1950 Italian Grand Prix with Giuseppe Farina walking alongside and looking unusually cheerful, as well he might – three hours later he had won the race and become the first World Champion driver.

exciting sound than a Ferrari or a Honda engine on full song.

Even now, after all this time, when I pass through the gates into the *Autodromo Nazionale di Monza* I feel I want to park the car instantly and run to the wire fence, just to see a Grand Prix car going past at its absolute maximum, even though I know it will be going past again, and again. At Monza there is always a feeling that you must not miss a single glorious moment of speed.

The start/finish straight at Monza has always been the most significant part of the circuit, being very wide and very long, with vast grandstands on the outside and the pits and paddock on the inside, so the impression of noise and speed has always been amplified as the cars pass between the two structures. Today, Formula One cars are passing at, as near as makes no odds, 200mph. They appear into view going incredibly fast, and are still going fast as they disappear out of sight, to all intents and purposes lapping at 200mph on a banked oval like Indianapolis. A few years ago the Ferrari of Prost was fastest through the speed-trap at the finishing line at 199.04mph, and it would certainly have gained another 5mph before it passed out of sight. In the 1½-litre-turbocharged days speeds of 212 to 214mph were recorded, and those cars were still accelerating! As I have said, the principal atmosphere of Monza is noise and speed, and it has never failed to excite me.

If you walk around the infield there are a variety of corners to see, from really high-speed ones to comparatively slow ones through the artificial chicanes that have grown up over the years in attempts to control the lap speeds. In spite of these slow wiggles, the fastest lap made in 1991 by Ayrton Senna in the McLaren-Honda V10 during qualifying was 159.951mph, and his race lap record was 150.756mph. Monza has always been about speed.

The Italian Grand Prix has a long and honourable history, starting as it did in 1921 at Brescia and moving to Monza in 1922, where it has stayed ever since, apart from the odd deviation or two. All but five of the Italian Grands Prix have been held at Monza. In 1929 there was no Italian Grand Prix, and in 1937 it was moved to Livorno; the war put stop to the 1939 event and it did not reappear on the calendar until 1947, when it was run in Milan. In 1948 the *Autodromo di Monza* was in the process of being restored after the ravages of war, so the Italian Grand Prix moved to Turin, but in 1949 it returned to the rebuilt Monza. From that date to this the Italian Grand Prix has been held continuously, and apart from 1980, when it went to Imola, the traditional home of the race has been Monza.

To read down the list of winners of the Italian Grand Prix races is to read the history of Grand Prix racing: Bordino, Benoist, Varzi, Nuvolari, Caracciola, Farina, Moss, Clark, Stewart, Peterson, Lauda, Prost, Piquet and Senna. The famous manufacturers and constructors in the list is a Who's Who of the industry: Fiat, Alfa Romeo, Bugatti, Mercedes-Benz, Ferrari, Lotus, Honda, Renault, Porsche and Cosworth.

The first race was won at over 86mph and recent races have been won at close to 150mph, though the highest ever still stands to Peter Gethin in a BRM at 150.7mph in 1971 before the first chicanes appeared.

Monza has always been synonymous with speed, and many commercial enterprises have used the name to promote their products, the most significant being Alfa Romeo and Ferrari, and you cannot imagine an Alfa Romeo *Tipo* Monza not being red. In my collection of 'toys' I have a single-seater sports sidecar made by Watsonian, and it is called MONZA; as it is hauled by a fairly rorty 650cc Triumph it is adequate, but I despaired when I came up behind a caravan that was called MONZA. I just could not believe that any caravan could be of a 'sports' category, let alone a 'supersports' or 'racing sports'!

This sudden outburst of enthusiasm for the *Autodromo Nazionale di Monza* happens once every year, and as I write this I have just got back from the Italian Grand Prix and all that the name MONZA stands for. It won't be quite the same when I get back from Pembrey.

16

AN ACCIDENT

A bent 300SL

It never ceases to surprise me that even after 35 years people still want to hear about that great day in 1955 when Stirling Moss won the 1,000-mile race in Italy (the Mille Miglia) with a sports-racing Mercedes-Benz 300SLR at an average speed of nearly 98mph. Of course, the reason for asking me is that I sat alongside him throughout the 10 hours 7 minutes and 48 seconds that we spent on the roads of Italy between leaving Brescia in the early morning and returning in the late afternoon on Sunday, May 1, having been to Rome and back on the normal everyday roads, with no *autostrada* involved.

However, I rode alongside Stirling for some 12,000 miles while practising for the race, using the prototype SLR, a works 300SL and a 220a saloon, so a

The result of the accident with an army lorry near Forli. Though the truck was scarcely damaged, the 300SL was well and truly bent. But Mercedes team manager Neubauer declined to press charges against the military, much to the disappointment of the local chief of police, who was looking forward to throwing the book at them.

lot happened that has never been written down in detail before – some of it good, some of it bad, with some exciting moments and some dodgy moments.

One such happened on April 1, 1955, exactly one month before the race, when we set off from Brescia at 6.30am in a 'competition' 300SL Gullwing coupe. Across the top of Italy to Padova, then south to Forli, heading for the Adriatic coast, we had averaged 78mph. Leaving Forli we were getting nicely into our stride again when an army lorry turned across in front of us! Although Stirling did everything he could, the right front corner of the 300SL struck a front wheel of the lorry, and after the noise of the impact had subsided, there we were in a very bent Mercedes-Benz. Stirling's first words were: "Are you alright, Denis?" and my reply was: "Yes, but the car isn't."

For a few moments we sat there discussing the situation, for there was no way the Merc was driveable anymore and we were a couple of hundred miles or more from base. The question was, first to contact Herr Neubauer back in

Brescia, and then how were we going to explain another accident a month and a half after we had crashed the 300SLR sports-racer. By this time a large crowd had gathered and we realized they were getting very agitated, trying to get the doors open to get us out, naturally assuming that we were both injured. At that time very few Italians had seen a 300SL Gullwing coupe and they had no idea how to get the doors open. Deciding that first of all we had better find a telephone, then a breakdown truck, we both opened a door and as they rose up and over the roof the crowd leaned back in amazement.

A pleasant young Italian, who clearly knew what a 300SL was and who Stirling Moss was, latched himself on to us, speaking fluent English and offered to be our interpreter, for by this time the police had arrived and the army officer in the lorry and his driver were standing by looking very sheepish and guilty. Arrangements were made to get the wrecked Merc back to the Fiat garage in Forli. A middle-aged dark and swarthy man offered to take us in his Fiat *Topolino*, so Stirling got in the front and I got in the back. The man explained that he owned the Fiat garage and his breakdown truck would deal with the Merc; then he said: "You are practising for the Mille Miglia? I won the Mille Miglia in 1937 with Pintacuda". When I replied: "You are Paride Mambelli?", he smiled and said: "Yes", and drove us quietly back to his garage.

On the telephone Neubauer was wonderful as always; his first concern was that neither of us was hurt, saying: "We can repair a broken car, but we can't repair a broken Moss". Our instructions were to wait at the garage until a mechanic arrived with a 220a saloon, and the transporter would come and pick up the wrecked SL. Also, to avoid any complications, as no injuries or third party were involved, we were to tell the army that if they agreed to repair their lorry, Daimler-Benz would repair the SL and the whole affair could be forgotten.

Our Italian friend was aghast when he heard our instructions, saying: "I cannot tell the army officer that! Their damage will cost them 15,000 lire, yours will cost you 15 million lire; it is crazy". However, we insisted that those were our instructions from our Chief, so almost sobbing with frustration he told the army officer, who immediately perked up, because he was visualizing having to pay for the Merc out of his wages, so he agreed instantly. He shook hands all round and quickly disappeared, and when it was explained to the police they shrugged in amazement and also went away as no civil offence had been committed, nor had any laws been broken.

As we settled down with a coffee and sandwich to wait, our interpreter friend held his head in his hands in total disbelief. All we had broken on the army lorry was a front spring shackle and a wheel, while the SL was almost a write-off, and it had been the fault of the army driver. By now it was late afternoon, and we had a message that the Chief of Police of the Forli district wanted to see us.

Our interpreter took us to the fortress-like building that was the police headquarters, and after being escorted down endless corridors into the very depths of the huge building we were ushered into a vast office, and behind a large desk sat a very imposing gentleman in an immaculate pale blue uniform, with gold epaulets. We were beginning to tremble a bit because we thought we were in for trouble, driving too fast, a racing car on the road, driving without due care and attention, and everything else in the book.

The Chief of Police indicated us to take a seat and we sat there like two schoolboys in front of the headmaster. Putting his elbows on the desk, he placed his fingertips together in a most elegant fashion and said in perfect English: "The Mille Miglia is a wonderful race. I drove it myself three years

54

ago in a small 750cc Stanguellini. Unfortunately it broke down, so I did not finish. But I am proud to say I drove the Mille Miglia. It is a wonderful race." Stirling and I looked at each other and breathed a great sigh, and we then had a long chat with this imposing Chief of Police.

He knew all about the accident, and that the army were going to pay for their lorry damage and Daimler-Benz were going to pay for the 300SL damage. He told us he was very sorry to hear this because it would have been an excellent opportunity for the police to take action against the army. It seemed that this part of Italy had a big military activity and they were always causing traffic accidents, but being the army they were untouchable. But now that they had damaged 'foreign tourists' the police could have taken them to the cleaners. "A pity," said this fine fellow, "we have been waiting for something like this for a long time."

When we finally left he wished us every success in the race, "but behind the Ferraris, of course!".

By this time a Mercedes mechanic had arrived with Stirling's 220a saloon, and by the time we were back in the hotel in Brescia it was 1am on April 2. It had been a long day, and this was only practice! We never met the Chief of Police again, but we both hoped he wasn't too disappointed when we won the race.

17

THE NEW SILVERSTONE (AGAIN)

'Mickey Mouse' or 'Stop and Go'

On August 1, 1990 we all gathered at Silverstone to watch Tom Walkinshaw drive a Track Marshall digger on the infield of the circuit after Abbey Curve and 'turn-the-first-sod' to set in motion the end of the Silverstone airfield perimeter track circuit. To convince us that the BRDC and Silverstone Circuits were serious, Tom then moved the Track Marshall onto the pristine tarmac of the circuit at the exit of Abbey and proceeded to punch a great hole through the tarmac. Someone suggested that Mercedes-Benz had applied for a test-day on August 2, but in fact it was the official signal for work to begin on the building of a new Silverstone circuit on the site of the old one that has been going since 1948.

Exactly five months and nine days later we gathered again, on January 9, 1991, to witness the official opening of the new circuit and to drive round it. During that time over 100,000 tonnes of excavated material had been moved, a new shape had been created, a new surface laid and a New Silverstone had emerged. Indeed, the only part of the old circuit that had not been touched was Woodcote Corner and the pits straight. The circuit had been increased from 2.97 miles to 3.202 miles and lap times were expected to increase by 10-15 seconds, while the average lap speed dropped by 20mph, which meant that it would still be very fast.

Why was all this necessary?, you may ask. About six years earlier, Nelson Piquet was testing a Brabham on the old Grand Prix circuit and you could hear the car the whole way round. Gordon Murray was chief designer for

Brabham at the time, and at one point he had a look of bliss on his face as he quietly said: "He hasn't lifted his foot off the throttle for a whole lap". That was interesting food for thought, and I went away wondering about the idea of converting Silverstone into a Daytona or Talladega-type Super Speedway. If Piquet could take all the existing corners and straights on full-throttle, only losing speed by understeer tyre-scrub, why not go the whole hog and bank all the corners and have a really high-speed circuit? A year or two later Rosberg recorded his memorable qualifying lap at 160mph and I could see my Silverstone Speedway having a lap speed of 200mph.

When someone asked Rosberg how fast he was going down Hangar Straight, he said: "Straight? What straight? On a 160mph lap of Silverstone there are no straights, it's all high-speed curves." This, I thought, put things nicely into perspective. By a steady process of development, the original airfield perimeter track had turned into a Super Speedway. Many of us can still remember the excitement of the first 100mph lap at Silverstone. Today's Formula One cars can average 100mph down the pitlane to the exit [though of course it would now be frowned upon as being excessive and would incur a 'stop-go' penalty].

That Silverstone was a very fast circuit was beginning to penetrate the minds of officialdom in the FIA, and suggestions were being made about slowing it down. To the official mind that means chicanes, as exemplified by Le Mans, and the BRDC could see signs that a chicane would be demanded down Hangar Straight and another at Abbey. Not only would these slow the circuit by artificial means, they would spoil the 'flow' of driving the circuit, which has always been a characteristic of Silverstone.

Once Tom Walkinshaw got at the controls of his digger, Silverstone was 'slowed' by an acceptable amount, the process producing a new and very interesting circuit, both for drivers and spectators.

Woodcote would still be taken flat-out at 170mph, with speed rising to 180mph by the end of the pits, but Copse was to be realigned, having a tighter entry, with an earlier apex, but much faster on the exit. Maggotts would come into view at 180mph, but instead of heralding a left-hand sweep and heavy braking for Becketts, it would become the aiming point for a fast right-hander of the new Becketts, the old Becketts becoming a run-off area. From Maggotts to Chapel there was to be the fast right-hand entry curve, leading into a left-

The realignment of Copse, with the pit exit road making a tighter turn and only joining the main track well beyond the corner and well clear of the racing line.

All roads lead to Woodcote. It used to be a flat-out blind, then came a chicane to slow things up a bit, and when that didn't work there was that sharp left and an even sharper right. Now this was to be cleverly integrated onto the end of the new 'infield' complex which begins with the quick and testing Bridge right-hander towards the bottom of the picture. It has given Silverstone a completely new character.

right S-bend with a fast exit on to Hangar Straight. The entry into Stowe appeared the same, but instead of exiting on the fast straight down to Club, Stowe would now go on and on round to the right and drop down into a dip with a left-hand exit. Anyone who does not understand the term 'understeer' will soon find out on this corner. At a lower level than the old circuit, Vale curved along to a tight left-right to join Club Corner at about its midpoint, with a very fast exit and the fast run up to Abbey, which itself was for the time being to remain unchanged.

Anyone taking Abbey fast on the previous line would have been in real trouble. At the exit of Abbey you now needed to be well over on the left to take a flat-out dip under a new entrance road bridge, for as you came up out of this dip the new circuit peeled off right through a 140mph slightly banked corner, taking the circuit across the infield to join the Club Circuit straight, where a double-left took it back towards the old Bridge corner. In a slow car this double-left would be two distinct corners, but fast cars would need to take them as one, apexing on the exit of the second part. Luffield Corner, which heralded the start of Woodcote, would now be approached much faster, so that the run into Woodcote could also be faster. In Formula One qualifying in 1990, the faster cars were recording 170mph across the finish line; the changes were expected to raise this speed to around 175mph, and so it proved.

From the pits, or the grandstands opposite, Silverstone had not really changed, but a walk round the outside of the circuit revealed the enormity of the whole project. All the material moved to create the new circuit was used to build up banks on the outside of the new parts to enable spectators to look down on the action. From the top of the embankment on the outside of Becketts you could see the entry to Maggotts and the whole of the new fast S-bend. Coming out of the new Club Corner you became conscious of the fact that you had to look up to see the top of the embankment.

I didn't think many drivers would find the new Silverstone dull, nor even a 'modified old circuit', and it would keep them very busy, though I could anticipate a few complaints about strained neck muscles. Above all, the circuit still 'flowed', and drivers were still able to set up a rhythm, which has always been a characteristic of Silverstone. There was to be no 'Stop-and-Start' stuff for the BRDC. [PS: By 1994 I was proved wrong.]

18

ROYAL BLUE TO THE SEA

An epic journey

In the mid-1950s the town of Modena was very much the centre of Grand Prix racing, with the Maserati factory as one focal point and the Ferrari customer premises as another. There were numerous 250F Maseratis in private hands, with much coming and going through the customer service department, as well as owners of Maserati sports-racing cars. Among the 250F owners was BRDC member Bruce Halford, who hailed from Devon and had a converted Royal Blue coach as a transporter, the interior being gutted and doors fitted in the rear through which the Maserati could be inserted.

The Royal Blue coach line was famous in the south of England for the regular service they ran on the A30 road from London to Exeter and Plymouth. Anyone running a small saloon, like an Austin 7, knew the Royal Blue coaches well, as the quickest way to the west was to tuck into the slipstream of an Exeter-bound coach and achieve 55mph, or even 60mph across Salisbury Plain. In the coaching world they were very respected vehicles that pulled high axle ratios to enable leisurely high-speed cruising, in contrast to many coaches of the day.

Bruce's full-time mechanic was Tony Robinson, who had served his apprenticeship with Stirling Moss and Alf Francis and was a very resourceful character, able to cope with any country in Europe, any route and frontier, any circuit and any organizer, which was very necessary in those days before FOCA and travel agents. Bruce would collect his starting money and any prize money he had won from the race organizers, thrust a handful to Tony and say: "See you in Naples (or wherever) next week", and return to England to look after his private affairs.

If the Maserati needed any serious work to be done Tony would head off back to Modena, fettle the car in the *Assistenza Cliente* and then travel on to the next race. Occasionally there might be a gap between Formula One races which allowed for the odd day off and some relaxation, and if that coincided with a visit to the Maserati factory it produced some happy times in and around Modena, with the *Hotel Reale* as the centre point where the top floor seemed to be permanently filled with racing people. There seemed to be a standard European arrangement in hotels that the higher you went the cheaper it became!

In those days I was travelling all over Europe in a 356 Porsche, reporting on races, rallies and hill-climbs, and Modena was the centre of my crisscrossing.

This was the view from inside the Royal Blue coach as it made its way over the mountains between Modena and Naples in 1956. Compared with the twists and turns above Bonassola, roads like this must have been child's play for Tony Robinson.

Tony Robinson and I spent many happy times together, and occasionally I put away my notebook and pencil and helped him with the preparation of Bruce's Maserati. There was a continual flow of racing visitors to the *Hotel Reale* and a frequent one at that time was Herbert Mackay-Fraser, an American who had grown up in Brazil where his father was working. Mac was a happy-go-lucky fellow who came to Europe with a 3-litre sports Ferrari to join in some real open-road motor racing, his talent quickly getting him drives with BRM and Lotus. He lived with his wife Marga in a tiny village on the Mediterranean coast between Genoa and La Spezia called Bonassola, on the opposite side of Genoa to all the fashionable places like San Remo, Imperia or Alessio. Mac used to say: "Bonassola has the same sea and the same sand at half the price of the fashionable places".

On one occasion when there was plenty of time to get to the next race Mac left Modena to return home and suggested that Tony and I might like to call in on our way by and spend a day or two by the sea. "If I am not at home I'll be at the bank", said Mac as he got into his Fiat 1100. He wound the window down, grinned at us as he let in the clutch, and said: "The sand bank, by the rocks".

I left the following morning in the Porsche, leaving Tony to follow in the Royal Blue, estimating that he would arrive at about 7pm. The route from Modena was an interesting one up the via Emilia to Parma and then over the Appenines to join the coast road between La Spezia and Genoa, where it ran over the *Passo del Bracco*. Mac's instructions were quite simple: "You will see a signpost saying Bonassola, and that road leads right down into the centre of the village". After a super run over the mountains in the Porsche I joined the coast road and, sure enough, there was the signpost.

Mac had mentioned that Bonassola was about one mile from the main road, but he omitted to mention that it was a 'vertical' mile. The road was actually a gravel track a car-and-a-half wide, with hairpin after hairpin as it literally descended down the face of the cliffs, and I spent about half-an-hour in bottom gear with the brakes on before I arrived in Bonassola, but I must say it was well worth it.

After a leisurely afternoon we lazed about waiting for Tony to ring up and say how he was getting on. Darkness closed in, with no word from Tony, so we decided he must have been delayed in leaving Modena and we went off to a

No mistaking the heritage of Bruce Halford's racing car transporter. Tony Robinson is hard at work during one of his long trans-European journeys, when any passengers on board no doubt would have been ill advised to either tap windows or press bells!

trattoria to have dinner, settling in for a convivial evening and being joined by a couple of Marga's local friends.

It must have been well past 11pm when the door opened and in came Tony, his eyes bulging out on stalks with a look of complete exhaustion on his face. He staggered across to our table, totally incoherent for quite a time, until we plied him with some brandy, when he said: "Christ Almighty! I need another drink and some food".

While this was being arranged he explained how he had come down the cliff-face in the Royal Blue coach, in the dark and all alone, having to make as many as six reversing manoeuvres on some of the hairpin bends. We listened open-mouthed and Mac then said: "Jesus, Tony, you're telling us you came down the cliff path in the Royal Blue? That's impossible, nothing bigger than a Fiat 1100 has ever used that path". A still very shattered Tony said "It's outside". We all rushed out into the street and it was true, there was the Royal Blue parked outside with the 250F Maserati inside and most of the village population gathered round it in disbelief.

We went back into the *trattoria* and all needed some brandy to steady our nerves. Mac explained how he meant for Tony to park at the top and telephone us to come up and collect him, or to walk down, as most of Mac's visitors did. Tony had thought it a bit narrow when he started down the path in the dark and had misgivings at the first hairpin, and by the second one he was totally committed. He had no idea where he was heading as all his headlights showed was a black void of empty space. He lost all count of time or the number of hairpins he negotiated and how often the tail of the Royal Blue was sticking out over the edge as he made his to-and-fro movements to get round the hairpins, or the number of times he had to get out and see how close to the edge the rear wheels were.

After we had filled him up to overflowing and he was feeling no pain, we put him to bed. Before we all retired Mac casually remarked that the only way out of Bonassola was back up the cliff track!

At breakfast next morning a rather ashen Tony joined us as we were discussing the possibilities of hiring some sort of barge or tank landing craft and wondering where we could beach it in order to load the Royal Blue on it.

Tony was looking puzzled so we broke the news to him that the only way out of Bonassola was back up the cliff path. He didn't know whether to break down and weep or laugh hysterically.

It was a lovely sunny day, so after some strong *espresso* I took Tony up the cliff path in the Porsche to see where he had been the night before. He was very quiet as I drove up the cliff face, but at the top he decided there was nothing for it but to have a go, so we descended and made some plans. Some of the hairpins could be taken in one sweep providing nothing was coming down, while others would need three or four reversing manoeuvres. Back in the village Mac rounded up as many friends as he could find and we all stationed ourselves at strategic points on the track, some to wave all clear to help with the reversing, while Marga Frazer volunteered to go up to the main road and use her charm to prevent anyone trying to descend while our operation was in motion.

It all went splendidly, and giving a virtuoso display of driving and judgment, Tony took the Royal Blue up the track, needing full-throttle in first gear most of the way, but she came out onto the main road like a good 'un. When he stopped at the top Tony was giggling almost hysterically and said the climb was more hair-raising than the descent because in the dark he had had no idea what he was doing, but in the daylight..!

If ever you meet Tony at Silverstone, [he is one of the long service Associate Mechanic Members of the BRDC], don't ask him how he enjoyed his visit to Bonassola. All the time it was happening Bruce was blissfully ignorant of the fact that his Royal Blue and 250F were poised on the brink of disaster. If he had been forced to post himself as a non-starter "because the Royal Blue and the Maser are in the 'oggins, having fallen off a cliff path", nobody would have believed him.

19

DON SERGIO

A delightful man

In the centre of the old part of Modena there is a church, naturally a Roman Catholic one, and the resident priest is a small rotund man with steel-rimmed spectacles and a beaming smile. This is Don Sergio Mantovani, who looks after the spiritual needs of a large section of the people of Modena. We all know that Modena is where the 250F Maseratis were made, and where the Scuderia Ferrari was born in 1929, later moving about 10 miles away to the village of Maranello.

I cannot recall exactly when I first met Don Sergio, but I remember where it was; it was in the pit lane at Monza before an Italian Grand Prix in the days when the engines were at the front. Don Sergio was not there preaching about the evils of motor racing on a Sunday, he was there to see the new Maseratis and Ferraris, especially the Ferraris. It would have been during Saturday afternoon practice, and in our brief conversation he would lament that he could not be present for the race, "...but, tomorrow is Sunday and I am needed at the church, more's the pity. But I will listen to the radio...".

Don Sergio was, and still is, a rabid motor racing enthusiast, especially for Grand Prix racing. His knowledge of the cars and people in Grand Prix racing is truly remarkable, and to see him even today, in the pit lane, beaming at Senna or Prost, is a gratifying sight.

He has no need for an official pass, for everyone in Italy knows Don Sergio, and since the Italians 'arranged' things to hold two Grand Prix races every year, one at Imola in springtime and one at Monza in the autumn, Don Sergio never misses the opportunity for a visit; his beaming smile and long black cassock are all the credentials he needs to go anywhere. He cannot visit Grand Prix events in other lands, but he knows all about them, reading all the Italian sporting papers and magazines.

One year he added the 1000kms sports car race to his Monza visits, on the occasion when Mike Spence was to drive Jim Hall's Chaparral-Chevrolet. Just prior to this event Mike Spence had won the non-championship Formula One race at Brands Hatch, the Race of Champions, and on seeing Mike in the pits Don Sergio recognized him from photographs he had seen, and clutched my arm as he said, with great admiration: *"Mike Spence, vincitore della Corsa da Campione, a Brands Hatch?"*, to which I replied that indeed it was he.

Instantly Don Sergio went over and grasped Mike's hand and poured congratulations on him in rapid Italian, not realizing that Mike could speak no Italian at all. As he was looking a bit taken aback by the smiling priest, I joined them and explained to Mike what it was all about. A huge smile spread across his face, and even though he had no idea what Don Sergio was saying, he enjoyed the meeting. Later on he said to me: "I'm glad you came to my help; I thought that the priest was 'bible punching' and trying to convert me!".

When Modena was the centre of European motor racing and I spent a lot of time there, living at the *Hotel Reale*, and later at the *Palace Hotel*, it was a regular thing to meet Don Sergio out in the town, going about his business. He was always happy to stop for a chat, and usually had some interesting snippet of information like "...the new Ferrari engine was running on the test-bed last night". How did he know that, you may wonder? Quite simple, really, because one of the test-bed operators who had been on the night shift had been at early morning Mass at Don Sergio's church on his way home! If you could 'trade' a little piece of information from England, gleaned from the grapevine, about Jim Clark having tested the new Lotus at Snetterton, or something about BRM acquired during a phone call to England, it would make Don Sergio beam with delight as he went on his ecclesiastical way through the streets of Modena.

At one time Bruce McLaren built a Formula One car using an Italian V8 engine and the final assembly was being done in a workshop opposite the *Palace Hotel*, so naturally all the 'resident enthusiasts' of the *Palace* bar trouped across the road when we heard it was about to be started up. While we were gathered around watching the final preparations, who should pass by the open door but Don Sergio. He came in and joined us and I noticed that Bruce and his New Zealand colleagues looked a bit puzzled as the priest came in. The brand new car was painted in virgin white, preparatory to final sponsorship deals and corporate colour schemes, and inside the workshop it made a glorious sound when the engine ran for the first time.

Bruce switched it off with a happy smile on his face, and as the workshop fell silent Don Sergio's voice rang out, in Italian of course, and the McLaren lads had no idea what he was saying and thought they were being admonished for making an unholy noise in the town in the middle of the morning.

In fact, Don Sergio was saying: "How wonderful, a brand new racing car, and

If you had to nominate two people whose names were synonymous with the word Modena, many would choose Enzo Ferrari and Don Sergio Mantovani. My late friend Peter Coltrin took this picture of the two of them chatting to a third party at the municipal Autodrome one day in 1965. Don Sergio's love of motor racing and motor racing people made him a frequent and welcome visitor to the test track whenever there was some activity to be heard and seen.

it speaks for the first time. It is new and in white, but regrettably, I, Don Sergio Mantovani, do not have any Holy Water with me. I could have given it a blessing on its coming to life. What a pity," and he quickly left us and went on his way. When all this was explained to Bruce and his lads, I am not sure they really believed us, but we knew Don Sergio.

Some years ago the BBC made an awful television film about Stirling Moss and yours truly and the Mille Miglia, and someone had obviously heard about the famous priest of Modena. They interpreted him as a rather dull and lugubrious young man who gave us a fatherly talk over a cup of coffee, to the effect that if we believed in the Lord he would look after us on our perilous journey. When Stirling was driving the Maserati what Don Sergio actually said was: "*Dia, Sterleeny, in bocca lupo*", which, loosely translated, says: "Give it all you have, Stirling, put your head in the Wolf's mouth", which is an Italian way of expressing total confidence in someone and wishing them the best of luck. Only the fearless, the brave, the courageous and the master of all would put his head in the mouth of a wolf.

On a slightly sad note, at Don Sergio's church there is a monument to all Italian racing drivers who have lost their lives to the sport we all love, each one with a small plaque in remembrance. One of my boyhood heroes was our own A C Dobson, the ERA driver, and when I heard in 1938 that he had taken his famous white ERA to Modena for the *voiturette* race round the park in the centre of the town, not far from the church, I was most intrigued, for that was really taking an ERA into the lion's den. Naturally, the first time I visited Modena more than 10 years later, I made a point of driving round the park circuit to savour the occasion.

When Arthur Dobson died I explained my personal feelings to Don Sergio about him being one of my boyhood heroes, and asked if he could have a plaque on the monument. Now Arthur's one visit to the Modena circuit was long before Don Sergio's time, but he looked up the occasion in the archives of the Automobile Club of Modena and next time I met him he told me it was done, though he had spelt his name "Arturo Dobson". A truly sporting gesture from a truly sporting priest.

20

THE 1991 BRITISH GRAND PRIX

Landmark or watershed

Silverstone will always be Silverstone, the home of the BRDC and, so far as I am concerned, the home of British motor racing. Similarly, Silverstone has always been a name synonymous with speed, not quite in the way that Monza spells speed, but fast by any standards. In 1991 I explained how a new Silverstone had been built on the well-worn base of the Silverstone we had known since 1948. In an incredibly short period of time the transformation from the old to the new was accomplished in record time and on July 14, 1991 we had a very successful British Grand Prix on the new circuit, thus maintaining the unbroken record of the British Grand Prix that has never missed being a round of the World Championship series since its conception in 1950, a claim that not many countries can make for their major race.

The new circuit proved to be blindingly fast by the standards of normal people, and not slow by the standards of Grand Prix drivers, but more than that it seems to have been immensely enjoyable and satisfying to the drivers in the Grand Prix. There were the inevitable moans from the professional moaners about bumps, safety areas, lack of passing space and so on, but these people would moan if you gave them a million pounds to stop moaning. Come to think of it, some of the moaners do actually get more than a million pounds, but that is supposed to be for being a racing driver!

Anyone who watched the progress of young Bertrand Gachot in the Jordan after he was nudged into a spin at the start will have noticed that he found plenty of places to overtake as he speared his way up from 24th place on lap 1 to eighth on lap 21. My reaction was that I could see what he was doing, but what were all the other drivers that he passed doing? I know Nigel Mansell did a superb job out in front, but for me Gachot was the man of the meeting and, unlike some drives of his that had ended in disaster or a blown-up engine, he finished a well-won sixth behind Mansell, Berger, Prost, Senna and Piquet; most aspiring newcomers would be proud to be behind just one of those famous names.

The great thing about the new Silverstone is that it justified all the planning and thought that had gone into its layout. It is slower than the old circuit as regards lap speeds, but is still very fast and has a lot more challenging corners, and any racing driver worth his salt will rise to a straightforward challenge. It still retains the characteristic 'flow' that Silverstone has always had, but there is a lot more work to do when making a fast lap. I heard no complaints about the circuit being 'mickey-mouse', which is very satisfying because some new circuits and some old ones that have been revamped personify the term. Silverstone has always been a circuit on which a Grand Prix car could be used to the full, and I am pleased to say it still is, even with the fantastic advances that have been made in racing-car technology in recent years.

Nigel Mansell could always be relied upon to put on a show in his Williams, but the roar of the crowd seemed to lift him to an even greater effort at Silverstone. In 1991 there was no stopping him after he had recovered from too much wheelspin at the start and taken the lead from Ayrton Senna's McLaren on the first lap.

Back in the winter before the transformation was complete I voiced the opinion that cars would be crossing the start-line at 175mph, and bear in mind that the line is in the middle of a long, blind right-hand sweep. In qualifying Mansell clocked 172.5mph through the timing beam, and down Hangar Straight he recorded 180.4mph before braking heavily for the previously very fast Stowe Corner and dropping down into the new Vale section. On lap speed I had suggested that, given some practice and learning time, the pole position lap could be at a 145mph average. Mansell's pole-position lap time of 1min 20.939sec was an average of 144.42mph, so I was looking very happy and smug on that Saturday afternoon as I rode away from the paddock on my pedal cycle!

During the two morning 'test-sessions' I took the opportunity to cycle round the outside of the new circuit to view from the various public vantage points, and I found the new Becketts, Club, Abbey and Bridge corners enthralling. At the Becketts entrance, which is effectively the exit of the old Maggotts, you are impressively close to the cars, and the rear view of them taking a right-hander, then a left-hander, another right-hander and the final left-hander, which is actually the old Chapel, before screaming away down Hangar Straight, left me wondering where were the drivers' eyeballs.

Maggotts to Chapel must now surely be at an average of around 160mph, losing speed all through the swerves so as to judge coming out of the last one at the right speed for the blast down to Stowe. I saw quite a number of drivers who had to abort their planned pass through the Becketts swerves because they misjudged their entry speed and were going too fast to get back across the track to line up correctly for the second corner. At the exit it was the same; coming out of the last right-hander of Becketts too fast put them on the wrong line for Chapel and spoilt their run down to Stowe.

At the exit from Club I gained a wonderful impression of the acceleration of the modern Grand Prix car, because once through the tight left-right that is now Club Corner, full power could be used to accelerate out of Club and up to Abbey Curve, and the acceleration of a Formula One car from 100mph to 170mph is something that defies adequate description. I could stand on the top of the high earth banks and look down on all this. I read in one of the weekly 'comics' a letter from a professional moaner complaining about having to stand on 'slag heaps' all afternoon. I can only assume he longs for the 'good old days' when you stood ankle-deep in mud and if you were not in the front row you could see nothing at all.

Finally, the new Bridge Corner just has to be one of the best things to have happened in British motor racing. On the approach to Abbey Curve you can see nothing at all, and as you breast the brow you can see the new low-level access bridge, but you cannot see where the road has gone. It is not until you are diving into the underpass that you can actually see the entrance to the climbing right-hand 140mph corner, and by that time you are totally committed and should be knowing not only where you are going, but at what speed and from which side of the road. A true racing driver's dream corner, and I don't mean a nightmare.

There was much pressroom talk about drivers who could take the part from Abbey Curve, through Bridge without lifting off. While I was watching at the entry I was very conscious of bright orange glowing carbon-fibre brake discs, and sheets of flame from the exhausts of the front runners as rich mixture from the overrun burnt as the cars powered out of the dip under the bridge. From the outside of the exit to the new Bridge Corner it was fascinating because you could hear the cars coming, but you could not see them, and suddenly there they were in the dip and powering up and around to the right. It was impressive.

Personally, and I know I am not alone, I thought the new Silverstone circuit was a huge success, and it is a pity that we can only see it in use by the world's fastest Grand Prix cars once a year. We deserve more. Couldn't we revive the Dutch Grand Prix at Silverstone, or create the Milton Keynes GP or something?

It was interesting to see that the circuit lap speed table in the first programme after the changes only went down to 1min 20.0sec – 146.11mph. That, of course, was soon out of date, and who wants to bet on the first 150mph lap before the end of the century? Silverstone Circuits and the BRDC did a great job in slowing the circuit down to keep 'officialdom' happy.

But the best drives all too often fail to be rewarded with victory. In the 1991 British Grand Prix, the man of the race for me was young Bertrand Gachot, whose Jordan was nudged into a spin at the start and slipped down to 24th place. During the next 20 laps Gachot carved his way through the field into eighth place, which I thought was the most conclusive evidence anyone needed that all this talk about not being able to overtake in Formula One is a load of cobblers. In the end Gachot was rewarded with a World Championship point for finishing sixth, and he thoroughly deserved it.

21

PIGEONS ON MY PORSCHE

An old racer

During my motoring travels around Europe I had many chance encounters, meeting people unexpectedly and getting involved in things on the spur of the moment. One such happening was in 1957 when I was on my way down through Italy, going to Pescara, on the Adriatic coast, for the Grand Prix. Naturally I stopped off in Modena on the way, as one always did in those days when it was the centre of European motor racing, and there I met John Eason-Gibson, later to be the BRDC Secretary. After visiting Maserati and Ferrari, he was planning to go by train to Pescara, where he was meeting some friends who were on a motoring holiday.

I was on my own in my 356 Porsche Coupe so I offered John a lift for the 250-mile journey. A great enthusiast for Italy and Italian people, he suggested that we stopped off for lunch with his old friend Dorino Serafini. Before the war Serafini was racing motorcycles for the Gilera factory, and in my book of 'racing heroes' he had a special place for his lap record of over 100mph on the Clady circuit in Northern Ireland, riding a blown four-cylinder Gilera during the Ulster Grand Prix. After the war he took up car racing, and by 1951 he was the third man in the Ferrari team in the days of the 4.5-litre unblown V12 Ferrari that finally vanquished the all-conquering Alfa Romeo 158/159 team.

By the time of our visit he was retired and living quietly in a small town on the Adriatic coast. He was delighted to see us, and lunch began with a Campari or two, and before we started eating Luigi Villoresi arrived, also on his way to Pescara, so when we finally sat down we were well into a very pleasant afternoon, which finished about 5pm. Suddenly Dorino threw his hands up in horror and exclaimed: "The pigeons, I have forgotten the pigeons". John and I looked at each other and thought: "Oh no! We couldn't eat any more", but Dorino was saying: "They have to get to the railway station". Now I know we had partaken of the juice of the grape fairly adequately, but pigeons on a train was a bit baffling.

Serafini explained that these pigeons were no ordinary birds, they were purebred racing pigeons bred by him as a hobby since he gave up motor racing. His number-one team were entered for a championship event starting in Trieste, and when we had arrived in the morning he had been in the process of packing his team of birds into a special wooden crate for travelling by train. Due to the pleasure of our company he had forgotten to finish labelling the crate and telephoning the local carrier to come and collect the precious birds and take them to the railway station.

By now the carrier had finished work and gone home, so we helped Dorino offer-up the very large crate of burbling birds to his Fiat 500, but by no stretch of imagination would it go in. Villoresi had a Fiat 1100, but that wasn't big enough either, and there was no point in even looking at the Porsche 356 Coupe. The situation was getting serious, so Serafini telephoned around the village to various friends, but to no avail; nobody had a vehicle big enough to take the crate, and all commercial vehicles were either out on a job or the owner had gone home.

Suddenly we had a brilliant idea. My Porsche had a sliding sun roof. If we

"Molto veloce!"

By the time the war in 1939 had put a stop to racing, **Dorino Serafini** had made quite a name for himself in motorcycle racing and was a member of the Gilera factory team, riding the very powerful 500cc Rondine four-cylinder supercharged machine. He had left his mark on the British Isles when he rode in the Ulster Grand Prix on the Clady circuit in Northern Ireland. His record lap there was at over 100mph, and it was the first time that any road circuit in Europe had been lapped at over three-figures by a motorcycle.

During the afternoon recounted in the accompanying story, I talked to him about that record lap and told him of the story I had read many years earlier by Freddie Frith, the Norton works rider. Frith's 500cc Norton would reach 116mph on the seven-mile Clady straight with the rider flat on the tank, knees, elbows and toes all tucked in and head right down. That was the real terminal velocity of a works Norton. Freddie recalled how Serafini had drawn up alongside on the supercharged Gilera, without even having his head down behind the wire-mesh fly-screen ("almost touring," as Freddie put it!). Then Dorino looked across at him, grinned broadly, wound the throttle open and disappeared up ahead.

I asked him if the Gilera really was that fast. He chuckled, gave me a broad grin and said: "Oh yes," and with an expansive gesture with his right hand clenched, as if round a twist-grip, he wound his wrist back, as if opening the throttles, and said: *"Multo veloce!"*.

After the war he turned to car racing, driving both sports cars and racing cars, and eventually he joined the Ferrari team when they were running their 4½-litre Formula One cars. Like so many Italians, he loved racing on open-road events, and in 1949 he drove a High-Speed Frazer Nash in the Tour of Sicily and was leading the 2-litre class with it until he hit a kerb and damaged the steering.

Dorino Serafini (left) photographed outside the Frazer Nash factory early in 1949 when he came to negotiate his entry in the Tour of Sicily. His friend Count 'Johnny' Lurani (right) acted as interpreter and they were accompanied by John Eason-Gibson and his son Neil, who followed his father into a career of motor sport administration.

put the crate across the roof opening it would sit fairly level and an arm out of the window could reach up to the ends of the crate. A third person sitting in the space behind the seats could reach up through the roof opening and steady the crate fore and aft, so putting Dorino in behind the Porsche front seats, no mean feat for he was a big healthy Italian, John and I carefully lifted the crate onto the Porsche roof, leaving Dorino to steady it while we got in the front seats. By this time Luigi Villoresi had seen enough and set off for Pescara in his Fiat 1100.

Steering and changing gear with one hand, I had my other arm out of the window holding on to my end of the crate, and in the passenger seat John had an arm out of his window holding his end of the crate. With Dorino reaching up behind us, steadying his precious cargo and soothing the birds' shattered nerves with 'pigeon talk', I drove carefully along in first gear, avoiding using the accelerator or the brakes, for if the crate had slid backwards it would have gone down the smooth tail and smashed to pieces on the ground; if it had slid forwards it would have made a mess of the front of the Porsche and probably smashed the windscreen for good measure.

The 'racing team' were safely delivered to the station and loaded on the train for Trieste, and we then delivered Dorino Serafini back to his house.

By the time we left we were running very late and our plan to be in Pescara by mid-afternoon and have a swim in the Adriatic before tea had long since been cancelled. The journey down the Adriatic coast road, long before there was an *autostrada*, was enlivened by a 70 to 80mph dice with an Alfa Romeo Giulietta, and it was 10pm by the time we got to our hotel. We had supper and soon went to bed, totally exhausted having 'just stopped off for lunch with an old racing driver friend'. At 1.30am all hell broke loose as a monumental firework display started out on the beach in front of the hotel; it was All Saints weekend and a national holiday, but that is another story.

22

THE TARGA FLORIO

Never a dull moment

I must have gone to the Targa Florio 10 or 12 times, the drive to Sicily always being a highlight in my year's motoring, and some of those journeys in Porsche 356, Jaguar E-Types and other cars will keep this column going for a long time. But this time I want to talk about the Targa Florio itself, or at least some of my own activities at that fantastic race round the Sicilian mountains.

The great joy for a spectator, or journalist, was that the circuit comprised the normal everyday roads so that you could always drive a lap of the 44-mile circuit in your own car, or go with someone else in their car. More exciting was the fact that there was no limitation on the competitors using the roads with their racing cars, though the roads were open to the public and you had to obey the normal rules of the road, more or less. There were no traffic lights, traffic bollards, one-way streets, pedestrian crossings, unmarked police cars, speed limits or any other hinderance to fast motoring. All you had to be sure of was not hitting someone coming the other way, but the general

It was a long drive to Sicily before the autostrada was extended to the toe of Italy, but it was a lot harder work in a transporter. This is Ferrari's travel-stained Fiat-Bartoletti at Cefalu with three of the team's battle-scarred cars from the 1960 Targa Florio already on board and ready for the long haul home.

notion was that anyone going the 'wrong' way round the circuit was a fool and deserved to be hit!

Almost as soon as you arrived in Sicily you checked into your hotel, dropped your luggage off and set off for a quick lap of the circuit. During that initial hour you could be sure of being overtaken by a raucous Alfa Romeo Giulietta, an Abarth or a 250GT Ferrari, and if a works Ferrari sports-prototype or a factory Porsche went by on full-song, it made your day. It was Targa Florio time and '*Il primavera di Sicilia*', with flowers and trees in full bloom, a most satisfying time if you had just left an English winter behind.

Whichever hotel you were staying in you could guarantee there would be some competitors there and there was always a chance of cadging a ride round the circuit in something interesting or with a leading driver. Most drivers seemed pleased to have a maniac accompany them on the 44-mile lap because if they had an accident or the car broke down you could be stranded out in the mountains for a long time, and it was nice to know you had someone to talk to. There were no radios or 'in car' telephones, or searching helicopters in those days.

One memorable trip round the circuit was with Graham Hill. He was just about to set off on a couple of unofficial practice laps in a Porsche 2-litre Carrera 356 production model which the Porsche team had with them as a practice 'hack' when I came out of the hotel where we were all staying. Seeing he was on his own I nipped across and said: "Can I come with you?". Graham looked at me and said: "Of course, but I'm not going to hang about, you know". I replied: "Good, I would not come with you if I thought you were going to drive like an old woman". I think I detected an evil smile under that famous moustache!

For the first time in my life I used a seat belt; they were not mandatory in those days, but Porsche fitted them as standard anyway. The reason for 'belting up' was not a question of safety in case of an accident, because the thought of Graham Hill having an accident never troubled my mind. The reason was that the Porsche Coupe had normal seats rather than close-fitting racing seats, and by strapping myself in I could be sure of not rolling about on the seat and disturbing the driver or getting in his way when he was working hard through all the corners.

The 2-litre Carrera Porsche Coupe was one of the ultimate GT cars of the time, born and bred for use in events like the Targa Florio and the ideal 'practice hack', so I need hardly bother to try to explain what a couple of laps of the Targa Florio circuit with Graham Hill was like. I find there are two reactions from my friends and colleagues about such trips; one lot say: "You must be mad" and the others say: "I'd give my right arm to take your place".

Every year there was the possibility of a ride round the Targa Florio with one of the competitors, either in a practice car, such as the 300SL Gullwing Mercedes-Benz with Stirling Moss, when he was practising for the race in 1955 with the SLR sports-racer, or with a private owner making his first visit and needing help and direction to make his way round on a reconnaisance lap in his transporter.

A lap with Phil Hill in the coupe Chaparral, with the big air brake across the roof, was really interesting. The 'grunt' from the big Chevrolet V8 was incredible and Phil could throw that large car through the corners as if it was a little Porsche. The Chaparral team were garaged in the village of Cerda, where the circuit used the main street (indeed, the only street) through the centre of the village. When we returned we stopped outside the garage and sat in the car discussing its technicalities.

It was a very advanced car in so many respects, constructionally, suspension-wise, handling, aerodynamically, automatic transmission, you name it and Jim Hall had thought about it. The big aerofoil across the roof did two important things: it generated down-force to improve tyre adhesion, in the days when few people had ever heard the expression 'down-force', and it could be raised to the near-vertical to become a very effective airbrake.

This aerofoil was mounted on two structural pillars on which it pivoted, and its movement was controlled by a mechanical linkage operated by a pedal by the driver's left foot. With the two-speed automatic transmission on the Chaparral the driver had his left foot as a spare. A sensitive driver like Phil

The Chaparral 2F in which Phil Hill and I scared off the inquisitive natives while we were parked and chatting in the car having done a practice lap before the 1967 Targa Florio. A quick dab on the pedal for operating the airbrake sent them scurrying off in all directions. A puncture put the car out of the race, but there was no holding it when Hill and Mike Spence won the BOAC 500 at Brands Hatch.

Hill could operate the 'wing' from horizontal to vertical to suit a number of conditions, enabling him to effectively balance the car through fast bends by a combination of throttle opening and aerodynamic drag and down-force.

Round the wild and woolly Targa Florio circuit it was used mainly as a pure airbrake, but it was a fantastic crowd-puller and had the Sicilians in a perpetual state of awe. To see a blood red Ferrari racer going through the mountains was one thing, but this futuristic white car was something else, and some of them actually saw it move its great 'wing', and you can just imagine the stories being recounted in the bars and cafes in the evenings.

While sitting in the car chatting we became aware that it was getting dark outside, not from natural causes but because a large crowd of brown Sicilians had surrounded the car and were getting braver and closer. They had found the big white 'bird car' at rest, looking all 'peace-and-quiet', and as they cautiously approached it did not get agitated and attack them, so they came even closer, peering in at the occupants of the strange machine with wide, inquiring eyes.

After a time some of the braver ones began to touch the Chaparral, not knowing quite what to expect. Phil and I sat fascinated and watched them get braver, and when it got to the point of us not being able to see out anymore, Phil gave a quick prod on the 'wing' pedal. Without a sound the great white wing above the roof gave a huge flap and in two seconds flat the whole area was deserted. If you know Sicilians you will know how quickly they can move, and when the Chaparral flapped its wing they were gone. With a deep grumbly, rumble the big white bird trundled off to its 'nest', with Phil and I roaring with laughter.

There was never a dull moment at the Targa Florio.

23

A BLIND ALLEY

A glimpse of what might have been

In my Grand Prix files I have a lot of material covering all aspects of Grand Prix and Formula One racing from the first French Grand Prix in 1906, which started it all, to the most recent Formula One event, and from early Fiat, Panhard and Mercedes to this year's Jordan-Peugeot. One section is devoted to Grand Prix or Formula One cars that were unorthodox rather than successful – though some were both – but the important factor for this file is that they fascinated me by their conception and audacity of design.

One of my favourites is the Lotus 56B, of which only one example was made, and it raced in a purely experimental manner as a probe for what might be coming. After the Granatelli brothers showed the potential of a turbine-powered racing car for use on the Indianapolis Speedway, they co-operated with Colin Chapman to produce the Lotus 56 specifically for Indianapolis. The gas-turbine unit came from Pratt & Whitney for the Indy project, and when Colin decided to build a Formula One version of the car, to be designated the Lotus 56B, the Canadian engine firm provided all the help they could.

The first obstacle to be overcome was to modify the engine so that it

Emerson Fittipaldi studying the unfamiliar dials on the Lotus 56B's instrument panel. Exhaust gases from the Pratt & Whitney turbine emerged vertically through this large-diameter 'funnel' immediately behind the cockpit.

complied with the Formula One rules, which at the time were restricted to cars with 3-litre capacity piston engines, normally aspirated. The FIA technical commission drew up 'equivilancy rules' to equate the gas-turbine with a piston engine, effectively putting a limit on the air entry to the gas generator. Pratt & Whitney made the necessary modifications to their STN 6/76 engine and looked after all the engine work, actually retaining ownership of the engine under the deal done with Lotus.

The chassis was virtually the same as the Lotus 56 Indycar, with double-wishbone suspension on all four corners of the 'bathtub' monocoque chassis. The driver was mounted well forward, with the gas-turbine unit behind him, which had the gas generator in the rear half of the unit and the power turbine in the front half, the unit being known as a 'two-shaft' because the gas generator and the power turbine were not connected mechanically. From the power turbine the drive was stepped sideways, and shafts running fore and aft down one side of the car took the drive to front and rear axles, providing four-wheel drive.

Ducts on each side of the cockpit fed air into the gas generator, and the spent gases left the power turbine by way of a 'chimney' behind the cockpit. The sides of the chassis tub contained tanks for the kerosene fuel, and because it was a very thirsty unit some 75 gallons were necessary to cover a Grand Prix distance.

These were the days of Team Lotus being sponsored by Gold Leaf cigarettes, with the cars painted red, white and gold, and early in 1971 the 56B was shown to the press and media at a gathering at the *Royal Lancaster Hotel* in London. Not many people understood the working of a gas-turbine, let alone four-wheel drive, and most of the media men called it a Jet Car, which was totally inaccurate. In the midst of the ballyhoo that we used to have to suffer in those 'good old days' of lavish publicity functions, Colin looked across the cockpit at me with a twinkle in his eye and said: "Want to hear it run?"

I hardly needed to reply, and he lent in the cockpit and pressed the electric starter. Of course, the gas generator was not going to actually fire up, but the whirring sound as the generator turbine was wound up to astronomical rpm with a noise few of us had ever heard before was truly intriguing. It was some seconds before the assembled gathering realized this fascinating noise was coming from the Lotus, and before anyone moved Colin switched off and quickly moved away into the assembly.

It was a day or two later that I first heard the Pratt & Whitney gas-turbine running in anger, and I could not drag myself away to listen to boring things like Cosworth DFVs. A whole new world seemed to be opening up, but most people were going around saying it was going to ruin Formula One, there would be no spectacle in a bunch of turbine cars going round a circuit with very little noise, just the woosh of hot gases exhausting skywards.

As so often happens, I formed a very small group of one who was enthusiastic about the Lotus 56B, though needless to say the whole of Team Lotus were as enthusiastic as Colin Chapman, but most of all it was the enthusiasm of Emerson Fittipaldi that impressed me. He was having to learn a whole new technique of driving, let alone of racing, and he loved every minute of this new challenge.

It had only two pedals, a power pedal and a brake pedal, the brake pedal being applied by the left foot. There was no gearbox or gear-lever and no rev-counter, and temperature was all-important and figures in the region of 800 degrees centigrade had to be appreciated by the driver. The actual speed at which a gas-turbine is revolving is of little importance; it is the percentage of its output at which it is working that is important.

With the Pratt & Whitney two-shaft unit there were two percentage gauges, one for the gas generator and one for the power turbine, marked N1 and N2 respectively. Between the two parts of the unit was the annular combustion chamber into which the kerosene was injected, and the fuel/air mixture burnt and expanded into the power turbine. It was the temperature in the combustion chamber that was all-important, and the gauge monitoring this temperature was the ITT (inter-turbine temperature) gauge reading from 0 to 10 (x 100°C) with a danger line at the figure 8.

With the gas generator running and fuel burning in the combustion

While Fittipaldi went back to his Lotus 72 in a vain attempt to reduce Jackie Stewart's points lead in the 1971 World Championship, the 56B was entrusted to Reine Wisell in the British Grand Prix at Silverstone, but a throttle problem reduced it to a crawl before the finish and the Swede was unclassified.

chamber the driver had to keep his foot on the brake pedal to stop the car creeping. It would be reading 0 while N2 would be rising, depending on how much fuel the control pedal was allowing into the combustion chamber, and naturally the ITT gauge would be rising.

Standing in the pits with Colin, I was fascinated as we looked into the cockpit as Emerson prepared to take off. With the N2 gauge rising, so did the ITT gauge, until things reached a point where the brakes did not really want to hold the car back anymore. The moment Emerson let the brakes off with his left foot the N1 gauge began to chase after N2 and the ITT figure eased back a bit and the car just wooshed away with all four wheels driving, no wheelspin and very little noise. As the car came by at the end of that first lap accompanied by a whine and a heat-haze above the exhaust 'chimney' and a rumbling from the tyres, I said to Colin: "We are looking into a new world", to which he replied: "Exciting, isn't it", and he radiated satisfaction.

Once under way the driver kept things 'on the boil' by reading his three important gauges, and at full speed he was getting equal readings of 10 on each gauge, indicating that both parts of the gas-turbine unit were working at 100% efficiency, and with the ITT gauge reading 8 it meant the car was 'Harry Flatters', like pulling maximum rpm in top gear on a conventional racing car.

In that first race, the non-championship Race of Champions, the 56B was forced to retire with suspension trouble, caused by the car continually bottoming on the Brands Hatch dips and bumps due to the unusually heavy fuel load it had to carry.

There was a lot of development work to be done to adapt the turbine car to circuit racing, and to adapt the driving methods to the different situations that did not crop up in speedway racing, and in addition to Emerson Fittipaldi, who gave the 56B its racing debut, Dave Walker and Reine Wisell assisted with the development.

Sadly, Formula One was not really ready for such an innovative Grand Prix car, and trying to win the World Championship with conventional cars took too much of the potential from Team Lotus, and by the end of the year the project was shelved, not because it was a failure, but because the whole project was too complex to be tackled half-heartedly, and Lotus resources were unable to cope.

Colin often used to say: "I wish we could call a truce in Formula One for a year so that we could all catch up on the things we would really like to be doing technically", but then he would grin and say: "I don't suppose it would really help. We would still be working against time when the truce ended, wouldn't we?" I had to agree that he was right, for the brain of a genius would never stop.

The only 56B built can be seen in Tom Wheatcroft's Racing Car Collection at Donington Park. The Pratt & Whitney engine is not 'live', so the car will never run again, but it is a fascinating example of what might have been. The penultimate race in which it ran was the 1971 Italian Grand Prix at Monza, and because Team Lotus were in the throes of a legal battle over the Jochen Rindt accident of the year before, and it was deemed prudent for Gold Leaf Team Lotus not to be seen at the 1971 race, the 56B was painted Gold and Black and entered by World Wide Racing, a Lotus subsidary company.

Before returning to England, Emerson also raced the 56B in a non-championship event at Hockenheimring in which he finished second and recorded the fastest lap. The car is still in its Gold and Black livery today.

24

DRIVERS

A remarkable standard for all

Just after winning his first Formula One Grand Prix in 1985, a future World Champion said to me: "Excuse me, I don't know your name, but I see you at all the races and I know you have seen many Formula One races and seen many drivers. What, in your opinion, are the main requirements for a first-class Grand Prix driver?".

Now this is a subject that really interests me, and I have studied it long and hard for over 30 years, my interest being really galvanized in the mid-Fifties when I got to know Stirling Moss and his contempories at very close quarters. I was in the fortunate position of being able to analyze what they did, why they did it and the way they did it, with a very willing master to give me practical demonstrations of what I knew in theory.

I gave Ayrton Senna a list of five or six requirements, all of which you have to be born with; things like eyesight, depth of perception, judgment, anticipation, natural reflexes, and so on, and after each one I was aware that he wasn't looking at me, he was looking through me and self-analyzing each faculty, and by the look on his face I could see that he was not lacking any of the important factors. These factors were not sharply defined, and one could overlap another, and he agreed that if any of the natural faculties were not 100 per cent then it was possible for a neighbouring one that was very strong to make up a slight deficiency.

I told him there was a bonus point that you either had or you had not. If you did not have it, it was of no great importance, and you could not develop it, but if you had it by nature, you were lucky and it would help you along the path to the top.

This was the natural and genuine extrusion of confidence in your own ability that inspired everyone around you, especially your team personnel. It is a slightly intangible thing, but when a driver has it by nature you can see its effect happening on all sides.

When Fangio appeared with a Mercedes-Benz the whole team knew he was going to win. The same with Stirling Moss when he arrived at Maserati. Over the years I have seen a lot of drivers displaying this natural aura without them being aware of it: Jacky Ickx, Niki Lauda, Nelson Piquet, Gilles Villeneuve, to name a few. The important natural faculties must come first, of course, and while talking to Senna I knew he had this bonus point even before he won his first Grand Prix, for prior to the race I was aware that the members of Team Lotus were walking on air, and even though Senna had only just joined the team they were smiling and saying quietly: "We've got a winner". It really is the best thing for team morale and you can see it a mile away.

During that 1985 race Senna had had a big moment on the rain-sodden track, just near the point where I was watching. The Lotus had gone off onto the grass verge with all four wheels, missed the barriers by an inch or two and speared back onto the track and continued down the hill at unabated speed. I mentioned this moment in our conversation and he smiled and said: "They said it was brilliant car-control, but that is bullshit". The "they" he referred to were the people in the pit lane watching the incident on television. He went

The combination of Jim Clark and a Formula One Lotus was usually so dominant that many Grands Prix quickly developed into a battle for second place. Here is the familiar scene, shortly after the start of the 1966 Monaco GP, but this was a circuit where victory would always elude him; on this occasion rear suspension breakage late in the race halted his majestic drive.

on: "I was totally out of control. I lost adhesion on all four tyres and when that happens there is nothing to do. It was pure luck that I did not hit the barriers, and that when there was some grip the car came back on the track. In this game you need a little luck", and he smiled.

I added that it was also important never to give up, even if you are out of control, because then you are ready for the moment when luck helps you. As the car had slid back across the road there was a fleeting moment when there was some grip available, and a brilliant touch on the steering wheel and the accelerator pedal enabled him to catch the car at that moment and carry on racing. Had he not been totally at one with the car, even though it was out of his control, he would have missed that opportunity and slid right across the road and off on the grass on my side of the track.

It all happened in an incredibly short space of time, but it was fascinating to watch, and even more so to discuss and analyze it after the race. For a driver who had just won his first race his calm introspection of a 130mph incident was worth listening to.

Since that time I have had numerous occasions to discuss 'The Racing Driver – What he does and why' with Ayrton Senna and I have never been disappointed with what I have heard. Jimmy Clark was a driver I could listen to with wrapt attention, as was Gilles Villeneuve. Some drivers put me off with their first sentence or first answer, especially if it is an answer to a serious question that doesn't make any sense, or it is obvious that not only are they trying to delude me, but they are deluding themselves. If you cannot be honest with yourself you might as well keep your mouth shut and just look pretty.

There was one occasion when quite a good private-owner had a real 'on' day and was mixing it with the leaders with their works machinery. It was a good bit of inspired racing, but it was unreal, and after 10 or 12 laps this chap began to drop back. He finished out of the points, and then a journalist, complete with tape-recorder, went up to him, seeking a tale of woe and sympathy, and said: "What happened? What went wrong?", expecting to hear complicated stories about tyres 'going off', or the engine starting a misfire, or the gearbox playing up, and he was a bit perplexed when this chap said: "Christ! I couldn't keep that pace up, I was knackered". An honest racer, and one for my book.

Nelson Piquet has always been one of my sort of drivers. When he first appeared in Formula One he drove an Ensign and one was instantly aware that an Ensign had never gone so fast or been so high up on the grid. Shortly after this Piquet was interviewed by a French journalist, who asked: "Do you hope to be World Champion one day?". Piquet looked at him, almost in disbelief, and replied: "Why do you think I am in Formula One?". Over the years he became World Champion three times!

Another driver, whose name I will keep to myself, did little to endear himself to me when, after about three races, I asked him how he was getting on in his new environment, expecting him to say something like "not too bad", or "it's harder than I expected", or "I'm pretty pleased with progress so far". Not a bit of it, all I got was how other drivers were cheating, how they were bending the rules, how certain engines must be illegal, and on and on, all aimed at trying to tell me why he wasn't on pole position. No question about his experience and ability not being as good as those of Senna or Prost or Mansell *et al*. I didn't talk to him much after that opening broadside and, oddly

I never turned down the chance of a drive with a top driver, and they never came better than Jim Clark. Here he is about to show me how he tackles Brands Hatch in a Lotus 40, Colin Chapman's far from successful Group 7 sports car.

enough, he never won a race, or even looked like winning one.

There have been drivers who look at the race winner and say: "To think we used to race wheel-to-wheel in Formula Ford". No sour grapes, no ill-feeling, a sensible acceptance of the situation and a simple statement of fact. These sort of people may not become great drivers, but they are invariably nice people, and even after they have retired from Formula One are always a pleasure to meet and have a chat with.

Jimmy Clark was probably the greatest racing driver of all time, yet in all sincerity he could not really understand why he was so great. Often, in a very serious moment, he would say: "Why don't the others go as fast as me?", and he really meant it.

25

RUNNING REPAIRS

Lancia Aprilia – a good car

In the early days of my European wanderings, covering motor racing events as the reporter for *Motor Sport*, I used a pleasant little 1939 Lancia Aprilia as transport. For its time it was a very advanced little car, with a V4 engine and a lovely four-speed gearbox mounted in a unitary-construction chassis/body unit that now we would call monocoque.

It was a four-door saloon with no centre pillars, and had independent suspension to all four wheels, inboard rear brakes and a very good steering lock. The gear ratios were matched perfectly to the engine torque curve and it really came into its own in mountain country. This was not surprising as the Lancia factory in Turin is within sight of the Swiss, French and Italian Alpine passes. It was not particularly fast, about 80mph downhill with a following wind, but it would cruise at 60-65mph on secondary roads across France or Germany.

In one particular week I had a busy time, being at the Belgian GP on the old circuit that ran to Stavelot and back on the Sunday, on Monday messing about with some film people who were using the Francorchamps circuit for background to a motor racing 'epic' which extended into the Tuesday, and I finally set sail in the Aprilia on Wednesday lunchtime. My objective was Milan, to attend a sports car race the following Sunday, so I allowed myself a comfortable day and a half for the trip.

The run from Spa down to Reims was enjoyable enough, and next morning I set off early to put in a full day of motoring and get to Milan that night. Down the N74, the main road in those days, the Aprilia was humming along nicely and I enjoyed the feeling of running down a good wine list, through Gevrey Chambertain, Nuits St George, Beaune and Meursault, on to the N6 and down through Macon to Lyon.

All was well with the world until I was leaving Lyon, when the Aprilia made an awful noise from underneath. I stopped, and the noise stopped, which instantly ruled out engine trouble, so I got underneath and found that the fabric disc of the front universal joint on the propeller-shaft had disintegrated in a terminal fashion and the two spiders were clanging against each other. I

tied the whole thing up solid with wire and found I could drive gently along in second and third gears, so decided to try and get to Italy where the chances of getting bits for a 15-year-old Italian car would be more likely than in Citroenland.

I struggled painfully along to the foot of the Mont Cenis pass and decided that was enough for one day, especially as the hotel in Lanslebourg was one of my regular 'stopping off' points. The journey from Lyon at low speed, driving carefully and avoiding putting any reverse loads on the wired-up universal joint, hadn't done any harm, so next morning it was a question of 'up and away'.

By looking a long way ahead and reading the road it was possible to keep a pretty constant cruising speed of about 30-35mph, always keeping the engine pulling, even when the brakes had to be applied. The run from Susa to Turin was pretty easy, and once in the middle of the city I pulled into the service road running alongside the main street, where there was unlimited parking.

A closer inspection of my trouble revealed that the cause of the fabric coupling tearing itself to pieces was that one of the engine mountings had broken, letting the engine sag to one side and the U/J to run out of line. I always travelled with a pretty good tool-kit, so it did not take long to jack the front end up onto some blocks of wood and remove the broken engine bearer and the bits of the fabric disc and, armed with these, I made inquiries about a Lancia agency. By sheer luck there was one barely five minutes away and I was soon back at the car with the new parts.

It was not yet midday and the sun was shining, so I set to work at the kerbside; there were no parking restrictions in those far-off happy days of freedom, and I worked away untroubled. In four hours I was mobile once again with a new engine bearer and a new universal joint fabric disc. While I was under the car I changed the flexible exhaust pipe mountings as well, simply because the Lancia shop I had found had some nice new reinforced ones.

Now all the foregoing is not particularly special when you are living on the roads of Europe with an old car, but what was special, and so Italian around midday, was that on a bench on the grass strip between the service road and the main road, an old man had been asleep throughout the whole four hours.

I noticed him asleep on the bench when I first arrived. When I got back from the spares shop he hadn't moved, and throughout the time I was working on the car, occasionally getting out from underneath to do something, he still never moved. I packed the tools away in the Aprilia's boot, washed my hands and took my overalls off, and still there was no movement.

Deciding that an audience of that duration was pretty exceptional, I got my camera out to record the fact, bearing in mind it was in the middle of a bustling city. As the shutter clicked the old man opened one eye, looked at me and then shut it and went back to sleep, and I still have the photo to prove it!

After that it was a simple thing to bowl along the *autostrada* from Turin to Milan at my usual gait of 60-65mph and get to Monza in time for dinner and ready for the Saturday practice. The sports car race was the *Trofeo Supercortemaggiore* (or AGIP, as it is better known today) for sports cars up to 3 litres, over a distance of 1,000 kilometres on the Monza track. It started at 4pm on Sunday and finished at about 10pm, the last hour-and-a-half being run in darkness. It was won by Mike Hawthorn and Umberto Maglioli in a 750 Monza Ferrari, the 3-litre four-cylinder 'thumper' that was good for 7,000rpm. A heroic age!

26

"FAN-TASTIC"

Too good to be allowed

I suppose the first time I realized that Gordon Murray was 'up to something' with the flat-12-cylindered Brabham-Alfa Romeo was when I called in at Silverstone to assist with some midweek testing of an Historic racing car. We were fiddling about in the paddock prior to going out on the circuit when, by chance, I decided to wander round to the front of the pits. There was no sound of activity, so I was surprised to find Gordon Murray and the Brabham test team with a Brabham-Alfa doing some experimental work.

The whole of the rear of the car beneath the rear wing was covered by a fabricated aluminium 'potato-chipper' grille. There was obviously some very detailed research going on with reference to the airflow over the top of the Alfa Romeo engine and out through this grille. When I moved in to have a closer look Gordon gave me a quizzical look of surprise and said: "What brings you here?". I explained I had come to mess about with an old vintage car, and I realized that he would appreciate it if I returned to my purpose and did not ask any questions.

I have always been diplomatic with racing people whom I admire and want to stay on good terms with, and Gordon Murray has always been one of those people, so I discreetly made myself scarce and left the small Brabham group

The Brabham BT46B, with its ingenious extractor fan, was an intriguing development, but when it won the 1978 Swedish Grand Prix it earned the wrath of every driver who had followed it closely and been peppered by dust and debris sucked up from the track and ejected through the fan! The device was promptly banned, but the victory was allowed to stand.

to get on with their business.

Some time later, when the Brabham-Alfa Romeo appeared at the Swedish Grand Prix at Anderstorp with a device on the rear of the car, I was not unduly surprised. This device consisted of a multi-bladed ducted fan, driven by gearing off the back of the gearbox, and was mounted vertically under the rear wing. The official team explanation was that it was to assist the cooling of the flat-12 Alfa Romeo engine. That idea looked plausible because there was a large flat radiator mounted above the engine and the ducting and cowling was such that the extractor fan on the back was going to draw air up through the radiator and expel it out the back.

The important question was where was the air coming from before it was sucked up through the radiator? The answer to that required a closer look underneath the car, but Murray and Bernie Ecclestone discouraged people from trying to insert mirrors under the car, and the Brabham was so low that even the smallest journalist had no hope of seeing underneath it. The other question that really needed answering was the fact that the fan was driven from the gearbox, so while the car was stationary the fan was not rotating, yet the engine did not overheat!

There were two of these intriguing Brabhams in the Anderstorp paddock, one for Niki Lauda and the other for John Watson, and these were the days of virtual free-thinking on ground-effect and under-car airflow experiments, when everyone was trying to gain an aerodynamic advantage and the FIA technical people were not really keeping up with the times.

This device had been accepted by the FIA in pre-race inspection, when it had been considered to be primarily a cooling system for the Alfa Romeo engine. But when Niki Lauda first drove off down the pit lane, interest by the other teams turned to indignation because it was obvious by the way the car sat down on its suspension that the fan was creating a large low-pressure area under the car. The faster the car went the greater the air pressure differential between the area above the car and below it, thus improving the tyre loading and subsequent adhesion, or in simple terms 'improved ground-effect'.

This was in 1978, and we already had rules regarding 'movable aerodynamic devices'; anything that affected the airflow around a car could be adjustable, but while the car was moving it had to be fixed rigidly.

While Lauda and Watson were circulating, the cars looking very stable on the fast swerves of the Swedish circuit, there was heated discussion behind the pits as to whether Gordon Murray's 'cooling fan' was primarily for cooling, with a secondary ground-effect advantage, or was it the other way round? It was quite obvious that the side skirts of the engine bay were sealing nicely, and there just had to be an air-dam across the car, though you could not see it. The whole ducting between radiator and fan was beautifully executed, and when the fan was running the Alfa Romeo engine was in a virtual vacuum.

The Swedish Grand Prix as such seemed to take second place in the pits and paddock, and complaints came in from other drivers that the 'Fan Car' was blowing dust and debris out the back, causing an unacceptable hazard! It reminded me of Le Mans in 1955, when Mercedes-Benz arrived with a huge air-brake across the tail of the SLR sports cars. The Jaguar team complained that when following a Mercedes-Benz when its driver raised its airbrake, their own driver's vision was seriously impeded.

My comment at that time was too simple for most people; it was to the effect that if they were leading the German cars they would have had no such problem! In Sweden I viewed the bleating in the same light; if they were in front of the Brabham there would be no problem!

The outcome of the BT46B, as it was officially known, was that it raced and won, using the fan as primarily a cooling device, though everyone knew its secondary ground-effect purpose was much more effective than the cooling element. The other teams protested Lauda's victory, but the Swedish organizers decided not to adjudicate and referred the whole affair to the Sporting Commission of the FIA. After much investigation and discussion they finally decided that such 'fan devices' would be banned from Formula One racing, but as this decision was made after the Swedish Grand Prix, Niki Lauda's victory with the 'Fan Car' stood. As far as that race was concerned, it was never declared to be illegal, nor was it officially disqualified from the Swedish Grand Prix. It was banned from Formula One after the event.

Gordon Murray and Bernie Ecclestone were pretty philosophical about the whole affair after it was all over, but they were not too enamoured of the way their various 'friends' in Formula One had reacted at the time. It was an interesting experiment and was sailing very close to the letter of the law, but that Swedish Grand Prix victory can never be taken away from the Brabham-Alfa Romeo BT46B.

27

DRIVER SAYINGS

The printable ones

I have a collection of 'off the cuff' remarks by drivers that I have gathered over the years that either make me smile, or at the time I thought 'Good lad'. These are not dull platitudes that are trotted out at press conferences (introduced to European racing from America!), or the specially prepared spiel so beloved of the PR world, nor the official 'corporate words' put into a driver's mouth as soon as a TV camera appears.

My collection are things that drivers have said on the spur of the moment after getting out of a racing car, either in practice or after a race, before he has had time to be got at by the Team Manager, or the sponsor's PR men, or the media. Sometimes they have been said to me personally, and other times they have been a general remark to anyone who happened to be around.

Some years ago, at the height of the 'keep the sponsor happy' campaign led by a man who was winning most of the races, dear old 'Clay' Regazzoni did a super job at the old Nurburgring to win the German Grand Prix. He climbed up onto the winner's rostrum, looked around with a great beam on his face and said: "I dedicate this victory to myself." The press and PR world were aghast, expecting him to dedicate it to Mr Ferrari, or Firestone, or AGIP, or the people at Maranello, or Uncle Tom Cobbley and all.

A driver with an impish sense of humour as far as Formula One press conferences are concerned is Nelson Piquet. After being without a win for quite a long time, he lucked into an unexpected victory. When he appeared before the press, before anyone could say anything he said: "My name is Nelson Piquet, remember me?"

In one race Alan Jones was driving for Frank Williams and in the opening kerfuffle he ran into someone and bent a nose fin down so that it scraped the ground and was pretty ineffective. He drove a good race, seemingly unperturbed by the handling, and afterwards said that from the cockpit you can't see the nose fins anyway and he had no idea one was bent. He said: "Hell, I was racing hard, and when you are racing that hard you haven't got time to worry about handling, you just get stuck in." As he walked away he looked back and grinned and said: "If that had been practice I'd have come straight into the pits and bellyached."

In the early days of Porsche Formula One racing, Dan Gurney was driving the air-cooled flat-eight 1.5-litre and not really making good progress during practice. The Porsche engineers were doing their best to improve things, but Dan was getting a bit irritable. Just before the end of practice he went out and threw caution to the winds in one of those laps you can do once, and probably never again. The time put him in a reasonable place on the starting grid and

The ever-popular Dan Gurney performed wonders with the eight-cylinder Porsche in practice for the 1962 French GP at Rouen, and when congratulated by his team he remarked: 'Yeah, not bad for a Volkswagen'!

the Porsche people were delighted. When he came into the pits they all gathered around, saying: "Well done", "Very good", "Congratulations", and so on. Dan took off his helmet, not looking particularly pleased with himself because he had not enjoyed driving the car at that pace, and said: "Yeah, not bad for a Volkswagen."

Ronnie Peterson was always good for a smile, though most times he was being quite serious and did not really see the funny side of his remarks. When he was doing some testing for Lotus he kept saying that the car had "too much understeer on the fast corner out the back". At the time, Peter Warr was Lotus Team Manager, and at one point he had to drive out through the back gate of the circuit on an errand unconnected with Ronnie's testing. He took the opportunity to stop at the fast corner to see how bad the understeer was. Ronnie went by at a prodigious speed and all the way round the corner the Lotus was in violent oversteer, with the tail about 45 degrees out of line!

When he returned to the pits he said: "Ronnie, I thought you said the car was understeering. I have just seen you go around with monumental oversteer, with the tail hanging out." Ronnie was very serious when he said: "Oh yes, that is the only way I can get round the corner, the understeer is so bad that I have to throw the car sideways before I get to the corner and power through, otherwise I would go straight on."

Jochen Rindt was a pretty outspoken driver, but he had a sense of humour. It was at the time when the German bath-foam product Badedas was all the rage. Practice was very wet and Jochen was driving a Cooper-Maserati that wasn't very good in the dry, let alone in the pouring rain, and it tended to fill its cockpit with water. Rindt came splashing down the pit lane, water everywhere, and his pit crew just knew he was not happy. He stopped, switched off the engine, raised his visor and said in a loud voice in German: "Do you have some Badedas, please?"

When Mario Andretti won his first race with the 'ground-effect' Lotus he came up to the press stand with Colin Chapman, to accompanying applause and congratulations, and said with an open heart: "Jeez, a monkey could have done what I did; congratulate Colin." It was always good to listen to Mario, he has such a simple way of putting things. Talking about different cars and circuits, he says: "If you can drive, you can drive". When a well-known World Champion found Mario running round the outside of him on a corner, he said afterwards: "We don't do that in Formula One." Mario's reply was very simple – it was: "I've got news for you, kid."

Mario Andretti grew up in the hard school of American oval-track Midget racing on loose shale, where discipline is all-important if you are going to survive. He tells how when you do your first dirt-track Midget meeting it is made very clear that if you transgress the racing rules, you have done your last meeting as well.

When the Indianapolis drivers came to Monza back in the 1950s, to race on the newly built banked track, they found European cars with rear-view mirrors. "What are them for?", they inquired. They were politely told that they were for seeing if another driver wanted to overtake. "Hell", said one of the Indy drivers, "if Jimmy Bryan wants to come by he'll stick his front wheel under your elbow; we don't need no mirrors."

One very grizzled old professional in the Indianapolis world used to listen to a sprightly young new driver who was going on a bit, look at him, and say: "That ain't hayseed, that's dandruff', as he brushed imaginary specks off his shoulder.

This year's Formula One flyer, Michael Schumacher, endeared himself to me when he drove his first Formula One car. He came into the pits and the team engineer asked him what he would like to have altered – spring rates, shock absorbers, brake balance, or whatever. "Nothing", he replied, "I have never driven a Formula One car before, so I don't know how a Formula One car should handle. Let me find out first and then you can start altering things." It did not take him long to find out, as we can all see.

Finally, the classic Andy Granatelli remark: "Luck! What's that?", and I think he really meant it.

28

TO THE ARCTIC CIRCLE

Holiday motoring

Recently a colleague lent me a video about the life (and death) of Count Wolfgang von Trips, the young German nobleman who drove for Porsche, Mercedes-Benz and Ferrari in the mid to late Fifties. In this video of contemporary archive film were some scenes of a 300SL Gullwing Mercedes-Benz being driven very fast on loose-surfaced roads in the north of Sweden, with some shots looking back from the car at the enormous dust cloud following.

I realized that they were films that I had taken while on a motoring 'jolly' with von Trips in 1955, some 37 years ago. It is a sobering thought that not many of today's racing drivers were born that long ago, let alone able to go on a journey to the Arctic Circle just for the sheer hell of it, and in a 300SL that had just finished a couple of races.

It all started earlier in 1955 when I met Wolfgang after the famous Mille Miglia, in which he had driven his own 1,300cc Porsche into second place in his class. He had been leading until the throttle cable broke, which he solved by wiring the throttle wide open and driving on the ignition switch for the last 250 miles. My introduction to this likeable, handsome young German Count was through a mutual Porsche-owning friend, for I was driving about Europe in a Porsche 1500 at the time, so we had a lot in common.

By mid-season von Trips had been taken into the Mercedes-Benz sports car team, his drive in the Mille Miglia and events on the Nurburgring with his own Porsche against factory-supported ones having not been missed by the Stuttgart firm. By the middle of August he was being actively 'groomed' by Mercedes-Benz with the loan of a factory-prepared 300SL Coupe for some minor German events, and accompanying the team to important events to soak up the atmosphere. [It sounds as though I am writing about Michael Schumacher, doesn't it!]

The Swedish Grand Prix was run on a circuit near Stockholm and was for sports cars, so Wolfgang went along. Our Porsche-owning enthusiasm meant that we kept in touch during the racing season, and following the race at Kristanstaad some of us went into the middle of Sweden for a small club meeting on the Karlskoga circuit. The Mercedes-Benz team had gone back to Stuttgart, but von Trips stayed on to do a delivery job for the factory.

There had been three racing versions of the production 300SL Coupe at the 1,000-kilometre race and local drivers had then used them for the Karlskoga meeting. Wolfgang's delivery job was to collect one of these cars from the Swedish driver after the race and drive it to the Mercedes-Benz dealer in Stockholm, then fly back to Stuttgart. On the Saturday afternoon after practice, von Trips said: "I have a problem. The Swedish agent tells me his firm is closed for holidays, and he does not want the car until Monday week. He says I can use it for a holiday. Do you know anyone who has a week to spare and would like to come with me?" He did not have to look very far.

I gave my Porsche to a friend, who would take it to Denmark where I would pick it up in 10 days' time, and after the Sunday race at Karlskoga I joined Wolfgang and we drove out of the paddock to go on holiday, the car being just as it finished the race, on racing tyres, numbers on it, hard plugs and nothing in the way of tools or equipment. Happy, carefree days!

We looked at a map of Scandinavia and it did not take us long to come up

Gullwings aloft. We paused to take the left-hand picture of the 300SL because we thought the Swedish scenery at that spot typified so much of our trip. Later on, Wolfgang took a breather as I snapped the Mercedes coupe, with the headlamps still taped from its last race.

with a plan. We would go to the Arctic Circle, motoring right up the centre of Sweden to the last marked town, then head west over the mountains into Norway, and north up the only marked road to cross the Arctic Circle. At that point we got a bit carried away, and looking at the map decided we would go right to the top of Norway, cross over into Finland, run south down Finland, and take a boat across to Stockholm. The fact that we were going to use a race-prepared 300SL Coupe never posed any problems in our minds, nor did we think of telling anyone what we were going to do. So while the rest of the world got on with their business we disappeared 'on holiday'.

It would take forever to recount all the happenings of our week of motoring. Suffice to say we got to Stockholm the following Sunday night, washed the car and delivered it to the Mercedes-Benz agent first thing on Monday morning, having covered about 1,000 miles. Due to a number of unforeseen problems we were unable to carry out our plan to drive right round the top of Sweden and return from Finland by boat, but we did get to the Arctic Circle, and spent a night at the tiny seaport of Bodo, about 200 miles into the Polar Regions, where night lasts from 11.30pm until midnight. During that 30 minutes we drove the 300SL around on sidelights, just to convince ourselves about the lure of the midnight sun. Our whole journey had been done in the most glorious summer weather, Scandinavia being in the throes of an unusual heatwave.

While at Bodo we had a look around the 300SL and were a bit taken aback to find the rear tyres very bald. We had been cruising at nearly 100mph on the dirt roads up through Sweden and had never given a thought about tyres. More important was the fact that our route to the very top of Norway now involved crossing about 25 Fjords, each involving a ferry, and from information gleaned from people in the hotel it was going to take a very long time, more than we had available. There was only one thing to do and that was to return the way we had come to the Arctic Circle-crossing point, and we decided to then continue on south in Norway and cross over into Sweden as

We just had to stop right on the Arctic Circle for a spot of film making and happy snapping of each other, if only to prove to the world that we really had been there with the Gullwing!

far south as we could get.

During our journey north we had made various deviations and asides, and many of these I had filmed with Wolfgang's Bolex cine camera, this being one of his many hobbies. We found the SL was quite happy to be driven at 60 to 70mph with both gullwing doors open, and with all the air vents open it was quite pleasant in the heat.

We were driving stripped to the waist and realized it must have been an unusual sight, so I recorded the fact on film from across a small lake; as Wolfgang drove the car along the lakeside road, it looked very weird when he disappeared behind bushes and shrubbery with just the door in view! On some of the dirt roads in Sweden you could go very fast, for the base of the road was smooth and firm under the dust and gravel. At one point we got up to 110mph, but at that speed the car was beginning to waltz about a bit, so we settled for 90mph as being a comfortable cruising speed.

In those days Sweden was like Great Britain in that their rule of the road was to drive on the left. When we crossed into Norway at a very remote frontier in the mountains we were taken aback to find a notice telling us to drive on the right. The actual demarcation between Sweden and Norway was on a desolate country road, with only the notice board to tell us we had to change side. There were no road markings, buildings, or other traffic, so it was a bit eerie, and while Wolfgang went back into Sweden for a couple of hundred yards and drove towards the frontier line on the left, I filmed him coming towards me and then he swerved sharply from the left of the road across to the right of the road as he passed the notice board.

We had a lot of fun making our own private little films, and at the Arctic Circle, where there was a notice-board to pinpoint the line, Wolfgang play-acted a scene, which I filmed, pretending to arrive at the Arctic Circle on foot, triumphant but totally exhausted. Some of the film we took through the rear window of the 300SL of the dust clouds behind the car at 90-100mph was most impressive.

On our way back south to the Arctic Circle line we had our first setback when the right-rear tyre punctured. We fitted the spare, which was virtually new, and continued on our way, but just as we arrived back at the Arctic Circle line the left-rear tyre punctured, and I filmed Wolfgang astride the line, with the driver's door up and open, and him looking gloomily at the flat tyre. It was still gloriously hot and sunny, so we opened our 'iron rations' box and had a sandwich while we contemplated the fact that we had two punctures, only one spare wheel and no puncture outfit, and we were 'astride' the Arctic Circle. Wolfgang said: "We must do like Sir Henry Birkin with the Bentley at Le Mans, we must take the tyre off and drive on the rim".

This we did and found we had about an inch of clearance on the left-rear corner, and we managed to crawl about 12 miles like this until we found a tin-shed garage and were able to patch the tubes. Going at a much reduced pace, we crept our way south until we reached Norwegian civilization where we bought some new tubes, and the journey across Sweden to Stockholm was comparatively uneventful apart from running into torrential rain, which made driving a bit dicey on our bald tyres.

However, all was well, and the Mercedes-Benz agent was delighted to take delivery of this special Competition version of the 300SL. He assumed we had been to some fashionable Swedish sea resort to lay in the sun for a week. "You have had a nice holiday?", he asked. "Oh yes, very nice, thank you", we said.

29

DID IT REALLY HAPPEN?

The Tyrrell six-wheeler

When 'Uncle' Ken Tyrrell rings you up and says: "Can you come over, I've got something to show you", you don't ask: "What?" or "Why?". One thing about Ken, and I have known him for 40 years, is he has never called a spade a shovel; you know exactly where you stand with him, right or wrong. So one morning in September 1975, having just got back from Monza, I got on my motorcycle and rode over to Ken's house in West Clandon, and after a welcoming cup of coffee he said: "Come out into the garden". Totally unprepared for what to expect, I followed him out on to the lawn and my mouth fell open, and a look of total disbelief came upon my face. Ken roared with laughter as I stood there, speechless, and to this day he still has a chuckle at the memory of 'Jenks speechless'.

There, in the middle of the lawn, stood Project 34; this was the unconventional Tyrrell six-wheeler, designed by Derek Gardner. Taking a normal Cosworth DFV-powered car, with Hewland transmission sticking out the back, it was more-or-less cut in half at the cockpit and a completely new front-end grafted on, the like of which we had never seen before. In place of the normal pair of front wheels were four tiny 10inch wheels shod with special Goodyear racing tyres. Each wheel had its own little disc brake, hub assembly and wishbones and coil-spring suspension unit, and they were in pairs, one behind the other, like a Bedford motor coach chassis. Ahead of the forward pair of front wheels was a typical Gardner full-width nose cowling, but much lower than anything we had seen before.

My first reaction, after recovering from the initial shock, was to say: "Ken, you're having me on", but he assured me he wasn't and went through the design and thinking and construction of this remarkable vehicle. Effectively, there were two front axle layouts, and all four wheels steered, the geometry and linkage to the rack-and-pinion being fascinating to behold.

At this private preview the car had yet to run, and after a good look round it we went to the Tyrrell factory and Derek Gardner explained the theory behind the concept. It was all about control of the front end of a racing car by spreading the rubber 'footprint' to give more adhesion for cornering and braking. Admittedly, there was also the advantage of a lower frontal area, but

When Ken Tyrrell invited me out into his garden, this was the surprise he had waiting for me. For once in my life I was almost speechless!

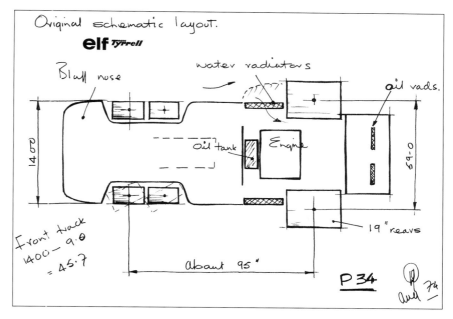

This was Derek Gardner's free-hand schematic layout drawing, dated August 1974, of his P34 concept. A great idea, which was overtaken by events.

this was rather negated by still having the same area presented to the wind at the back of the car, as with a conventional four-wheeler. Gardner was a great believer in penetration, and his small-wheel concept improved this commodity, though I never really understood how it was measured.

As we looked at various components of the P34's front end I began to think that Ken Tyrrell was going into the model car business, but the following week, when a huge press 'junket' was laid on at the *Heathrow Hotel*, I began to realize it was serious.

The design and construction of this prototype had been kept remarkably secret, there not having been a word through the normal 'grapevine', and ELF had given it their full backing. After my personal preview I was asked to maintain a silence until after the unveiling, which I readily agreed to, and I went to the *Heathrow Hotel* with a more than usually blank look on my face. Francois Guiter, of ELF, arranged to bring a group of journalists over from Paris, and when the coach arrived at the terminal to take them to the hotel it turned out to be a twin-front-axle Bedford.

As the French journalists climbed aboard, Francois was beside himself with glee, for nobody had an inkling of what they were going to see, and he said: "I am glad to see that the French press are travelling in a vehicle of the latest concept".

The car was completely covered on the stage, the blue cover being supported at the front to take the shape of a normal four-wheeler. After the introduction and description of the new Tyrrell there was not a suspicion of anything unusual, and the press were standing around impatiently for what they were going to see.

The cover was taken off from the rear first, and when it was finally off the assembled press were as stunned as I had been. The secrecy that had been maintained by everyone concerned was not only impressive but totally effective and successful, which was rare indeed in the world of Formula One. The impact on the racing scene was amazing, and even if the car had never raced ELF were more than satisfied with the publicity that accrued from the initial introduction.

In the first week of October 1975 I was at Silverstone to watch the first running of the car, and the whole project began to take on a serious air of reality. The Tyrrell drivers at the time were Jody Scheckter and Patrick Depailler, and while the former was a bit sceptical about the project, the latter was bubbling with enthusiasm. As Ken said recently: "Patrick just loved cars, not only racing cars, but any sort of car, and he loved the experimental things".

The whole six-wheel experiment had been in the nature of a research vehicle, hence the P34 number rather than one in the Tyrrell Double-O series. If this first prototype car showed promise and it was decided to go ahead with the project, serious team cars would be built. Naturally, the support of Goodyear in making the 10in front tyres was vital to the whole project, but an enormous factor was the very positive and enthusiastic approach of Patrick Depailler, and today Ken is quick to emphasize that the real impetus to race the P34 came from Patrick.

Team Tyrrell raced a pair of six-wheelers during 1976, and Jody Scheckter, as team leader, scored a memorable victory in the Swedish Grand Prix at Anderstorp, with Depailler in second place. This 1-2 by Project 34 made a lot of people look closely at the idea, but no-one actually copied it.

At the end of the season Scheckter departed to join Ferrari, and Ronnie Peterson joined the team for 1977. As always, Ronnie drove his heart out, but victories eluded him, and I never felt that he really grasped the thinking behind Project 34, indeed sometimes I wondered if he was really aware of those four little wheels out ahead of the cockpit! Patrick was still working hard with the team on development, but there were two important areas in which this development was hampered.

Goodyear were at full pressure with their normal race-tyre programme and were finding it difficult to spend enough time on development of the special tiny 10in tyres. Consequently, the six-wheeler was not really keeping up with the latest and best in tyre technology, especially with rubber compounds. The other problem was that the front brakes were having trouble dissipating the heat generated, the tiny discs having to work overtime.

Project 34 with the three people most closely involved with it. Although his Tyrrell team-mate Jody Scheckter was fairly lukewarm about the whole idea, Patrick Depailler's enthusiasm for the six-wheeler did much to encourage Ken Tyrrell and Derek Gardner to press on with the car's development.

Although Scheckter's enthusiasm for the P34 was muted, it fell to him to score the car's only Grand Prix victory – in Sweden. The 'inspection windows' cut into the cockpit surround offered outsiders a rare glimpse of the modern Grand Prix driver at work.

The only solution available was to use thicker discs, but this put the project onto a vicious circle of weight-chasing. Had carbon-fibre been available in those days the P34 may have kept ahead, but as the second season progressed the Tyrrell lost ground and was finally abandoned.

It had been a brave attempt to try something different and it wasn't a failure, because Scheckter won a race and Depailler scored five second places, but it wasn't as successful as had been hoped and it did not lead to any further developments. I never did remember to ask Ken Tyrrell what Project 33 had been, or 32 or 31 for that matter.

30

THE TURBO YEARS

Exciting

I make no secret of the fact that for me the most exciting years of Grand Prix racing were from 1977 to 1988, the exhaust-driven turbocharged era of racing. The first time I saw a turbocharged installation was about 1942, when I was working at the Royal Aircraft Establishment at Farnborough. I was in the engine research department, and the particular section I was in was busying itself with exhaust flame damping – nothing to do with fire-prevention, as you might think, but concerned with flames coming from the open exhausts of aero-engines.

In the daytime this was no particular problem, but when flying in the dark, the bright blue and yellow flames from the stub-pipes of a V12 Merlin engine, for example, lit up everything around the plane. Up in the inky blackness of a

moonless night the flames made the plane a sitting target to anti-aircraft guns and other aircraft. The problem had been fairly well solved for Merlins and Bristol radial engines, but research on the subject was continuous, the findings being passed on to new engines and new aircraft.

Eventually, the Boeing 'Flying Fortress' came into our province, and when the first one arrived at Farnborough I was intrigued when I looked around it, and at the exhaust systems, under the wings, of the four Wright Cyclone radial engines. From the collector ring, instead of a single exhaust pipe squirting out more or less sideways, the big-diameter exhaust pipe ran rearwards to a large circular pancake affair, in which there was a turbine/compressor, and then a short stub-pipe carried on rearwards. It was an exhaust-driven turbocharger.

How it worked and what it did was not really the affair of our section. What we were interested in were the flames coming out of the four exhaust systems and their vulnerability visually in the dark. The first thing to do was to organize some 'ground runs' to weigh up the situation, and being midsummer, with the wartime 'double British summertime', it was after 11pm before we could justify a gathering on the tarmac, and nearer 11.30pm before we ran-up one of the engines (imagine doing that today – the telephones would never stop ringing and police would be on their way!).

At full-power against the chocks and anchor cables the first thing that surprised us was the turbo unit becoming incandescant and glowing like the sun. The amount of flame from the exhaust and the noise being considerably less than we expected, what we didn't expect was when the whole of the engine nacelle dissappeared in a mass of flame!

Everything was instantly shut down and the fire extinguished and it was agreed that the aircraft would be left where it was and we would inspect it in the morning. It was now nearly midnight, and none of the technical staff were on 'overtime', we were just getting on with the job. Next morning we found one of the cylinder heads split in two, right across the centre-line, through the twin sparking plug holes. The ground-crew who were running the engine learnt a lesson about cylinder head temperatures and boost pressures from an over-speeding turbocharger unit.

When the aircraft was repaired we organized some low-flying passes across

The people who helped to change the face of Grand Prix racing. Renault unveiled their prototype turbocharged Formula One car on May 9, 1977, and had to wait a long time for their inspiration to bear fruit with a Grand Prix victory, but they were absolutely right to spot and then exploit the loophole in the F1 regulations.

the airfield, around midnight, to observe the four glowing turbines, even with a 180mph wind blowing across them, and decided that exhaust flame damping wasn't really relevant to the 'Flying Fortress'. Thinking about it all rationally, the relative lack of exhaust flame was obvious, for the gases had dispersed most of their heat while passing through the turbine. Many of our systems designed for normal supercharged engines used a form of flat fishtail in order to dissipate the heat before it came out of the end of the system. The turbocharged layout had its own heat dissipator, but at the cost of a glowing turbine casing.

When Renault introduced the exhaust-driven turbocharger to Grand Prix racing in 1977 I moved in as close as I could, for from that first day with the Boeing B17 I was fascinated by the principle of using the latent power in the exhaust system of an internal combustion engine to supply the pressure for the in-going charge.

Many people thought the Renault had no future, but mostly they were people who did not understand the principle, or had no access to a turbocharged engine. Renault took on a monumental task, starting a whole new era of thinking in Grand Prix racing, and when Ferrari took an active interest in turbocharging the total breakthrough was made. By 1984-85 turbocharging had reached its peak, and from a mere 1,500cc, more than twice the horsepower of the then current 3,000cc engines was being achieved. The turbo/compressor units had started off at a fairly conservative 1.5-bar delivery, but once intercooling and anti-detonation fuels developed, the pressures rose dramatically, to 4bar for racing and a lot higher for qualifying.

Engine design was struggling to keep pace with the possibilities available, and the four-cylinder BMW became known as the 'hand-grenade'; you pulled the pin and it needed a Nelson Piquet to get in one qualifying lap before the explosion came! One engineer once said to me: "Do you want to see our crankshaft?", and he took the engine cover off his car and there was the crank in full view, still in its main bearings. Both sides of the crankcase casting had gone!

This era of almost uncontrollable power kept the tyre companies on their toes, the chassis designers were getting left behind, and the aerodynamicists

When Brabham took on board the BMW M-power turbocharged engine, Nelson Piquet was in his element with the BT52. With the wick turned right up for qualifying, the four-cylinder engine could produce more than 1,300bhp, becoming known as the 'hand grenade' due to its tendency to explode spectacularly as soon as it had reached its sell-by date, which was usually after – and on some occasions during – its first flat-out lap.

were having a joy-day with a surplus of power to utilize downforce ideas. There was very little whinging and whining from the drivers about 'no power'.

From a rather dull era of kit-car racing, in which almost anyone and everyone was building 'bitzas' around a Cosworth DFV engine and Hewland transmission, the Grand Prix world took off technically once Renault had done the groundwork and shown the way forward. Ferrari, BMW, Honda, Porsche-TAG, Alfa Romeo, Ford-Cosworth and Hart were all in it in a most exciting period of engine development and power production.

Unfortunately, the rule makers, who were not really very close to the subject, panicked at the power outputs and strangled development by limiting fuel consumption and compressor outputs, and by 1989 the turbocharged engine was banned. I was fascinated by a remark made by the head man at Honda when he said that it was a pity that the FIA panicked, because Honda were developing two-stage turbochargers and had as their aim 1bhp from 1cc of engine capacity! Since the introduction of the normally aspirated 3,500cc engines there has been a lot of good work done on engine development, but most of them need nearly 5cc to develop 1bhp.

They were heady days, from 1977 to 1988, for anyone who was obsessed with engines and sheer power as I am.

31

SICILY

Love it or hate it

Sicily, that big island at the very end of Italy, you either love it or hate it; I've not met many people who say: "Oh yes, it's alright". Any Italian born north of Naples tends to regard Sicily (or Sicilia, to give it its Italian name) as 'Garibaldi's Dilemma', but that's local prejudice. Me, I love the place. It is more than an island, it is a whole country and not a small piece of land surrounded by sea, like the Isle of Wight or the Isle of Man.

One of the good bits of 'the old days' which are long gone was that each year there were three big motor races that were worth attending. The *Giro di Sicilia*, which ran right round the island, starting and finishing at Palermo, was a 600-mile open road race that acted as a 'warmup' event before the serious 1,000-mile event on the mainland, from Brescia to Brescia via Rome. Then there was the Grand Prix at Syracuse, a very fast event on a triangular road circuit just on the edge of the town, and the famed Targa Florio, on the 44-mile mountain circuit in the Madonie. There were other events, like the 10 hours of Messina, the race round the lake at Enna, and one or two mountain hill-climbs.

I used to limit myself to three trips a year, and in the days before the *autostrada* went beyond Naples it was a good four-day trip from London to Palermo. Even when you had crossed the Straits of Messina it was still half a day's motoring along the coast road to Palermo. The recommended ferryboat crossing was from Reggio Calabria to Messina, which could take nearly an hour, but I used to cross by a similar boat from Villa San Giovanni, north of Reggio, which was a bit of a problem finding the boat in a small dock hidden by railway lines, and was more of a 'commercial' crossing, but took about half the time.

It did present interesting happenings at times like the occasion when we boarded the boat to become aware that it looked brand new, very large and very luxurious. The normal boats would charge out of the small harbour in reverse, do a sort of 'handbrake turn' and be away to Messina, but not this time; it took half an hour to get out of the dock, then it made a slow and stately progress across the water while we enjoyed the luxurious facilities. A chat with the Captain revealed that indeed it was a new boat, though 'ship' would be a more correct description. It was due to go into service on the Brindisi-to-Greece crossing of the Adriatic Sea and was doing a week of 'breaking-in' on the 5-mile Italy-to-Sicily crossing.

Docking at Messina took forever, but before we drove off we asked our friendly *Capitano* what the problem had been with manoeuvring into the berth. "No problem", he smiled, "but if I had marked this beautiful new ship, by bumping other smaller craft, or grazed the side on the quay, I would not have much in the way of prospects in the Italian Mercantile Marine." I bet a year later that impressive ship was bumping and boring its way round the Mediterranean with the best of them.

In planning my journeys to the Sicilian races I used to time things so that I caught a ferryboat at about 8pm and booked into the *Jolly Hotel*, one of a chain of such hotels throughout Italy, owned by the Marzotto family of Mille Miglia fame, on the Messina sea-front. This permitted a comfortable break, with a run to Palermo next morning to arrive in time for a seafood lunch. On one of these evening crossings I had a lady-friend with me, and we were on deck watching the sun go down into the Mediterranean. The Captain arrived quietly at our side and, looking at us and at the wonderful sunset, he said with great sincerity and feeling: "*Molto suggestivo*". We knew exactly what he meant, and agreed wholeheartedly.

On another occasion, while stopping in Messina we saw a very sleek cabin cruiser leaving the dockside. It was red, white and green (naturally) and looked to hold about 15 to 20 people and had a glorious exhaust note, but there was more. It soon got up to speed and then rose up onto two enormous

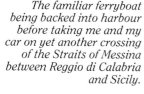

The familiar ferryboat being backed into harbour before taking me and my car on yet another crossing of the Straits of Messina between Reggio di Calabria and Sicily.

skis and planed across the sea with the entire hull out of the water and just the propeller immersed. It was the first time we had seen a hydrofoil. It took 10 minutes each way on the crossing to Reggio Calabria and back, so leaving the Porsche 356 on the dockside, we boarded it for its next trip.

The pilot showed us with some pride the big Mercedes-Benz diesel engine that powered it and explained the hydraulic system that swung the skis outwards once speed was up and raised the hull up out of the water. It crossed the Straights of Messina at 60mph, and when it arrived at Reggio Calabria it lost speed very rapidly and arrived at the keyside settling down like a great duck, burbling quietly up to the landing stage with its skis folded underneath. To us it was quite an experience, but to the rest of the passengers it was just a 'water bus' that they used to go shopping or to go to work. It was named proudly *Freccia d'Oro* (Golden Arrow).

Over the years I used a variety of vehicles for my trips to Sicily, the first being a little Lancia Aprilia saloon. This was to the *Giro di Sicilia*, and when I went to the organizers to see about press plates they thought I wanted to enter the event and could not understand why I had come all the way from England and did not want to race. I had great difficulty stopping them filling in an entry form on the spot and painting a number of the car. I did not understand about Sicilian racing at the time, but looking back a few years later I regretted my foolishness at turning down the chance of driving in the *Giro*.

I suppose it was partly due to my lack of knowledge of the Italian language at the time, but while making big efforts to learn Italian I had a nasty setback on another trip in Sicily. My friend was briefing me about simple things like differing between one cup of coffee and two cups of coffee, and small ones against large ones. We stopped at a wayside bar on the way to Palermo and in my best Italian I said: *"Due cappuccini alto, per favore"* (two coffees with frothy milk, large, if you please). The man behind the bar looked at me without saying anything and then turned his head towards the waiter at the coffee machine and said, in a flat gravelly voice: *"Dos Kaputch"*. I threw my Italian textbook in the sea after that.

For most of the Targa Florio races I attended I used to spectate at a road junction high up in the mountains, where quite a large number of Sicilians used to gather. Every year a chap used to arrive on one of those little three-wheeled Vespa pickup trucks, with civilized saloon coachwork surrounding the rider.

On the truck platform he used to set up shop, selling peanuts. Weighing them out on a pair of hand-held scales was an art only surpassed by watching a similar Sicilian ladle out a scoopful of ice-cream into a wafer cornet. Across the top of this peanut-carrying Vespa windscreen was beautifully painted *"Freccia del Sud"* (Arrow of the South). See what I mean about Sicily? You either love it or hate it.

32

BIMOTORE ALFA ROMEO

A fascinating monster

Since these 'chats' of mine began I have featured various unusual racing cars of recent times, so it would do no harm to look back to the dark ages, when I was an enthusiastic schoolboy, to one of the most audacious racing cars of all time. It is brought to mind by the appearance in 1994 of a complete and running recreation of the original car.

It is the Alfa Romeo *Bimotore* (pronounced Beemotory), and that year Tom Wheatcroft produced the result of something like 14 years of work by most of the skilled specialists in the old-car restoration business, with a total ability to make anything that was once made and is now gone. Among these people nothing seems to be impossible. Their motto must surely be: "If it was made, it can be made again". This remarkable car is in the Donington Park Racing Car Museum for all to see, and the lucky ones have been able to actually see it in action on the track and hopefully will be able to do so many times in the future.

In the 1930s Enzo Ferrari was running a very professional racing team from his premises in Modena, long before Maranello was thought of, and using cars and material supplied by Alfa Romeo in Milan for the exclusive use of the *Scuderia Ferrari*. By 1935, the Scuderia was being knocked off the top of the Grand Prix tree by cars from Mercedes-Benz and Auto Union, and Ferrari was dependent on the Milan research and development department to produce new models for Grand Prix racing. A new car with all-independently sprung chassis and supercharged 4-litre V12 engine was promised, but it was a long time coming. This was not due to a lack of interest, but there were more important engineering projects to attend to connected with Mussolini's military arm that was spreading south into Africa.

Ferrari's sole business was motor racing, and he could see the 1935 season approaching and no new cars on the horizon. Two very important races were due to be held which would be open to Formula Grand Prix cars, although they were not to be run to Grand Prix rules, but to *Formule Libre* instead. One of these was in Tripoli and involved huge amounts of prize money, and the other was in Berlin – wealthy enough for contemporary racing teams, but very strong on prestige. This was on the Avus high-speed track, and both events called for speed above all else, which was simple to translate into horsepower.

The *Tipo* B Alfa Romeos, even in 3.2-litre form, were hopelessly outclassed on horsepower against the new German cars, so for these two important races Enzo Ferrari and his Chief Engineer, Luigi Bazzi, built two 'specials' that made strong men blanch and solved the horsepower problem for all time.

They took a current Alfa Romeo *Tipo* B, the front-engined slim single-seater, lengthened the chassis and wheelbase, and installed a second engine in the rear, behind the driver. The Alfa Romeo engine of the day was a beautiful straight-eight with twin superchargers on the nearside, and after being raced in 2.9-litre form the latest version had been enlarged to 3.2 litres. In the normal Grand Prix Alfa Romeo the fuel tank was in the space behind the driver, so now that he had an engine in that space the fuel tank had to go elsewhere. In addition, the tank had to be of twice the capacity now that there were two engines in action, so long tanks were arranged on each side of the car, filling in the space between the front and rear wheels.

A single gearbox was mounted under the driver's legs and the output shafts from the two engines met in this central drive train and then ran rearwards in twin shafts in the form of a vee on each side of the rear engine to two crownwheel-and-pinion units, one to each rear wheel. That describes the layout in very simple and basic terms. As the American saying goes: "If you are going to be a bear, be a Grizzly", so Ferrari built two of these cars, one with two 2.9-litre engines (making 5.8 litres) and the other with two 3.2-litre engines (making 6.4 litres) with a total of well over 500bhp, which was very impressive for the times.

Imagine today if Renault decided to run in a *Formule Libre* event and got Patrick Head to build an FW14X with one V10 in the normal position, and another ahead of the driver in a lengthened nose. It wouldn't half go, but would probably be a bit uncontrollable and play havoc with the rear tyres.

That is precisely what happened with Enzo Ferrari's special-to-end-all-specials. At Tripoli the cars were immensely fast, but they tore their rear tyres to bits, and Avus wasn't much better, but to prove a minor point the 6.4-litre car was used to set new International Class records at just over 200mph; the *Bimotores* were then put away and the Scuderia got on with serious Formula

Tazio Nuvolari at speed in the Scuderia Ferrari Alfa Romeo Bimotore at AVUS, Berlin, in 1935. With a total of 16 cylinders giving a combined engine capacity of 6.2 litres, the car was tremendously fast, but it ate its tyres at a frightening rate.

The Bimotore when in Austin Dobson's ownership in 1937. Both front and rear engines drove the rear wheels via an ingenious coupled-drive mechanism.

Grand Prix racing with single-engined Alfa Romeos.

The whole concept and thinking behind the twin-engined project can only be viewed as 'a bit of a lark', but if motor racing people did not do such things life would be very dull. I would love to know just how fast a twin-engined Williams-Renault would go in a straight line on a record run where cornering and braking downforce, and resultant drag, would not be important. I must ask Patrick Head and Adrian Newey sometime.

In 1937, one of the *Bimotore* Alfa Romeos came to England, bought by an English racing driver with a view to racing it on the Brooklands banked track. In those days I had no money to pay the spectator entrance fee, even on weekdays, but I went to the track on my bicycle in the hope of seeing something interesting by standing on the saddle and looking over the corrugated iron fence. I was not disappointed because I actually saw the *Bimotore* go past while it was being tested. A memorable day, for I had read about it in the motor magazines and had seen photographs of it.

It was no more successful in English amateur hands that it had been in the Scuderia Ferrari drivers' hands, and eventually it was cut in half and made into a front-engined *Monomotore*. After the war years it was quite active in National racing, and then was sold to a New Zealand enthusiast, principally for its engine to act as a spare for an Alfa Romeo; eventually, about all that survived was the whole front end of the car and the two side members of the chassis.

Tom Wheatcroft acquired the remains in 1978 and started the prodigious task of recreating this incredible piece of machinery, and when you look at it now you can only shake your head in disbelief at the size of the task and the incredible workmanship that has gone into its recreation. People who saw the original car in 1935 probably feel the same.

33

THE BEST DRIVER

Ever controversial

Whenever I find myself among a group of motor racing enthusiasts, one inevitable question I am asked is: "Who was the best racing driver?" Before trying to give an answer I have to alter the question to "Who is..." rather than "Who was...", and then ask what we mean by racing driver. Older people, living on nostalgia for the past, tend to judge drivers by their versatility and results, both factors ignoring the fact that today there is little room for versatility. The scope of racing today allows a wide choice of type of racing, to which drivers can be involved in their quest for success; the choice being theirs to choose the type of car or the type of racing that appeals to them.

All drivers in any form of open-wheeled single-seater racing must surely have an obvious aim, which is Formula One, and ultimate World Championship status. No matter what category we look at there is a championship at the end of it for the successful driver, and the possibility of moving up to a higher grade and eventually to the pinnacle of Formula One.

Surely everyone who races wants to win. I don't believe anyone has started in racing without the desire to win, otherwise why bother to compete? After that first event it may become obvious to the competitor that he is never going to win, and he may give up all ideas of winning and carry on just enjoying driving under racing conditions, or he may simply give up and play

I had many conversations with Innes Ireland during his driving days and they were invariably enjoyable, even though we agreed to disagree about things from time to time.

This signed photograph of a group of highly talented people was taken as part of the publicity build-up for the 1955 British Grand Prix at Aintree. Moss, Fangio, Kling and Taruffi would finish 1-2-3-4 for Mercedes, while engineering director Rudolf Uhlenhaut, on the left, could so easily have been a distinguished Grand Prix driver in his own right had he chosen to do so, such was his ability behind the wheel. On the right is Alfred Neubauer, the company's famed team manager.

golf. Even so, he will still want to win at golf! The human being is a basically competitive animal, and if not he is a 'cabbage'.

So the initial question of the best driver cannot be readily answered, and anyone who poses the question in such a simple form doesn't really have much of a grasp on the motor racing scene of the second half of the 20th century. With the 21st century beginning in eight years' time [as I write this], those who want to think forward should start planning now.

At the moment some people have just realized that the Formula One Drivers' World Championship has served its purpose and that the year 2000 should see the start of the Formula One Team World Championship, because winning is a collective effort by dozens, if not hundreds, of scientists, engineers, mechanics, electricians and key personnel, only one of which has the status of driver.

Formula One only leads the way in motorsport; in the outside world there are many examples of where the human being seems to be going, and not all of them are healthy for those of us who like old-fashioned 'driver racing'.

The next question is: "How do you rate driver A to driver B?", but I have to qualify this question by pointing out that I am only prepared to evaluate drivers that I have seen racing, otherwise you are dependent on reporters and journalists, or myths and legends. For me, the important thing is 'how' a driver wins a race, not the mere fact that he has won. If he wins simply because there is no opposition, then I say: "Good luck to you", but the win is not significant as far as I am concerned. If the circuit itself is challenging and he wins without any opposition, then that is a different matter, though challenging circuits are few and far between these days.

In today's hi-tech Formula One cars, the real challenge lies in being totally under control at the limit at all times, for the limits of everything on today's cars can only be appreciated by those who have been there, and only a handful of BRDC members can honestly say they have been to those limits. There is no real place today for the 'natural hazard', let alone the 'unnatural' one.

If driver A and driver B are in near-equal and identical cars, if that could be possible, then it is fairly easy to form an opinion about their relative abilities. If there is nothing to choose between them, then they are both very good, or both very poor; it can be either unless a third factor can be found to act as an eliminator.

None of the driver questions are easy to answer satisfactorily, which is why I prefer mechanical questions rather than human ones; a simple question with the use of a dynamometer test-bed facility. I always regret that no race organizer took up Keith Duckworth's suggestion: If racing was purely about engines, he suggested a test-rig in the middle of Wembley Stadium, with two competitive engines pulling against each other on full throttle and full load until one of them blew up! The next engine would be brought in and the competition started again. This would go on until the strongest and most powerful engine would be left running on its own. The sound and tension would be greater than all the pole-position laps put together, providing you liked engines and noise.

To pose the question of 'the best racing driver' to the BRDC membership would be foolish in the extreme, with its membership of active and successful racing drivers. If I were brash enough to ask: "Who is/was the best driver?", I would be very disappointed if I did not get simple answers spontaneously, such as: "I was", or "I am", or "I am going to be." My questioners are usually people who have never raced, or at best only done a little mild competition, but are keen observers of the overall scene and love the whole idea of the sport of motor racing. The enthusiasts.

More than 30 years ago I was in the throes of one of these sort of discussions with a group of colleagues and I was 'banging on to the troops' with my ideas of who was a good Grand Prix driver and who wasn't, and who had good possibilities and who was hopeless, when a relative newcomer to the Grand Prix scene was passing by. He stopped, and out of curiosity joined the group, and it wasn't long before he began to question some of my arguments.

We had a bit of a verbal battle, while my colleagues listened with great interest, until he turned away to leave, and his parting shot was to say: "Do you think you are God?", and my reply was: "Yes". He stopped in his tracks, completely lost for words, and I am very happy to be able to say that our late President, Innes Ireland, and I were good friends ever after, though we still argued about this and that.

34

EUROPA TO SICILY

A chance meeting

In 1969 the Lotus Europa had just been released for sale on the home market, after being 'For Export Only' for a couple of years, and it was a car that obviously interested me, having been championing the cause of the mid-engined GT car for some time. Eric Broadley's Lola-Ford V8 really made my

Having taken the bold decision to drive all the way to Sicily in a Lotus Europa (their reputation for fragility at the time caused many people to believe that any destination south of Dover was courting trouble), the last thing I expected to come across when I was almost there – after a completely troublefree run – was another one, which had made an equally uneventful journey from Austria.

adrenalin flow just looking at it when it appeared at the Motor Show. The subsequent development into the Ford GT40 set the seal on a whole new world.

Colin Chapman's mid-engined Europa was a sort of 'mini' GT40 that was affordable, providing the same fun at a lower level. The concept was similar, with a two-seater cockpit area and the engine between the cockpit and the rear axle. The big difference was that the GT40 had a great lump of Detroit horsepower to push it along and the Lotus had a tiny little Renault 16 engine to propel it. I said it provided similar fun at a lower level, and this it certainly did.

Lotus made noises about me doing a road test of the new UK-market Europa, but I said I would want to do a serious bit of motoring in it, not just a squirt up the bypass and back, or a few laps of Brands Hatch. At the time I was driving all over Europe to sports car and Grand Prix races in a 4.2-litre E-Type Jaguar, so I suggested doing one of my trips in a Europa. "No problem," said Graham Arnold, who was looking after Lotus press and publicity. "How about a trip to Sicily for the Targa Florio?", I suggested. "NNoo problem," said Graham, rather nervously. I made one stipulation, which I considered reasonable, bearing in mind that my presence in Sicily to report the race was very important to the well-being of *Motor Sport*. "If it breaks down I shall leave it by the roadside and get a taxi to the nearest railway station or rent-a-car service and go on my way", and generously added: "I'll send you a telegram telling you where it is." When Colin Chapman heard this he laughed and said to Graham: "That's alright, it won't break down. Just have faith." So that was it, a 4,000-mile road test from London to Palermo and back.

My friends thought I was mad. "It probably won't get to France," they said. "Sicily, you must be joking." Being an avid Chapman fan, I had the faith, and had had it since I first met him in about 1947. I was due to leave London at 7am on Monday morning, April 28, which gave me four days at 500 miles a

day, a normal European journey in a Jaguar E-Type.

The day before I was due to leave there was no sign of the Europa, so I began servicing the E-Type ready for the 'off'; it did not amount to much, just changing the oil and checking the tyre pressures, the incredible reliability of the Jaguar being one of its strong points providing you used it hard and never let it get really cool. I was going round the corner to a small, quiet little West London restaurant when the phone rang. It was the man from Lotus. "Where will you be at 10.30 this evening?", he asked. I gave him the name of the restaurant, and he said: "Right, I'll be with you", and rang off. I could only assume he was bringing the Europa, though he did not actually say as much. At 10.30pm almost on the dot, as I was having coffee, the door opened and the cheery Graham Arnold came in, put the keys on the table and said: "She's outside, there are the keys, there are some rubber bands, a roll of insulating tape and some wire in the glove-box, you'll be alright. Have fun!", and at that he disappeared out into the night and hailed a taxi. He wouldn't even stay for a coffee!

Sure enough, out in the street was TNG 10G, a white Lotus Europa with a GB sticker on the tail, fully taxed and insured (or so the paperwork in the door pocket said). I climbed in and settled down into the reclining seat and said to myself: "This is going to be a riot of fun."

Next morning, on the dot of 7am, I motored away towards Lydd and the channel crossing. Once out on the open French roads (no *autoroutes* in those days) the Europa really was a riot, a riot of fun and satisfaction, and 500 miles later I stopped for the night, as planned. Next day I was through the Mont Blanc tunnel and down the Italian *autostrada* to Modena, where I picked up a friend at 3pm and then went straight on south to Orvieto for the night. Another 500 miles. This second day had been memorable, the little Lotus cruising happily at 6,100rpm, virtually 'on full-noise' the whole way and

Outside the Hotel San Lucia in Cefalu, Jonathan Williams, due to drive a Porsche in the 1969 Targa Florio, uses the Europa as a seat as he chats to me and my photographer friend Geoffrey Goddard on one of the practice days.

singing to itself quite unperturbed.

I knew it was going to be a good day when I entered Italy, for the sun was shining and the *carabinieri* at the frontier took a keen interest in the Lotus. "Where are you going?", they asked. *"Sicilia, perlo Targa Florio"*, I replied. *"Concorrenti?"*, they queried. *"Non, giornalista da Londra, Inglese"*, to keep them happy. "Ah, *The Times*", they said. I left it at that and went on my way. While having dinner at the hotel in Orvieto the waiter volunteered the information that he had seen me in 1955 *"con Steerlini Moss, Mille Miglia, con lo Merchadees"*. He had been a waiter in an hotel in Acquapendenti, actually on the Mille Miglia route, 14 years before!

On Wednesday we got into the mountains of Calabria, and the Europa really was fun, loving every minute of being thrown about on the winding, twisting roads without a care in the world. Now and then I would try to behave myself and conduct a serious road test approach, as befits a serious motoring journalist, but I soon got bored with that and returned to enjoying my motoring, as Chapman had intended. Another 500 miles, about 350 of them on mountain roads, and we arrived at Gioia Tauro right on schedule, almost within sight of the Messina ferryboat to Sicily.

Next morning, Thursday, we set off to cover the last 50 miles to get the boat at Villa San Giovanni. We had come down this last bit of the route on the west coast of Italy, on the Mediterranean side. The alternative route is to travel down the east coast on the Adriatic side, but it means a longer route as you have to go right round the bottom of Italy and up the west side to get the boat from Villa SG. There is a road that crosses the mountains, but it takes longer than going south all the way round the foot. Where this road joins the Mediterranean coast road there is a T-junction so you can imagine my surprise as I approached this junction to see another Lotus Europa coming in from my left, down off the mountain road.

It was nothing to the surprise we gave the other Europa driver, and as the T-junction was wide and deserted we both spontaneously flashed our headlights and did a 360-degree spin-turn to stop side-by-side in the middle of the junction.

Shaking with laughter, we got out and welcomed each other. He and his wife had come from Vienna in their red Lotus Europa, and I had come from London in our white one, never having seen each other before. We were both going to the Targa Florio and a chance in a million brought us to that road junction at precisely the same moment.

We ran in convoy to the boat, and talked Europa motoring all the time during the crossing to Messina. Then we ran in convoy along the coast road of Sicily, to Cefalu, where we were staying, and they went on to Palermo. We never saw them again! I said it was a chance meeting, and luckily my friend who was with me took a photo of the two cars together in the middle of the junction near Bagnara Calabria (where the hell is that, you might well ask). Otherwise, no-one would have believed our story.

The Europa not only got to Sicily on time, but got back to the Belgian Grand Prix the following weekend, and back to London on schedule. So impressed was I that my road test absorbed three full pages in *Motor Sport*, in the days when the magazine was very full of words.

35

FERGUSON PROJECT 99

Very advanced

In 1961 the Ferguson-Climax single-seater, with four-wheel drive, won the Oulton Park Gold Cup race driven by Stirling Moss. This is a fairly unspectacular statement of historical fact, but there was much more to it than that. The Coventry-based firm of Ferguson Research, started by Harry Ferguson, the Ulster tractor magnate, had been concentrating on the problem of four-wheel drive for a long time, with Tony Rolt leading the research team. By the late 1950s they had finally got the concept of 4WD for road vehicles into the minds of the big manufacturers.

Harry Ferguson had always wanted to put the concept into a racing car, but the opportunity never arose, and obviously he would not have needed to ask Tony Rolt twice. In 1962 a new Formula for Grand Prix racing was due to start, and in the spring of 1960 Harry came away from the May Silverstone meeting deciding the time was ripe. He gave the go-ahead to Ferguson Research and orders were issued under Project 99: 'A High Speed Lightweight Vehicle'. Up to this point Ferguson Research had built a number of experimental one-off saloon road cars for research purposes, some being right up to production specification, but had never shown any sporting interest, their whole effort being aimed at the motor industry.

Claude Hill, who had designed the first postwar Aston Martin, had long been working for Ferguson and was Chief Engineer in charge of Project 99. To the outside world it was just another Ferguson Research design project, except that all drawings emanating from Claude Hill's drawing office were printed on green paper instead of the more usual white paper. This was an indication to everyone on the 50-strong manufacturing staff that Project 99 was important.

The factory was very self-sufficient as far as engineering and manufacturing facilities were concerned, and was geared to a normal outlook in R&D that 100 per cent accuracy was paramount in everything it did, but that 99.99 per cent would be tolerated in some things and would be acceptable. A part laid out on green drawing paper was something special, and 100 per cent was not only expected, as was usual, but nothing else would be acceptable, and this applied to everything 'in house' as well as from outside suppliers.

For a long time, the outside world, and especially the motor racing world, knew nothing of Project 99. It was August 1960 when the project officially started, and during the winter of 1960-61 work was intense, so much so that by March 1961 the P99, as the car had become known, was standing on its wheels. By April the car was ready to run, using a 1.5-litre four-cylinder Coventry Climax engine, and on April 5 Tony Rolt drove it under its own power for the first time, at Silverstone. The racing world sat up and took notice, for here was a car that was in opposition to all the racing car concepts forged by Cooper and Lotus, and eventually followed by everyone else, which was basically the engine behind the driver and weight concentration over the rear wheels to aid adhesion and power use for acceleration, even though it brought about problems of oversteer in handling.

The P99 had the engine in front of the driver and had been designed from scratch, using no proprietary components apart from the engine. The aims that were achieved were no weight penalty compared to more orthodox cars with a rear engine and only the rear wheels driven, no overall loss of efficiency through driving all four wheels compared to driving only the rear wheels, and consistent handling characteristics, weight distribution being studied minutely. The resultant car was long, lean and low, and every detail had been designed from the word go for a four-wheel-drive project, not adapting the four-wheel-drive concept to an existing design.

The use of the Coventry Climax engine was a shrewd move because much of the opposition at the time were using the same engines, so the rest of the car could be compared directly with the rest of the world. Although it was built as a pure research vehicle, and spent much of its life gaining data for the Ferguson four-wheel-drive concept, it was the first time that Ferguson Research were going to perform 'on stage', so to speak.

The Ferguson P99 was an intriguing technical exercise which embodied several advanced features, although the concept of a front-mounted engine for a Formula One car was already out of date. Nevertheless, despite the complication of four-wheel-drive transmission, they claimed there was no significant weight penalty or power loss compared with conventional rear-engined cars with two driven wheels.

The P99 laid bare to show the drive line from the Coventry Climax engine to the rear wheels running down the left side of the tubular chassis and the inboard mounting of the disc brakes on the driveshafts.

109

The beautifully designed tubular spaceframe could accept either a 1.5-litre Coventry Climax engine, or the 2.5-litre version, the smaller unit being necessary for Formula One events and the larger being available for free-formula events and for research and test purposes. Before it appeared in its first race, which was the July Silverstone International Trophy meeting, Rolt and Jack Fairman did an intense research programme at Goodwood and at the Road Research Laboratory test-track at Crowthorne, particularly with regard to high-speed handling and steering of 4WD and the Dunlop Maxaret anti-lock braking system.

That first outing was so inconspicuous that some race reporters of the time did not even mention it, even if they actually saw it! Jack Fairman drove, albeit briefly, and Stirling Moss was seen taking a great interest in the concept. The next appearance was at Aintree for a depressingly wet British Grand Prix, with Fairman once again doing the driving, but with Stirling nominated as reserve driver. The water got into the Climax engine and after a long pitstop the mechanics inadvertently push-started the car, which broke the racing rules and entailed disqualification.

Trying to be helpful, the organizers merely announced that no further lap times would be recorded for car number 26, not actually saying that it must stop. Fairman carried on with what amounted to a test and research programme as far as Ferguson Research were concerned, as the car was going well. When Moss had to retire his Lotus, the Ferguson was still running well, so Stirling replaced 'Jolly Jack', and those who were watching closely, and were not in the Aintree bar, were able to see the true potential of the Ferguson P99 on the streaming wet track. Eventually, other teams began to view car number 26 as an unnecessary and illegal hazard on the track, considering it had been disqualified officially, and the Stewards 'black-flagged' it.

The rest, as they say, is history. Stirling was convinced about the car's ability and drove it in the wet and dry conditions of the Gold Cup race at Oulton Park. He scored a great victory for Ferguson Research and put the first race win for a car driven through all four wheels into the record books. The point about 4WD had been made, but this was back in 1961. Today, in the 1990s, most enterprising hi-tech manufacturers build cars with four-wheel drive, and I am sure there are many members of the public driving about in their family or executive cars with four-wheel drive and not having the slightest idea what the words mean. I am sure few of them know how the concept was first demonstrated to the public.

Before putting Project 99 away it was loaned to various drivers to use in alternative competitions, among whom was Innes Ireland, our late President, who drove it in the Tasman races. My personal involvement, apart from writing a very detailed story in the November 1961 issue of *Motor Sport*, was to attend a very busy test and research day with the Ferguson engineers watching Tony Rolt carry out exhaustive tests on the anti-lock braking system, and evaluation tests of acceleration and braking at the Road Research Laboratory proving ground.

Today, the Ferguson-Climax is on display in the Donington Park Racing Car Museum, and anyone making a visit to Tom Wheatcroft's incredible collection should not miss an opportunity to pause and have a good look at P99.

36

TAKEN FOR A RIDE

Graham Hill and Speedwell

Not being a very fast or brave driver, it was never very difficult to find someone who could do it better than I could, so that if there was something interesting to be driven I was always happy to sit in the passenger seat and watch what was going on at close quarters. I always found this more satisfying and instructive than standing about 'outside'. Over the years I seem to have amassed a large collection of photographs of interesting vehicles in which I have been driven, and one or two that I have actually driven myself. The former category are in a bulging file marked 'DSJ being taken for a ride', and obviously pride of place goes to the Mercedes-Benz 300SLR sports-racer of 1955, in which Stirling Moss gave me a ride to remember!

Rummaging about in this photographic file, looking for a Ferrari actually, I came across the accompanying photograph which caused me to say: "Good Heavens! I'd completely forgotten about that". It was taken on the Belgian *autoroute* just outside Antwerp on a day when the *Royal Automobile Club de Belgique*, with the co-operation of the *gendarmerie*, closed one side of the motorway so that the firm of Speedwell could establish some officially timed speeds for the flying-kilometre and the flying-mile. In the picture is my Porsche 356, which dates it as pre-1965.

Speedwell was a London tuning firm specializing in small BMC engine tuning, and was run by Graham Hill and George Hulbert. Graham had been doing heroic things in Club events with a Speedwell-tuned Austin A35 and Speedwell Sprites were the thing for 'the lads'. They had two cars in Belgium, the little Sprite hardtop and a special streamliner. This had a smooth all-enveloping body with the passenger side of the cockpit faired over and a plastic bubble-top over the driver's side. The hardtop coupe was going to set some baseline speeds, somewhere in the mid-90mph range, and the streamliner, running on racing fuel and prepared for straight-line speed, was aiming at speeds of over 110mph, all from highly-tuned BMC A-series engines.

In those days I was a completely free spirit, wandering through the European sporting scene, so I joined the Speedwell team to watch what was

going on. Both Graham Hill and George Hulbert did some test runs in the two cars, and then the serious business of a timed run in each direction began. While final adjustments were going on with the hardtop Sprite, Graham suddenly said to me: "Do you want to come with me?". George agreed, as the added weight was not going to affect the speed because the length of run-in to the measured-mile was more than adequate, and a passenger was not going to affect the frontal area or the aerodynamics.

There was no passenger seat, but that didn't matter, so I climbed in and curled up on the floor alongside Graham. The little Speedwell 'screamer' was revving to over 7,000rpm and away we went. The noise and bumping seemed to go on forever as we made our way along the *autoroute*, and naturally I could not see anything, lying on the floor as I was, so I spent the time looking at the driver. As always, Graham's face was completely relaxed and placid, but his eyes were burning brightly, looking ahead down the empty *autoroute*. His right foot held the accelerator pedal hard down on the stop and we just went on and on at a speed not far short of 100mph in this tiny buzz-box.

Eventually he lifted off, so I knew we had finished our timed run, and we gradually lost speed until we reached the turn-round area. Then it was back the way we had come, up through the gears to peak in top and then the constant scream of the engine through the measured distance again, Graham still sitting there, implacable as ever, but enjoying the fact that Speedwell were proving their claims on engine tuning.

Lying there on the floor of the car I did wonder why I was doing it, for there was nothing to see and nothing to do, but I felt that it was better than standing by the side of the road watching the car go by. It was the old, old feeling that I have always had, that somehow I must get involved. I am the world's worst spectator, and always have been. If something is going on I just have to be part of it, no matter in how small a capacity. On this occasion it was a case of being 'unnecessary ballast', but there was no way I was going to refuse Graham's invitation.

When we got out of the little hardtop Sprite the 'streamliner' was being made ready for George to make his timed runs, and I suggested that I'd like to go with him. Unfortunately it was impossible to find any room under the metal fairing over the cockpit into which I could conceal myself. There were pipes and tanks and things on that side of the cockpit that could not be moved or dispensed with, so reluctantly I had to stand about with Graham and watch the runs of the 'streamliner' as a spectator.

When Graham Hill invited me to climb aboard the Speedwell Austin-Healey Sprite for the record attempt in Belgium it seemed too good an opportunity to miss, even though from where I would have to crouch I would see very little of what was going on!

112

Like the little hardtop coupe, the 'streamliner' ran perfectly and achieved its target speeds, so the Speedwell team returned home well satisfied with their day. I got into my Porsche and drove off to other things.

37

THE BRITISH GRAND PRIX

1948 to 1993

By sheer chance, while I was looking for something else, I turned up the programme for the first Grand Prix to be held at Silverstone and it made interesting reading. The first page said it was the 'Programme of the Royal Automobile Club International Grand Prix at the R.A.C. Silverstone Circuit, Saturday, October 2nd, 1948'. Under the title 'Officials' it said that Flag Marshals were members of the British Racing Drivers' Club. It also said that the Fire Party were members of the Midland Automobile Club, and there was a High Speed Patrol comprising A.J.Bell Esq, M.Cann Esq, F.L.Frith Esq.

Pits were described as 'Depots', and one of the Chief Depot Marshals was F.G.Craner Esq. Now this was the jovial but fiery Fred Craner, Secretary of the Derby and District Motor Club, who had run the Donington Park races from 1931 to 1939. In the programme blurb it said that thanks to the Air Ministry making the Silverstone airfield available to the RAC, our august governing body were about to stage the first International Grand Prix race to be held in England for 21 years. It was true that the RAC had not staged a Grand Prix event since 1927, when the 2nd RAC British Grand Prix was held at Brooklands, but, as everyone knew, Grand Prix races had been held at Donington Park in 1935, 1936, 1937 and 1938. If full factory teams from Auto Union and Mercedes-Benz did not constitute a Grand Prix, then those of us who went to Donington Park in those far-off days must have been duped by dear old Fred Craner!

No doubt Fred snorted a bit when he read the programme, but the RAC were writing about the RAC, not a lesser body called the Derby and District Motor Club, who had organized two of the greatest races seen in Great Britain in prewar times. Added irony was caused by the fact that the War Office had commandeered Donington Park for wartime purposes and in 1948 were still refusing to return it to the rightful owners, and we were having to 'make do' with an old airfield.

If Donington Park had been released in 1946 one wonders what would have happened. Would the RAC have staged their first Grand Prix for 21 years at Donington Park, and would the interesting road course have become the Home of British Motor Racing, and would the BRDC have joined forces with the Derby and District Motor Club, and would Tom Wheatcroft have eventually come into the picture? 'Ifs' are lovely things to while away one's thoughts on, because 'if' Donington Park had been released, would Brooklands have returned, and would the BRDC have found a permanent home in Surrey? After all, the BRDC 500 Mile race was a major annual fixture at the Surrey track, and was run at a higher speed than the Indianapolis 500 Mile race. Where would we be now?

By the time I had scanned that old 1948 Grand Prix programme, price 'One Shilling', when 20 shillings made a pound sterling, it was time to head off to the Home of British Motor Racing, at Silverstone, and peruse the £5 programme for the 1993 British Grand Prix.

Since the first postwar Grand Prix race in England in 1948 there has been a Grand Prix in England every year without a break, and some years we have had two, and not many countries can make a claim like that. Not all our Grand Prix events have been at Silverstone, but the majority have. If you go every year it is easy to overlook the changes that have been made to the old airfield, and a friend who had not been to Silverstone for a number of years exclaimed: "What happened to all the corn fields?"

From having one major race (the Grand Prix) and a small support race, there are now six major races in the two-day Festival of Speed and Excitement, and Race Number 5 is considered to be the important one, with the title of British Grand Prix, but if your interests lie elsewhere it could be Race Number 1, or Race Number 6, which is your idea of being important. If racing was not your scene, then over the weekend of the 1993 British Grand Prix there was plenty to keep you entertained, either publicly, or you could bring your own entertainment with you into the camp-sites.

For those interested in the Grand Prix the keynote seemed to be the progress of Damon Hill in the Williams-Renault team. In his first season of F1 with a front-line team he had made good progress, still lacking actual racing miles in which to gain experience when compared with Alain Prost, Ayrton Senna or Riccardo Patrese and others. With the 1993 season at its mid-way point a lot of people hoped that the Williams-Renault team had such a grip on the scene that they could afford to 'arrange' for Damon Hill to finish ahead of Alain Prost in his home Grand Prix. Others thought that Hill was capable of beating Prost without any team 'assistance', and Damon himself was determined to do his best to try and win anyway.

Before the race there were people recalling the 1955 British Grand Prix, held at Aintree that year, when Stirling Moss won by a few feet from Fangio, both being in the dominant Mercedes-Benz team. While I was chatting to Stirling in the paddock, someone asked him about that Aintree race, saying: "Did Fangio let you win that one?" Stirling replied: "I honestly don't know, there were no team orders as far as I was aware." What he said was true, but the person asking the question had clearly not read Fangio's autobiography. It was entitled *FANGIO – My Racing Life*, and published in Spanish, and I had the great honour of supervizing the scrupulous translation from Spanish into English by Michael Bayley.

On page 254, Fangio's chronicler says: 'That season (1955), Stirling Moss won only one Grand Prix: the British. The young Englishman had recently triumphed in the Mille Miglia, the first Briton to do so, and the Mercedes-Benz team wanted to take advantage of this and reward him on his own ground with a Formula 1 victory. Juan Manuel Fangio had orders to let Stirling Moss win, and to be quite sure of this there was a secret change of gear ratios the night before the race. Even so, Fangio managed to lead some of the way, and followed his team-mate closely to the finish.'

On page 262 Fangio himself is talking about team tactics at the German Grand Prix and the possibility of a German driver winning his home Grand Prix. He says: 'They wouldn't have dropped any hints, as they did in England, that I should let Moss win. That hint didn't come straight from our manager (Herr Neubauer) but from Artur Keser, the public relations manager for Daimler-Benz. It was clear that something had been said to him, and that's why he came to speak to me. "Let's see how things go in the race", I replied. It did not matter to me that Moss won, because I was already certain of the Championship when we went to Aintree. In any case, they gave me very low gear ratios for fear that I should disobey and win the race. I made a lot of headway in the last lap.'

At that British Grand Prix, Mercedes-Benz really dominated the Grand Prix scene, entering four cars and finishing first, second, third and fourth. Nobody thought it was boring in those days.

This year Williams-Renault and Alain Prost did not have to show their hand as poor Damon Hill retired with a broken Renault engine, so the team did not even have a first and second, let alone a 1-2-3-4 in a British Grand Prix.

There were plenty of fun and games in the supporting races and classic of the weekend was the Toyota team in the saloon-car event. Will Hoy and Julian Bailey had a 'misunderstanding' and collided in full view of the BRDC's own grandstand. Will Hoy finished upside down and unhurt, and Bailey retired with a flat tyre. The incident prompted some wry smiles and the catch-phrase became: 'The car on its roof is a Toyota.' Good publicity stunt, but a bit dicey and expensive to my way of thinking.

As always, Silverstone provided a very full four days of entertainment, and I benefited from BRDC membership by settling into the Members' camping site with a comfortable caravan hired from Walford Leisure, bringing everything

Juan-Manuel Fangio made Stirling Moss work hard for his first Grand Prix victory at Aintree in 1955. Here the two of them are nose-to-tail through Anchor Crossing, their Mercedes W196s already pulling clear of Jean Behra's Maserati 250F in the opening laps.

(except the kitchen sink, which was supplied) with me in my Escort van, including a folding bicycle, umbrella, derry boots and Barbour suit, as well as a Club tie and a suit for the Club's annual Grand Prix Dinner on the Friday evening. Somehow there was so much going on that I did not get to the end of Hangar Straight this year, but by all accounts the front-runners of Formula One were going very fast, which is what Silverstone has always been about, and I hope it always will be.

I never did read the programme and the entry booklet of facts and figures, because had I done so I would have missed most of the racing, there was so much in it. I'll keep it for some quiet winter reading.

38

FERRARI

A passion or a cult?

There is a general feeling in the sporting world that everyone loves a Ferrari, but personally I do not subscribe to this myth. I love some Ferraris, it is true, but by no means do I love all Ferraris, nor do I love everything about Ferrari.

My formative years were in the 1930s, when Alfa Romeos were raced by the *Scuderia Ferrari*, operating from workshops in Modena, so that any Alfa Romeo with the *Scuderia Ferrari* 'Prancing Horse' emblem on the bonnet was a 'real' Alfa Romeo, and they were invariably a rich red in colour. Alfa Romeo, with their beautifully slim 2.6-litre, eight-cylinder supercharged *Tipo* B *monoposto* cars, ruled the circuits of Europe, that is until the Mercedes-Benz and Auto Union from Germany joined the Grand Prix scene. Enlarging the engines to 2.9 litres and then to 3.2 litres was not enough to compete with the German cars, but I still remained an Alfa Romeo fan, and a picture of a single-seater with the *Scuderia Ferrari* emblem on the bonnet made the adrenalin flow.

In 1938 Enzo Ferrari fell out with the Alfa Romeo people in Milan, and built in Modena the wonderful little Type 158 *Alfetta* designed by Colombo. These were for what was effectively Formula Two, whereas the 'big boys' competing in Grand Prix races were the Formula One of the times. The potential of the *Alfetta* was clear from the outset, but the war put a stop to development. The *Alfetta* team was to return to the parent Milan firm and reappear after the war carrying the *quadrofoglio* (four-leaf clover) of the Alfa Romeo factory team. Enzo Ferrari severed all connections with the Milan firm and started building his own cars, carrying the 'Prancing Horse' badge and the Ferrari name.

It was not long before Ferrari cars began to appear in Grand Prix racing and soon began to challenge the *Alfettas*. During 1945-51 I followed the fortunes of the Alfa Romeo team, the beautiful little supercharged straight-eight *Tipo* 158 being one of my all-time favourite Grand Prix cars. As the new Ferraris began to challenge the Alfa Romeos I looked on with distaste as the 'postwar upstart' Ferrari grew stronger. When Ferrari finally beat Alfa Romeo I was mortified; my boyhood favourite team was being destroyed before my eyes by the man who had kept Alfa Romeo on a pinnacle for so long.

The sad day when Alfa Romeo suffered their first defeat at the hands of

Being such an avid Alfa Corse enthusiast, it was a dark day for me when Froilan Gonzales won the 1951 British Grand Prix in his Ferrari 375, bringing to a close an era during which the supercharged Alfettas had been supreme. The Ferrari steamroller was on the move.

Ferrari was at our own Silverstone in l951, when Froilan Gonzalez in a 4.5-litre V12 Ferrari beat Juan-Manuel Fangio in the best car that Alfa Romeo could muster. I'd had the bottom knocked out of my motor racing world.

Enzo Ferrari is quoted as having said after his first victory over Alfa Romeo: "I have killed my mother". For me Enzo Ferrari was a villain, and in the ensuing years I enjoyed watching his cars being beaten by Maserati, Mercedes-Benz and Vanwall, especially the last-named. Since beating Alfa Romeo, Ferrari has been a power in Grand Prix racing the like of which has not been matched. Ferrari cars have played a major part in Grand Prix racing for more than 40 years, and the factory team has never missed a season; nobody else can make that claim.

Some Ferrari victories I have enjoyed, but I have revelled in watching the rest of the Grand Prix racing world doing their best to destroy the red cars. Many marques have achieved this, but few have stayed the course for long. Ferrari is always there, a natural target for anyone trying to prove their worth in Grand Prix racing. There has been the odd race devoid of Ferraris, but as races they did not count for much. With Enzo's death at the age of 90 years the flame seemed to flicker and die and the Scuderia has not found a leader to replace 'Zio' Enzo, with the result that the racing team is at its lowest ebb ever, with little hope of it ever making a full recovery.

But what of the other side of Ferrari, the sports and production cars? For years they were very expensive and very exclusive; now they are merely expensive. In the 1950s the only way to get to drive a Ferrari road car was to buy one, and indeed the late Mike Parkes, when he was an engineer at Maranello, actually said that to me. I had been lent factory Mercedes-Benz 300SL Gullwings, Maseratis, Porsches, even a Lamborghini, but had never driven a road-going Ferrari 250 GT coupe. One day I said to Mike: "What do I have to do to drive a Ferrari?". He smiled and said: "You'll have to buy one".

On one of the very rare occasions when I met Enzo Ferrari at his Maranello factory I was having a bit of a 'nose around' with Peter Collins when he was driving for the factory. Ferrari looked down his nose when Peter introduced

Most Ferrari road cars certainly looked the part, but they didn't always go as well as their appearance promised. The trouble was, back in 1956, when this picture was taken, the only way you could get to road test a Ferrari was by buying it.

me and said: "A Maserati spy!". Peter gave me a ride in one of the 3.7-litre four-cylinder Mille Miglia cars one day; it was awful, and I reckoned anyone who raced them was a real hero.

Mike Hawthorn gave me a ride round the Nurburgring in a 2.3-litre V12 coupe, but I was not overly impressed, though I was by his action when the driver's door flew open going round the *Karussel*! Still on a wide throttle and a lot of steering input, he reached out and pulled the door shut without batting an eyelid. Other racing friends gave me rides out to circuits in sports Ferraris, but there was no regret that I wasn't able to drive, for they were all top-flight racing drivers and I could learn and enjoy from a trip with them much better than trying to drive myself.

Eventually I got the opportunity to drive a road-going Ferrari, and what a disaster it proved to be. A friend had bought a 330 GT two-plus-two and he offered me a drive while in Modena. At the time I was driving a 4.2-litre E-Type Jaguar coupe, not the world's best car, but excellent value for money, and lively and fast providing you treated it as a high-speed tourer and not as a sports car. In comparison with the 330 GT the E-Type was a jewel. Mr Bugatti is said to have called a Bentley "a fast lorry"; I called my friend's pride and joy "a truck", and it seemed as wide as a bus compared with the E-Type.

In later years, when Ferrari road cars got into serious production and Maranello Concessionaires developed in the UK, a number of Ferrari production cars were loaned to me, and I must say I was left with some gratifying experiences. The Dino 246 was not only one of the prettiest mid-engined cars to look at, it was a sheer joy to drive, the little V6 engine revving its head off in happiness. A 308 coupe was a good all-rounder, not short of anything, but the Boxer flat-12 was just too much for me. Its performance made me stop talking and take some deep breaths. I need not go on, for every new Ferrari seems to be more fantastic than the previous one, but it was not always like that.

The Scuderia Ferrari racing team may be on a 'low' at the moment, but nobody under-estimates them, even top engineers in rival teams, and in the world of supercars all the other manufacturers still have them as the target to try and shoot down.

But I am still not a real Ferrari fan, though the automotive world would be a lesser place without the 'Prancing Horse' emblem. Enzo Ferrari killed his mother, and I can never forgive him for that.

39

INNES REMEMBERED

Need I say more

Anyone who knew Innes Ireland will have fond memories of him, some hilarious, some thoughtful, some embarrassing, many of them unbelievable, but all of them enriched life itself. Hackneyed journalists would describe him as being "larger than life", but I would never subscribe to that view, because to me Innes was life. If you could not accept that fact it meant that you were pretty dull yourself.

I got to know him when he moved out of Club racing into International racing and was soon in Fl and Grands Prix. Over the years of travelling about Europe to all manner of racing events we spent a lot of time together, not only in the pits and paddock, but eating and drinking together at the events and generally relaxing away from 'work'. Best of all was when we met on the road between races, for Innes was never one of those 'professional driver' types who stepped out of the cockpit and scurried off to a business appointment clutching a briefcase.

One year, after a sports and GT race in Austria, I made a leisurely start on the Monday morning with a friend in my E-Type Jaguar and toured gently through mountain and lake country towards Germany. It was 'picture postcard' time and we stopped well before midday for a leisurely lunch at a *Gasthaus* alongside a lake. We were sitting on the verandah relaxing in the sun when we saw an 'apparition' approaching along the winding road around the edge of the lake. You could only see the top of it over the bushes and undergrowth, but it was unmistakably a Ford GT40. "What the hell is that?", queried my friend. "That is Innes Ireland", I said.

Innes had got a last-minute entry for this friendly Austrian event and had borrowed a GT40 from Bernard White's Team Chamaco Collect, but their transporter had been out of action, so Innes had borrowed a trailer and hitched it up behind his DB4GT Aston Martin and driven non-stop from England to Austria to be in time for first practice; he had told me all this at the race, extolling the virtues of the Aston Martin as a tow car! A GT40 riding at hedge-top height just had to be on a trailer, and as the tow vehicle was below the hedge-line it could only be the GT Aston Martin.

Sure enough, this incongruous sight hove into view and I was just about to go out into the road to hail Innes when I saw that his 'winkers' were indicating that he was turning into the *Gasthaus* car park.

It was Innes alright, and he was agreeably surprised to see me there, saying: "Hallo lad, what brought you here?" I explained that I was having a 'touring' day after the race, with no hurry to get to my next port of call, and that this *Gasthaus* looked a likely place for lunch. "Yes", said Innes, "I noticed it on Thursday on my way through to the race, and marked it down for a visit." He then added: "That lake looks as though it could produce a very nice trout." He was absolutely right. We had a very nice lunch, and that afternoon I followed the fine sight of a 'Gentleman Racing Driver' in his GT Aston Martin towing a trailer carrying a Ford GT40. Racing in the grand manner.

Innes liked Austria a lot and made many friends there, and would recount happy times to races in Austria when friends took him out into the mountains on night-time hunting expeditions. It was always a source of disappointment to him that he was never able to shoot a wild boar.

During the times of the great races on the Osterreichring we used to stay in the village of Judenburg, just south of the circuit. Our hotel was very old and a bit primitive, but it had a lovely atmosphere, and just across the square was *Grubers*. Herr Gruber ran a delightful restaurant where eating and drinking was an art form, not a necessity. We did not need many visits to 'get our feet under the table' and Gruber became a very good friend. He was very correct and always greeted us formally as Mr Ireland and Mr Jenkinson, and we always responded with Herr Gruber.

When we got to the end of the evening and suggested we should get the bill, Gruber would pull up a chair and join us for a chat and a nightcap. He would produce a bottle of very powerful white fluid, made at his farm in the foothills of the nearby mountains. It was invariably after 1am before we left the restaurant, the last to leave, and Gruber would call his very large black Alsatian to come and bid us farewell.

Quite often the evening before a race would get a bit rowdy in Judenburg, but never in *Grubers*. If Herr Gruber sensed troublemakers thinking of coming into his restaurant he would give a quiet low whistle and without a sound this fine black 'wolf-dog' would be at his side, not barking or snarling or making a fuss, but standing alongside his master and just 'looking'. Trouble just melted away. Gruber had been in the restaurant and hotel business all his life and had spent time in England and a lot of time in Switzerland in St Moritz, and would keep us enthralled by his stories about life in a professional kitchen. Sadly, Mr Ecclestone and the world of Formula One decided that Austria and the Osterreichring could not support their scene, and our visits to Judenburg came to an end. They were great days.

When he stopped active racing – I can't say he ever officially retired – Innes joined the ranks of journalists, first with *Autocar* and later with *Road & Track*. Like me he was going deaf, and when he returned to what one might call 'the modern scene', where television commentators became more important than journalists, and everyone in the paddock carried a briefcase and talked in whispers, he found the atmosphere very alien to him. For a time he worried about this, not really hearing or understanding what other journalists were whispering about, and he asked me how I coped with it. I explained to him that I had given up worrying about it years ago, because most of the time when I did listen carefully I found it wasn't worth listening to, and if I did not understand I would ask questions only to find out that it was of little importance.

On one visit to the Hockenheimring we were staying in Heidelberg and Innes took me out to the circuit in his car. We were in no great hurry to get back after one practice so I suggested we went back to the hotel 'the pretty way' instead of joining the rat-race on the autobahn. This way was twice as

A youthful Innes Ireland in the cockpit of his works Lotus, which he invariably drove right on – and often over – the limit. He was always entertaining to watch.

120

long and took twice the time, but involved a very pleasant drive through some lovely countryside and small villages and along the side of the great Neckar river, so that we arrived back in a relaxed frame of mind and 'all was well with the world'. On the way, alongside the river, we were discussing where we would eat in the evening and felt that there should be some pleasant restaurants along the way. Heidelberg was an interesting place to spend an evening, but it could become a bit of a crowded 'bun fight', especially the night before a race.

Innes looks well in control during practice for the 1961 Monaco Grand Prix, but it was about to go dreadfully wrong. On the next lap he selected the wrong gear coming out of the tunnel and crashed spectacularly, doing himself an injury. But the tough Scot was soon on the mend and he went on to score Team Lotus' first Grand Prix victory at Watkins Glen, USA, at the end of the year, and then got sacked from the team!

While Innes drove leisurely along I was casting around, and through the railing of a small private garden I glimpsed a *Gasthaus* that looked interesting. There was no obvious direct entrance to it, but we decided to return that evening and see if we could find it. It proved to be in the small village of Ziegelhausen, a few miles east of Heidelberg, and the *Gasthaus zum Goldenochsen* was down a little cobbled cul-de-sac with a view out onto the mighty Neckar.

Owned by Lothar Teichman and his English wife, this proved to be an excellent replacement for lamented *Grubers* in Austria. In addition to being an artist in the kitchen, Lothar enjoyed ending his evening's work sitting with his favoured customers and rounding off the evening with a glass or two from the inevitable bottle containing the home-made clear fluid that settled very comfortably on a well-balanced gastronomic meal cooked by the owner himself. Such meals are the products of men whose hobby and profession are

bound together as one, to the extent of being an obsession, just as driving and racing was to Innes.

I may be giving a different view of Innes Ireland to that expounded by the media and the popular journalists, but it was an aspect of him that I relished and enjoyed. His more lurid aspects, especially with regard to racing, have all been published many times, mostly culled from his autobiography *All Arms and Elbows*, the title of which says it all.

Many of the events that he recorded in his book happened very close to me, and some I was part of, but I shall always retain fond memories of him while spending time with him in European countries among people of the country. Some thought of him as a wild hooligan, and at times they were right, but for all his natural tendency to be a hell-raiser, he did it with decency and dignity and knew when 'enough was enough'.

On our last trip to Heidelberg we set off across the city heading for the *autobahn*, he in his Sierra 4x4 to head for Calais and home and me in my rent-a-car Opel heading for Frankfurt airport. I was leading the way when a big blustering BMW came elbowing its way by in the traffic, driven by a large similar type of driver. As luck would have it he was not very good at traffic driving, and by a bit of planning and looking ahead I managed to box him in behind a tram that was just stopping. Innes was behind watching all this and rose to the bait, and being on the same driving wavelength he supported me brilliantly.

The poor blustering BMW driver hadn't got a hope. As fast as he thought he had out-manoeuvred me he found Innes in the way, and at times we had him totally boxed in, with one each side, and I am sure he did not realize he was up against some good 'teamwork'. Once clear of the town we joined the *autobahn* and he went by my Avis car blowing his horn and waving his fist, carving me up and giving me a brake-test. He had just got all that off his big fat chest when a Ford Sierra 4x4 just blew him into the weeds, the driver smiling and laughing.

I met Innes a week or two later and he said: "I did enjoy our little fracas crossing Heidelberg." Dear old Innes, we shall miss him.

40

ARENA DI VERONA

A night at the opera

It was a Wednesday in Modena, we had recovered from the excitement of the race the previous weekend, and the build-up for the race on the following weekend had not started. A leisurely lunch had been taken in the *Albergo Reale* and we were sitting around in the restaurant when one of the group said: "Why don't we go to the opera this evening?" It seemed like a good idea and we soon mapped out a plan. It was a Verdi evening at the *Arena di Verona*, a magnificent ancient colosseum in the middle of the town, which Mille Miglia competitors used to roar past flat-out on their way through the great city of Verona.

It was a mere 70 miles from Modena, there were four of us, so our two Porsches were adequate, but then Henry said: "Gee, I'd like to join you." Now Henry was a bit of a mystery. He had a permanent room at the *Albergo Reale* and had been left behind by a private American team that had come to Europe to take part in Grand Prix racing. Before mid-season they realized they were out of their depth and packed up and went home to rethink and regroup, leaving Henry behind as their 'anchor man' for when they returned.

Sensibly, they had bought one of the huge Maserati team transporters at the start of the season, which Henry drove and looked after. Having delivered the whole team to Milan airport they sent Henry back to Modena, saying: "Don't go away, we'll be back." Henry lived at the *Albergo Reale* and the big transporter lived in a side street, it being his only means of getting about.

This was our unlikely 'taxi' to the Arena di Verona! This Fiat-Bartoletti transporter had been bought in 1960 by the American Scarab team and in time would be passed on to Shelby American for transporting their works Cobras. Parking the beast in Verona called for a certain amount of 'persuasive bargaining'.

Having decided he'd like to come to the opera with us, the rest was easy. We'd all go in the Maserati transporter and would meet in the restaurant of the *Reale* for an early dinner and leave about 7pm as the opera did not start until darkness had fallen.

Over dinner Henry mentioned that one or two "other guys" would like to join us, and there was plenty of room in the transporter parked in the side street, with quite a crowd standing around. Before we all clambered in the count was about 11, the driver and two alongside him, three in the living compartment on a sofa and three on the fold-down bed and two more squeezing in somewhere. There may have been a few more, but they were all motor racing people, so it was a happy and jolly bunch.

From Modena to Verona was flat and across country before the *autostrada* was built, and we made good time so that in no time Henry was heading for a car park outside the open-air *Arena*. "No!", screamed the attendant. "Motor

The Arena by day and by night. An evening of watching and listening to Verdi provided an unlikely but very enjoyable interlude between rushing around Europe in pursuit of racing cars.

coaches are round the other side." Henry explained it wasn't a motor coach, it was a private vehicle containing about 11 people. If it had been a motor coach there would have been 63 people on board. The attendant was adamant, "Round the other side!" So we went to the coach park. "No!" Another car park attendant. "You don't have a commercial licence, you can't come in here." Henry explained again that it was really just a big private car with 11 people on board, but the coach park attendant didn't want to know, so it was back to the *Arena* again.

This time we waited until the attendant was a bit preoccupied and then drove straight in without stopping and kept going to the far end of the car park. By the time the man caught up with us we had all scrambled out and formed quite a large crowd around Henry as he locked the cab door. At 11 to 1 the poor chap did not have much chance, and a combined attack by everyone with what smattering of Italian they could muster caused a happy conclusion, especially as we all began waving lire banknotes. The attendant was not going to give us a car park ticket for one 11-seater car, and equally we rejected his idea that the transporter was taking up the space of 20 Fiat 500 cars so we should buy 20 parking tickets. But we now had some good bargaining facts, and the idea that the transporter should not be in his car park was forgotten.

We attacked his figure of 20 Fiat 500s, pointing out that there were only 11 of us, so how could we have brought 20 cars into his car park, adding that two of the girls did not drive, so nine cars was the maximum, and then went on to explain that one person in a car was uneconomical. Before he could reply, two of the lads had produced a steel tape and proved conclusively that the transporter did not take the same parking space as 20 cars, adding that it was specially built to take only three cars! We were beginning to make headway. We finally bought eight car park tickets and made our way to the *Arena di Verona*, where we had no problem buying 11 tickets for the standing area in the centre of the great circular building.

The *Arena di Verona* is possibly one of the best and most complete in the whole of Italy; it looks big from the outside, but inside it is really big and impressive. We found ourselves near one corner of the giant stage, and looking up at the tiers of seats and boxes they seemed to stretch up to the sky. The stage looked big enough to hold some hundreds of performers. The accoustics were superb, as you would expect, and the solo singers were simply amazing, their voices ringing out clearly, though when they were on the far side of the stage you could barely see them.

One scene was in a marketplace, with two or three hundred 'extra' performers milling about in the market creating a subdued hum and murmur of a busy place above which the tenor gave full voice to his love for the young maiden. Just above us was the 'edge' of the crowd, not singing, but talking amongst themselves, apparently oblivious to the love songs going on overhead. Two Italians intrigued us as they were in such deep conversation that we could not connect them with the overall performance. We wondered what they were talking about so earnestly; were they discussing the football scores, the price of spaghetti, their mothers-in-law, their wives, their girl-friends, or what?

Two of us were very intrigued by this performance and seriously considered climbing up on the stage and joining the 'market place crowd', talking earnestly to each other about Maserati, Ferrari, Monza, Targa Florio, and any other Italian words that would keep up a background of Italian murmuring. But before we could make the attempt the scene changed and the 'market place crowd' drifted away, which was probably just as well...

We concentrated on the rest of the opera, which lasted until midnight. It was a truly uplifting performance, and a memorable experience, the applause afterwards being tumultuous. As it died down, an opera-lover standing behind us threw his arms into the air, flung his head back and screamed: "Viva Verdi". One of our group murmured: "Poor Verdi, and he's been dead for a hundred years." It was a fitting end to a glorious evening.

Leaving the car park was no problem, once we had all packed in again, as no car driver was going to argue with the big Bartolletti transporter, and Henry drove us back to Modena with everyone singing or humming their favourite aria and with a full chorus at times. A couple of night-caps in the bar of the *Reale* when we arrived back and everyone agreed that our Night at the Opera had been a huge success.

41

REAL RIVERS

A watery aside

I have no particular love for the sea, but rivers fascinate me, and the bigger they are the more the fascination. When they become estuaries and disgorge into the sea I lose interest. During my years of driving around Europe, first in a Lancia Aprilia, then in a Porsche 356 and subsequently in E-Type Jaguars, river crossings always attracted me. There were very few motorways in those days, so if I was not in a hurry I would study my Michelin maps and take a route that involved a major river crossing, just to have a look.

In many parts of Europe the aftermath of the war had still to be cleared up, and many of the bridges were still unusable, being replaced by temporary affairs, some of which were pretty primitive, while others were quite ingenious. Some parts of Europe were lucky in having a military Bailey Bridge still in operation, these lattice-steel structures being erected by the army to temporarily replace the bridges that had been destroyed. Ten or more years after the war ended many of them were still doing yeoman service and there were two memorable ones on the route of the Mille Miglia in 1955, when Stirling Moss and I spent three months in Italy on intensive training for the Mercedes-Benz team.

One of these Bailey Bridges was across the river that flowed into the Adriatic at Pescara. The bridge across the river in the town had been rebuilt, but inland, where we had to cross it again at the town of Popoli before climbing up into the Abruzzi mountains, there was still a Bailey Bridge in use. My 'home-made' route map had a little three-dimensional drawing of the square-sectioned lattice box spanning the river, with the arrow showing that the route turned right into the bridge, and at the other end, on the other side of the river, we exited and turned left. These were details that were important to let Stirling know about. Much later on in the route there was a similar bridge, with a similar entry, but the exit was dead straight and we must have come out of the steel box at 100mph, confident in the knowledge that the road was straight.

The noise as we crossed these bridges was shattering to us, so what it was like for the spectators who happened to be around I cannot imagine. The floor of these bridges was of wooden slats laid crosswise, and normal traffic was supposed to keep down to about 20mph, but we could ignore such indications. The exhaust pipes of the Mercedes-Benz came out of the engine compartment, below my right ear (the car was left-hand drive) and the noise bouncing off the steel lattice work was quite something, while the racket as we pounded across the wooden boards was pretty impressive. We were not on a scenic tour, we were motor racing.

In another part of Italy, up in the north, and fortunately not on the Mille Miglia route, was a wondrous crossing of the mighty Po river. It was on a back-road route I used when going to Modena, and consisted of a vast number of concrete boat-like pontoons lashed side-by-side to each other stretching right across the river. A wooden floor was lashed to the 'boats' and at about 5mph you wobbled and wallowed your way across the river. I knew it for about 10 years, but I think it was eventually replaced by a concrete autostrada bridge.

The huge and vast *autostrada* building programme eventually got under way, with impressive concrete bridges spanning some very large ravines. For a long time in southern Italy you would wind your way down the side of a valley to a primitive river crossing at the bottom, and then climb up the other side. When the *autostrada* programme got that far south the first signs of activity were the growth of huge concrete pillars as much as 100ft tall. One in particular that I watched reach fruition over a matter of years, while making at least two trips a year to Sicily for the Targa Florio and the Syracuse Grand Prix, was eventually finished and as I wafted south at 100mph in the E-Type I passed over that familiar ravine without being aware of it. Such was progress: efficient, but nothing like as scenic or intriguing.

Germany is a great country for river crossings, and on one trip northwards from Stuttgart to the Nurburgring I forsook the regular *autobahn* and ran as close as I could to the great river Rhine, and crossed it as many times as I could, using bridges of immense age and historical interest, civilized ferryboats carrying quite a large number of vehicles, and tiny ones that only took a couple of cars.

One particular crossing in the Mannheim region was on a ferry that just had to be experienced. It only took two or three cars and at first I could not see

My Porsche 356 became very used to sailing on ferries. On this occasion it was all in the cause of duty, crossing the water between Sicily and mainland Italy. Sometimes, though, I would make a detour on my journeys and take in an extra river crossing or two just out of interest. It always fascinated me watching ferries being manoeuvred and seeing how much they had to be 'oversteered' to cope with fast-moving currents.

There are two things which intrigue me when I watch people handling heavy transport. One is to see a row of racing car transporters being parked inch-perfect in a crowded Formula One paddock, and the other is to watch river barges as somehow they are manoeuvred through canals with only about an inch of clearance on each side.

what was driving it. It transpired that the vessel was attached to a cable that ran up-river a very long way to a pylon in the middle. The river had a very strong current at this point, and while the ferry boat was tied up to one bank the current and steel hawser was trying to pull it into the centre of the river. When the ferryboat master let go, the boat accelerated towards the centre of the river on an arc, gathering sufficient speed so that when the cable was on the centre-line of the river the boat had sufficient momentum to continue on its way on the arc, losing speed so that it arrived at the opposite bank as it came to rest, whereupon the master skillfully tied it up to the jetty! Someone had clearly done some very clever calculations and probably some very interesting trial-and-error runs before putting it into service. I was so fascinated by the whole affair that I went on my way slightly bewildered; what I should have done was to have made a number of crossings to find out more about it.

The growth of the motorway network throughout Europe changed the whole aspect of European motoring, and while the prodigious feats of civil engineering were most impressive and interesting to watch as they bored through mountains and spanned enormous river valleys, they were changing a whole way of life. Journeys that used to take four days were cut to two days, and mountains that took an hour-and-a-half to cross now took a matter of minutes through a tunnel. River crossings by ferryboats disappeared and were replaced by impressive single-span bridges, and great Victorian 'transporter bridges' that swung their cargo of cars across a river between two huge steel pylons were made obsolete by new bridges. Historic, even medieval bridges only wide enough for one car at a time, fell into disuse when the small French towns were bypassed with a modern new bridge outside the town.

Most of these things took a period of 10 or 20 years after the dust of the Second World War had subsided to be accomplished and completed, and I look back with pleasure at having had the opportunity to experience Europe before it was tidied up. To cross the *Europabrucke*, on the Brenner Pass between Austria and Italy, makes me look down from its great height and think: "Did my little 356 Porsche really scuttle down to the bottom of the

It could only happen in Italy. The country's massive road modernization programme involved some of the most impressive examples of bridge building and major civil engineering work I have ever seen, yet alongside all the modern technology and materials usage there was still room for time-honoured techniques. This is how to drop a plumb line Calabrian-style – just dangle a couple of rocks over the side!

valley, and climb up the other side?" As you drive through the Mont Blanc tunnel you remember the days of mountain motoring and hairpins. It is all much easier and more efficient these days, but it is the inevitable result of progress, and soon we will be emerging from the Eurotunnel under the English Channel and will be thinking: "It wasn't all that long ago when cars were being lifted by crane onto a cross-channel boat, the only way off our little island."

42

ONE HUNDRED YEARS

1994 – a landmark

In July 1994 we were able to celebrate the fact that organized sporting motoring had been in existence for 100 years, with only two serious breaks in its continuity, the first during the 1914-18 war and the second in the 1939-45 war period.

The first recognized event was in July 1894 and was described as a *Concours*, which we can accept simply as an event. It was for *Voitures sans chevaux*, or horseless carriages, which could be driven by any means, some of them being known, like steam, electricity or petrol, others being unknown, like a system of levers, the weight of the passengers, or self-acting.

Speed was of no consequence, prizes being awarded for ingenuity and practicality, and the event ran from Paris to Rouen, with a civilized lunch stop on the way. Although a steam-driven tractor unit towing an articulated trailer was the most powerful and fastest entry, first prize was awarded jointly to Messrs Panhard and Levassor and the Peugeot brothers. It went to Panhard because they built the whole car in their own factory, even though it was a bit of an ungainly affair and had rather primitive steering gear, whereas the Peugeot was a better overall design. But the brothers Peugeot only made the chassis and the running gear; they bought their engine from Panhard-Levassor, thus creating what we nowadays call a hybrid, and this was not considered as meritorious as making the whole car, even though the end result was better.

This event from Paris to Rouen, often described as the first motor race, which it patently was not, has the distinction of being the start of what we now call 'The Sport'. This motor sport, which we all love, was a disease that spread like an epidemic, and as we all know is of worldwide proportions today. If you don't like motorsport then blame the French, they started it all over 100 years ago. If you love it like I do, then raise your hat and say: "*Merci, mes amis*".

As I have mentioned, motor sport has only been stopped by two world wars, but throughout the 100 years there have been numerous occasions of acute crisis, arguments, discussion, much dissatisfaction, plans to change everything, strikes and riots, rivalry, legal wrangling, and every other badness that the human brain can scheme up, yet through it all motorsport has survived and flourished.

In 1895 the French ran a marathon event from Paris to Bordeaux and back

Outside an earlier home of British motor racing. With the Club House in the background, Whitney Straight heads out towards the Brooklands track with the ex-Trossi/Scuderia Ferrari Duesenberg in 1934. After being driven by Seaman, Featherstonehaugh and Duller, this famous car eventually came into my possession and it has since given me many enjoyable hours of fettling work. Here it is again, parked outside the gates at Brooklands, which I hope one day will become its final home.

to Paris, and this was a pure motor race and was the very first. Speed, time and distance were all-important and the fastest was the winner.

On that day pure motor racing was born, and though motor sport developed over a wide variety of forms it was motor racing that became the major attraction in the world of motor sport.

It is interesting to realize that the BRDC has been deeply involved in well over half the life of motor sport, in fact for 66 years of the 100 we celebrate.

130

When the Club was formed in 1928, motor racing was not only firmly established, but had ridden the storms of disaster and turmoil, over-enthusiasm and apathy.

The year after its formation, the BRDC organized a 500 Mile race at the Brooklands banked track, not with the idea of challenging the well-established Indianapolis 500 Mile race that had started in 1911 and was still going strong, but as a major high-speed event of our own. Whereas the American race was a scratch event for cars built to a given formula, the BRDC event was aimed at anyone and everyone, providing they drove stripped racing machinery, as distinct from sports cars. The cars varied from tiny 750cc Austin Sevens to unlimited-capacity specially-built track cars, and a handicap system was arranged that allowed any car to win providing it was the fastest in its particular category of engine size.

The 500 Mile race became a regular annual affair, and while the faster cars, capable of over 140mph, caught the imagination and enthusiasm of most spectators, the 'tiddlers' capable of little more than 100mph were never ignored or forgotten; on some occasions they even managed to win. The BRDC have never ignored the 'tiddlers' and have always encouraged them as being the nursery from which greater things grow.

In the years immediately after the Second World War, which put a stop to motor racing, the newly-formed 500cc racing got great encouragement from the BRDC, even though the Club was busy organizing events of Grand Prix standard.

Today, formulae for beginners are legion, many of them to 'one-design' rules tied in with big manufacturers, and all get support from the BRDC. One of the original aims of the Club was: "To promote the interests of motor sport generally and encourage all those interested therein." Sadly, the famous BRDC 500 did not survive, like the Indianapolis 500 has done, and it was abandoned before Brooklands closed in 1939 through lack of entries and poor spectator support. It suffered from being too hard on the competing machinery, much of which comprised normal road-racing cars, not designed

After the loss of Brooklands and the military occupation of Donington, it was left to people like Charles and John Cooper to create rough and ready, but affordable (Formula Three) cars with which British drivers could go racing on former airfields. This was the start of the rear-engined revolution as the concept was extended into Formula Two and then Formula One, through which the talents of some outstanding British drivers were to be exposed. That superb driver Tony Brooks is smiling out of the cockpit of Rob Walker's Cooper in the foreground, with Stirling Moss' car carrying his favourite No 7 parked behind it.

131

and built for sustained flat-out running. An engine blow-up at peak rpm on full throttle was usually a pretty expensive affair. Some of the specially-built track cars were becoming so fast that continually lapping the small cars, even on the wide expanse of concrete of the track, was becoming a hazardous business.

The lack of spectator appeal was obviously due to the handicap arrangements that were necessary to encompass such a wide variety in the entry. It was not the easiest of races to follow unless you stayed glued to the railings, noting every change as it occurred. There were insufficient specially-built track cars available to fill a starting grid, for unlike America we had no other form of track racing to encourage the specialists.

All our racing was of the road-circuit type and there were plenty of cars available, which the BRDC had recognized back in 1932, long before the flat-out bash in the 500 waned. The Club ran a race for the British Empire Trophy on a simulated road circuit within the confines of the Brooklands track, for pure road-racing, or circuit-type cars. This event later moved to the Donington Park circuit, always organized by the BRDC, and this promotion of circuit racing has grown ever since, especially when the Club got settled into their new home at Silverstone in 1953, our 25th (Silver Jubilee) year, when the Duke of Edinburgh became our President-in-Chief.

In celebrating this centenary anniversary of the birth of motor sport, we can feel proud that the BRDC has done its fair share in this first 100 years.

43

SUPERCARS

Forerunner is 'matchless'

Almost every year we hear about a new Supercar that is more powerful, more accelerative, faster and more expensive than the previous one, and by the present-day standards of the 'popular press', if it is more expensive it must be better. Few of them do anything worthwhile to justify the journalistic wonder-claims, a timed flying kilometre at over 200mph for a brief moment, a flash photograph of a speedometer reading over 200mph, but not much else.

But it should not be up to the magazines and the journalists to demonstrate to the world outside how good a car is, it should be the job of the manufacturer. Jaguar gave a lead by clocking a lap of the Fiat-Nardo test-track in southern Italy at something approaching the designated title of the XK220, but no more than that. A long time ago Ford built a spectacular car, before the term Supercar became popular, and it was intended to be a factory GT racer. It was the Ford GT40. It was built for racing and it won races, and was so effective that a surprising number of people bought them, went racing and also won. In the end Ford built a few civilized road versions as 'production' models, but they were still essentially pure GT40 Fords.

A little while ago, while people were raving (on paper) about some new Supercar, I heard Willie Green say that all this journalistic talk bored him; didn't they realize that Ford built a Supercar over 30 years ago and nobody has made anything to match it in concept since? He was referring to the GT40, and

I agreed with him wholeheartedly. Of course, many of today's cars have more powerful engines, are faster and more sophisticated, but they have not presented the motoring scene with a new concept like Ford did with their GT40, and few have put on an impressive demonstration to back their concept.

Before we leave the Ford GT40 we should remember that the original concept came from Eric Broadley with his tiny little GT coupe with a Ford V8 engine behind the cockpit and ahead of the rear axle. That beautiful little Lola stopped everyone in their tracks when it appeared at a London Motor Show. It

Poetry in motion...

A few days after this piece was published in the *BRDC Bulletin* in July 1994, Jenks received a surprise letter from **Sir John Whitmore**. It read in part:

Dear Denis

Strange are the ways of this world.

Yesterday, for no reason other than that I had time on my hands and I was playing with my computer, I wrote the enclosed poem. It was an unusual thing to do for I seldom even think about cars these days, let alone do anything serious in them.

The poem was evoked by my all-time favourite racing photo, which was taken by Alan Mann of me GT40-testing at Goodwood...

Imagine my surprise when I received the BRDC Bulletin this morning containing your memories of the GT40, Goodwood and me. I, too, remember it well...

Learning that Jenks wished to publish the poem – and the picture, which was taken at Fordwater – in this book, a delighted JW wrote: "Since this is the only poem I've ever written, I'm thrilled to find myself as a published poet!"

Many years on, and still that familiar Whitmore grin is in place! John always looked as though he was having the time of his life, and that's exactly the way he drove his cars – foot to the floor, loads of opposite lock, the tail way out of shape and smoke pouring from the tyres. All a bit unruly, but the crowd loved it.

THE TEST OF A LIFETIME

by John Whitmore

July 1994

Long winter shadows,
afternoon chill,
life in the meadows
is dormant or still.
The neigh of a mare
cuts the crisp air,
dogs bark a reply.
"Give 'er a try."

The thunderous roar
of four hundred and more
wild horses unleashed
to power a great beast.
A knight in his helmet
slips into his steed
to search for the limit.
He has to succeed.

Trying and testing
to find the best setting
for engine and gearing,
suspension and steering.
The cuckoo has flown,
the crowd has long gone.
The driver's alone,
but still he drives on.

This is the test
of man and machine;
the watches are set,
he drifts like a dream.
That lap was the best,
or so it might seem,
the next must be better,
by a fraction, I mean.

And so it goes on,
the search for the Grail.
The circuit he's on,
it is but a trail.
It's already here,
it's already now,
that perfection he seeks
by the end of this week.

There's always a race,
that keeps us from grace.
If only we knew;
if only he knew,
that the track has no bends,
and nobody wins,
and the race never ends,
for it never begins.

just did not seem possible to squeeze a big American V8 motor into such a tiny car, but it was possible, and Eric Broadley proved it. At the time few people realized its potential, or that Ford were going to acquire the concept and develop it into such an important landmark in the sporting world.

All that was over 30 years ago, but my everlasting memories of the GT40 were a day at the Goodwood circuit, and a little later, a week on the road with a Mk3 production version. The day at Goodwood was a simple Ford Press Day, where a handful of favoured journalists were allowed to drive a factory GT40 racer round the circuit for a few laps. Few of us had any idea of how to handle such a potent device and probably didn't even approach the performance of a basic Formula Ford single-seater. After doing my allotted stint I thought to myself, "interesting, but a total waste of time as it was light-years beyond my capabilities", and I smiled as I listened to other journalists who were slower than me talking about oversteer and understeer.

John Whitmore was standing nearby, having been doing some test-driving with the car earlier. I persuaded him to take me out in the car and show me how a GT40 should be driven. It was wonderful. I just sat and watched everything with complete satisfaction, enjoying every second of those few meteoric laps, and returned to the paddock with a very good idea of the potential of the car.

It is on occasions like this that mere mortals like myself can see why some people become racing drivers and some do not. Afterwards John said he hoped he hadn't frightened me, but I said: "Good grief, no". He laughed and said I *should* have been frightened because he had frightened himself once or twice!

The week I spent with the 'civilized' Mk3 was in the happy days of no speed limits and very little traffic across the middle of England. Every day was memorable, and I seemed to always be doing 130mph on highways and byways, not on motorways. The precision and accuracy of steering and suspension set new standards in my experience, yet it could be used to go down to my local village, or potter around seeing friends. I lost count of the friends I took for a blast, but some of them came from a long way away just to have a ride in the GT40.

That may have been 30 years ago, but the memories have not faded. Over 10 years ago Porsche set a standard by which we could judge Supercars, but they did not use a 'media' Supercar, they used a 928S off the Stuttgart production line. Our own Peter Lovett was involved when Porsche took a 928S to the Fiat-Nardo high-speed test track, and he and two Porsche colleagues drove it round for 24 hours and covered 6,033 kilometres, which gave an average, including refuelling stops, of over 251km/h (156mph). Not for one lap, not even for one hour, but for *24 hours*! As a demonstration of high-speed reliability from a production car you could not argue with it, and that was in 1982.

I am still waiting for one of the Supercars to improve on that. Instant 200mph is all very well, and a single lap at that speed, or more, shows potential, but I want to see someone put 200 miles into one hour, then continue for at least another 23 hours. With the proliferation of Supercars and the lack of demonstrative proof, I feel my requirements to be impressed may well rise to 250 miles in one hour.

There was a highly encouraging sign in the wind as a Bugatti 110 Supercar was entered for that year's Le Mans 24-Hours race, and McLaren were showing interest in the 1995 race for their Supercar, the F1 [which was destined to dominate it]. When I heard that I felt they must hurry up because the year 2000 is fast approaching and by then we should be on the threshold of a new concept, as outstanding as the GT40 was when it first appeared.

44

ANNIVERSARIES

My international landmark

Anniversaries are popular things with most people because they keep coming round! I have always been more interested in doing things, or creating things, that will generate an anniversary in time to come for other people to enjoy. I have considered myself not old enough for nostalgia (whatever it actually means). People who seem to have little to do find nostalgic pleasure in celebrating something from the past, even if it isn't their own personal past. Mostly it seems to be for things that happened before they were born, which always seems a bit odd to me.

All this is not to say I am not interested in the past or in motor racing history; far from it, for it only needs someone to say: "Do you remember when...?" and my personal computer (my brain!) selects the memory programme and out it all comes, but I don't live full-time in the programme, like some people I know. Rummaging round amongst old photographs soon sparks off thoughts like "...I'd forgotten that..." or "...was it that long ago?".

One such was a photo of a race at the Norisring in Nuremburg, in the middle of Western Germany, not to be confused with the Nurburgring on the Eifel mountains, round the castle of Nurburg. Noris is the old German name for the city of Nuremburg, and here was built an enormous stadium in which vast rallies were held during the Nazi rising of The Third Reich. The main concrete edifice is still standing and the public roads around it are closed to form the Norisring for racing purposes.

But I get ahead of myself. I was talking about anniversaries, and recalling the Norisring made me realize that August 1994 was the 20th anniversary of the last time I did a serious motoring trip outside of Great Britain. Not an occasion to celebrate, nothing to get excited about, in fact August 1974 was not meant to be any sort of landmark to remember. Unwittingly it became a landmark for me personally which I didn't realize until many years later, so no nostalgia, no commemoration, no retrospective, just one of those occasions to recall.

Since 1948 I had been spending the summer months motoring around Europe, North Africa and Scandinavia following the racing and sporting world as correspondent for *Motor Sport*. My annual mileage was between 25,000 and 45,000, and by 1974 I was well organized with a 4.2-litre E-Type Jaguar Roadster. Crossing the English Channel, by sea or air, had become so simple since my early days that I frequently came home for a weekend off, to get involved in some local event.

On the occasion in question I left the E-Type in the car park at Brussels airport (it was free in those days) and returned to England to take part in the Vintage Sports Car Club's Prescott hill-climb. The following Wednesday I was due to 'return to work' at the Osterreichring, nearly 1,000 miles away, and I arranged for my friend and colleague Alan Henry to travel with me. Alan worked for *Motor Sport* at the time and was good company, so we were always arranging trips together (for the benefit of our readers, of course). I went up to the London office to meet him, and one of the lads took us to Heathrow to catch the 6.30pm plane to Brussels. There we picked up the E-Type and drove

During my run to the 1974 Austrian Grand Prix with Alan Henry in my Jaguar E-Type Roadster I made a detour to show him the Norisring at Nuremberg, which had been the scene of rather more sinister goings-on in the distant past. Here the E-Type is parked opposite the Nazi saluting base, many of the former occupants of which ended up facing a war-crimes trial in the nearby courthouse.

to a motel near Liege for the night.

Thursday morning we left at 7.45am, along the Belgian *autoroute* and on to the German autobahn network, and headed for Cologne and Frankfurt. We were in no desperate hurry, so there was no feeling of setting out on 'an epic run', we just set off on a nice full day of motoring, with the hood down and the sun shining. A typical E-Type day in my life, but a new experience for Alan.

Our route was by *autobahn* right across Germany and through Munich to Salzburg and the Austrian frontier. From Frankfurt we took the then comparatively new *autobahn* link to Wurzburg, Nuremburg and Ingolstadt and on to Munich. The E-Type, with its high rear axle ratio, lolloped along around the 100mph mark on minimal throttle and averaged 22mpg.

Approaching Nuremberg it transpired that Alan had never been to the Norisring, nor seen the huge Third Reich concrete stadium, so not being in a great hurry we turned off the *autobahn* and made a visit.

Back to our *autobahn* 'cruising mode', enjoying the very hot sunrise as we got into southern Germany, we became aware of our side of the *autobahn* being fairly traffic-free while the northbound side was getting very full; holiday-makers returning from Austria, Italy and the Alps. We had already seen one accident that caused a stationary log-jam on the other carriageway, and now there was another, while our side was clear. On one very long stretch of rolling open farmland we could see another stationary jam a long way ahead of us and we 'logged' this jam. It was 20 miles long, as we wafted by on our side at 100mph, and we wondered when it was going to be our turn.

We got all the way to Munich without trouble and breathed a sigh of relief. I had vaguely thought of stopping the night in the Salzburg area, leaving us a leisurely run through Austria and over the mountains to Knittelfeld and the Osterreichring in time for afternoon practice on the Friday.

It was a beautiful summer evening, the air crisp and clear, and the Jaguar was purring along perfectly. Alan was still comfortable in the passenger seat so I suggested we might carry on through the evening right to the Osterreichring, it was only another three hours and through some splendid mountain country. This we did and arrived at our hotel near the circuit at 8.45pm, 1,174 kilometres from the motel at Liege, having left at 7.45am and done some sightseeing on the way.

Looking back on this very pleasant trip I asked Alan Henry recently if he remembered it. "I do indeed," he said. "Until that trip I had only done 100mph 'up-the-bypass'. What sticks in my mind was the way we sat at 100mph for hour after hour after hour, and the only instrument on the E-Type panel that moved was the fuel gauge." I asked him if he remembered the Norisring. "The great Nazi stadium?" he said. "We climbed up to the top of it and sat in the sun and ate our ice-creams." I particularly remember him asking what the imposing building was across the lake, and I explained it was the courthouse where the Nazi criminals were tried and sentenced after the war. He was quiet for a while and then he said: "You can imagine them in there, looking out of the window at this great stadium, and saying to themselves: 'Where did we go wrong?'"

After the Austrian GP Alan flew back to London and I eventually returned home in the E-Type by a not very pleasant route, and by the time of the following Grand Prix it was more expedient to fly out and back by commercial airlines. During the following winter a lot of minor changes took place around me, over which I had little control, and the following season I went to a lot of events by motorcycle, but that is another story.

That memorable trip to the Osterreichring turned out to be the last piece of serious continental motoring that I did, but it was not intended to be, and I don't intend to do a rerun, a nostalgic journey or a retrospective. It was just part of life at the time.

45

FANGIO

A tribute

Fangio only raced in Europe for 10 years, from 1948 to 1958, yet he left memories and standards that have spread worldwide. Many of the 'benchmarks' that he carved with his own blade have stood the test of time and are still viewed with some degree of awe by all of us.

The record books speak for themselves: after a season driving cars paid for by the Argentine Government, to enhance the emergence of Argentina into the world outside, he was signed up by Alfa Romeo and there followed a succession of factory contracts. Gordini, Maserati, BRM, Mercedes-Benz and Ferrari all made use of his outstanding abilities. While he was engaged in Grand Prix and sports car racing with European firms, the FIA started their World Championship for drivers, and by the time he retired he had been crowned World Champion five times, the last four consecutively, and used Alfa Romeo, Mercedes-Benz, Ferrari and Maserati to achieve these results,

A World Champion – five times over – and a gentleman. Juan-Manuel Fangio brought a unique blend of aggression, fair play and dignity to his sport.

showing a dominant ability to drive anything at the limit and to set the pace all the time.

In addition, his record book shows victories in numerous non-championship events, in *Grandes Epreuves* before the World Championship was invented, in sports car races from small mountainous events in Italy to the great Pan Americana Mexico marathon. He never won the Mille Miglia, but he was a very strong second in 1953.

After he retired from active racing he lived in his native Argentina, a country that he always loved and supported strongly in everything he did. He toured the world, he always considered himself to be an unofficial ambassador for his country and for many years was Argentina's representative on numerous world committees dealing with the motor car and its inherent social problems. Juan-Manuel Fangio the racing driver is known to us all, but Juan-Manuel Fangio the diplomat and ambassador for Argentina on worldwide motoring matters was equally well-known in non-motoring circles.

His business and commercial interests from his Buenos Aires offices, with very strong connections with Mercedes-Benz, kept his name high in the industry, so it is no surprise that the name J-M Fangio is as strong as ever it was when he was racing.

The decision by the BRDC to honour Fangio's life-long devotion to the sport by awarding him a BRDC Gold Star was acclaimed by everyone, detractors of the name Fangio being non-existent. He had no enemies and many admirers, and even his most powerful rivals admired him and respected his innate sense of decorum and fair play. As a competitor none came harder, but there was never a word against him, and he raced against all nationalities. There were many who tried hard to beat him, there were those who *did* beat him, but win or lose they all admired and respected him.

This sense of what you could do and what you should not do he learnt in his formative years when he was racing in the long-distance open-road events in South America. He had many racing 'idols' to whom he looked up. When he raced against them and eventually beat them they did not disappoint him, and their 'code', which had been learnt when racing began, was absorbed and practised by the young Juan-Manuel until he retired at the age of 47 years.

Now rising 84 years, Fangio could not make the journey from Argentina to

Keen anticipation was just one of the many talents Fangio had in his racing armoury, as he demonstrated on this occasion at Monaco in 1950, when stormy seas soaked the track at the Tabac corner and sent cars sliding off in all directions. But not the Argentinian's – he threaded his Alfa Romeo through the carnage and went on to win by a full lap.

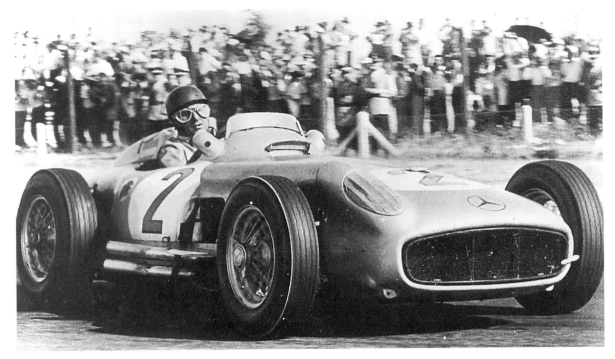

the Coy's Festival in order for our President to be able to present him with the Gold Star in person, surrounded by historic Grand Prix cars, many of which he raced when they were new. On his behalf his nephew Juan-Manuel Fangio II, who himself is a very active racer today, attended the meeting and collected the award for his illustrious uncle. The icing on the cake for the young man was to be able to drive round Silverstone in the actual 250F Maserati, chassis No 2529, with which his uncle created a lap-by-lap legend while winning the 1957 German Grand Prix. I have no doubt that when Juan-Manuel II told 'the maestro' about the unique experience, the old man's eyes narrowed and he smiled as he said: "That day I did things with that car that I had never done before, and never did again."

Among the many people at the presentation was, of course, our own Stirling Moss, one of Fangio's greatest admirers, and the man who beat him in 1957 with the British Vanwall. In 1955 Stirling joined the Mercedes-Benz team and automatically took on the role of No 2 to the great man, and he will tell you that he learnt so much from Fangio by following him that it surpassed all the knowledge he had accumulated to that point. But it was not easy, for Fangio was a hard taskmaster and made Stirling work for his knowledge. This was in 1955, the year Stirling won the Mille Miglia for Mercedes-Benz, so I was very close to the German team throughout the year, and often helped Stirling in practice.

At Monaco Fangio was always a fraction faster, and Stirling decided he was losing out on braking for the Gasworks hairpin (of fond memory). He quizzed Fangio on braking points, but the old man was a bit evasive, so I agreed to stand on the centre island and time them both round the hairpin. There were no stupid limitations on the number of laps they could do, like there is today, so I collected a pretty convincing number of times, and Fangio was consistently faster. We then decided to pinpoint where he braked, and it was consistently nearer to the apex than Stirling, so I then stood on the edge of

Fangio also had tremendous stamina, which he demonstrated most clearly in his own country in January 1955 when a heatwave so exhausted the drivers that all but two of them had to be relieved during the race. Here he is on his solo drive to victory in the Mercedes-Benz W196.

140

the track at Fangio's braking point and Stirling used all his skill and bravery to brake at the same point, but never managed it! When he stopped he said: "How does he do it?" and added: "You were at the correct point, weren't you?". I grinned and said: "You believed me for 1,000 miles when I told you where to go on May 1st in the Mille Miglia, you'll have to believe me now." Fangio was old enough then to have been our father!

He had great respect for Stirling's ability, and in the Dutch and Belgian races they had things pretty well sewn up and team orders were that Fangio would win and Stirling would be second. They ran round nose-to-tail and it all looked very easy, but it wasn't really. Just when Stirling was about to sit back and think it was all too easy, Fangio would put in a lap about 2 seconds faster than the pace they had been 'cruising' at. He would do this without any signal or warning, as if to make sure Stirling was 'on the ball', and afterwards Stirling told how hard he would have to drive to catch up. Looking through the lap times for the race afterwards it was quite clear when these 'fast' laps occurred.

Talking to Fangio much later in life I mentioned this little trick, and he explained that it was a way of monitoring Stirling's ability 'from in front' and Stirling came out with flying colours. He thought he was an excellent pupil and deserved every encouragement. When I asked him about Stirling's victory in the British Grand Prix at Aintree, he smiled and said that Artur Keser, the Mercedes-Benz press chief, had a word with him before the race, suggesting that it would be nice if Stirling could win his own Grand Prix. Fangio had shrugged and said: "Let us see how things go." As we all know, Stirling won that race by a bare car length. As always, Fangio made his young team-mate work for any favours he was granted, and as I have already recalled, he wrote in some detail about Aintree in his autobiography that PSL published in 1990.

This time it was his driving partner's turn to acknowledge the chequered flag, and Fangio was one of the first to congratulate Stirling on winning his first World Championship Grand Prix.

COMMERCIALLY SPEAKING

Thinking big

At this time of the year, either Christmas or the New Year, a lot of professional journalists, especially those normally engaged on serious road-testing and car analysis, let their hair down and indulge in a motoring fantasy. This means driving something way beyond their normal sphere of activity, or something hugely comical, and presenting the story as a serious road test, with tongue-in-cheek, for the festive season.

Looking through my motoring diary and photograph collection I realized that I seem to have indulged in fantasy motoring all my life – winter, summer, all weathers, all places – none of it really aimed at the end product to provide a good story. It just so happens that I enjoy any activity on wheels and always take the opportunity of widening my experience. Much of it has provided me with a good story that editors have been pleased to publish, and people have been pleased to read.

Thanks to friends in the motor industry, a lot of opportunities arose to look into the commercial vehicle world. This interest started in 1938, when at engineering college, and one Saturday morning the chance came to drive a giant Caterpillar tractor, complete with huge grader on tow. I found it as fascinating as driving a racing car, but not as exciting!

While Silverstone was being rebuilt a few years ago I had a chance to drive a similar D8 Caterpillar and, although it was 40 years old and had few creature comforts in the cockpit, it was as impressive as when I drove the first one. For such a big vehicle it was incredibly 'user-friendly', more so than some of the smaller modern brethren in use on that vast earthmoving project. They were more efficient and apparently more sophisticated, certainly more complicated and very clever, but that old D8 Caterpillar was more friendly. The young man using it for the job of work was so enthusiastic about it, even though he was not born when it was built. He just loved that old D8 and was so pleased that I was equally appreciative of its qualities.

Heavy vehicles have always fascinated me, and this one, photographed at Braunston, on the A45, was certainly heavy. I would rarely decline an invitation to broaden my driving experience, no matter how slowly it meant I would have to travel.

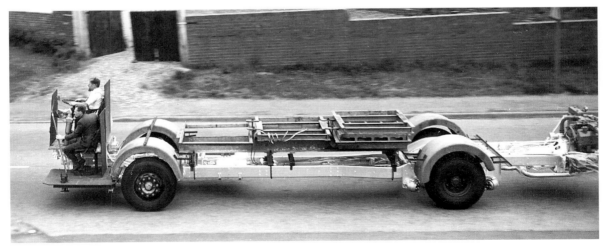

It was thanks to the late Andrew Whyte, Jaguar's PRO, that I came to 'play bus drivers' with this 50-seater Daimler Roadliner service bus. It came with a body by Marshall of Cambridge and had a 9.63-litre V6 diesel engine, an electro-pneumatic semi-automatic gearchange and air suspension. All went well until I made the mistake of stopping by a proper bus stop and opening the doors; my new 'passengers' were most annoyed when they were told they had to get off again!

I know track-laying vehicles don't run on wheels, but I enjoyed them. A vehicle that I spent a day on one summer had more wheels than I could count. It belonged to the heavy freight-moving firm of Wynns and they were moving a 250-ton transformer through my Parish. I rode in the leading tractor unit. We had a similar tractor unit hooked on our tail solidly, then came the multi-wheeled low-load trailer, and a third tractor unit pushing at the back. With full power on all three tractors and everyone in low gear it climbed gradients at less than walking pace. Speed was not important, it had to keep rolling, no matter how slowly, without faltering.

The fascinating bit on that trip was the way the driver of the front tractor set the pace and chose the 'line' at all times. At times there were as many as six men walking along with the outfit, seeing it through gaps, round corners, over humps and so on, they being in communication with each other by hand signals and whistles, all the information being transmitted to the leader of the gang who was walking along in front of us giving the driver signals that all was well.

It was all done without the slightest fuss or excitement and it was a pleasure to watch a professional team at work at close quarters. It wasn't the first time they had moved a big load, nor the last, and some time later I joined them again one night to travel with them as they threaded their way through the City of London, down to the docks, to deliver an enormous propeller for a ship. This was an 'all-nighter', and dawn was breaking before I left them.

The accompanying photograph of a single-decker Daimler bus was the occasion to visit Coventry and try something from another part of the Jaguar empire. They let me out on the local roads on the outskirts of Coventry with this urban version of the Daimler Roadliner. One of the Daimler engineers came with me and sat in the passenger compartment, having first let me drive it round the factory roads. It was powered by a 9.63-litre V6 Cummins Diesel limited to 135bhp for urban use. It was 36 feet long, with the driver at one end and the engine at the other end, controls being electro-magnetic and semi-automatic. It had air suspension and a 50-seater body built by Marshall of Cambridge.

The destination panel on the front read PRIVATE DAIMLER 00. Now 00 in European countries is the sign for a lavatory, especially in old-fashioned French towns and villages where the TOILET or REST ROOM (funny names!) is a shed out in the cobbled yard. In the suburbs of Coventry it made no impression, nor did the PRIVATE bit.

It was very docile and easy to control and manoeuvre, and being to urban specification it was happier stopping and starting than trying to get anywhere. Consequently I enjoyed myself 'playing at buses', pulling into laybys, opening and shutting the doors and so on. I completely forgot about the public outside, and at one stop I opened the doors and a crowd of people poured onto the bus. The Daimler engineer had his work cut out persuading them we were not an official bus and that they would have to get off. With others pushing at the back in a typically unruly bus stop mob, it took a long time to restore order! Clearly, none of them had read the front information panel – a bus was a bus, and a bus at the bus stop with the doors open was ready to be boarded! We drove off, leaving a rather angry queue of passengers, and my companion said: "I think we had better stop 'playing at buses' and go back to the factory."

Whenever I get involved with commercial vehicle movements I enjoy watching a really skilled driver reversing into a narrow gap with his rear-view mirrors as his only means of seeing where he is going. For a long time I practised with my normal road car, but was never convinced in what I was doing, probably because my cars were invariably GT coupes with unsuitable mirrors.

When the Renault F1 team gave some of us a day out at the Paul Ricard circuit, driving a little Formula Renault and then the current turbocharged Formula One car, I saw an opportunity to improve my skills. When the day was done my colleagues trooped off to find a supermarket and stock up with cheap booze, so I stayed behind, and once the 38-tonne Renault articulated transporter was loaded I persuaded the team manager to let me drive it on the airfield perimeter roads. Its rear-view mirrors were superbly situated for seeing backwards and I spent more time practising going backwards than forwards! There was nothing to hit on the airfield so I really enjoyed myself edging this monster along the grass verge and turning into laybys, and aiming it between self-chosen marks on the concrete.

I did not contemplate venturing forth on the open road, and Jean Sage would not have permitted it anyway, but he and his mechanics were highly amused by a serious English motor racing journalist enjoying himself with their workhorse, having driven the thoroughbred that was inside.

47

GRAND PRIX AT PESCARA

It was different

A friend of mine who has gone to work in Italy wrote to me recently from a small town on the Adriatic coast, just beyond Pescara, saying that as he was not far from Pescara, he was researching into the past history of the Pescara Grand Prix. He asked me about finding the route of the 16-mile circuit and queried: "Did I have any particular memories of the Pescara races?"

That started me off, naturally, and I recalled that my first visit was in 1954, when I was travelling about Europe in a 1938 Lancia Aprilia. This was in the days before the autostrada network had spread beyond Brescia, so the journey down the Adriatic coast seemed endless. Prewar, I had read about the Pescara circuit and studied maps and photographs, so I arrived with a small working knowledge of the event, but there was much more to learn!

Racing on the Pescara circuit started in 1924, when none other than Enzo Ferrari himself was the winner driving an Alfa Romeo. During the Mussolini regime the race was called the *Coppa Acerbo*, after Tito Acerbo, one of the Fascist leading lights, but after the war it resumed its true name, *Gran Premio di Pescara*.

My lasting impression of the whole affair was that it was *different*; I had seen sports cars racing on mountain roads and through mountain villages, in events like the Targa Florio, the *Giro di Sicilia* or the Mille Miglia, but the sight of pure single-seater Grand Prix cars like the Maserati 250F, Ferrari 625 and Gordini on mountain roads was something else. The 16-mile circuit was roughly triangular; the first leg, from Pescara up to the village of Capelle, was pure mountain road, the second leg was flat-out, slightly downhill to Montesilvano at sea-level, to a sharp right-hander, and then it was a long blast along the coast road back to Pescara.

The usual time for the race was mid-August, at the height of the Italian holiday season, and when the sun was at its best. In view of the heat, everything was finished by midday, so practice was from 9am until 12 noon, and the race itself was at 8am. No Bernie Ecclestone television schedules to adhere to in those relaxed days of Grand Prix racing. But the pit arrangements, now they were *really* different.

The start of a voiturette event at Pescara in 1934. The crowd in front of the clock at the side of the track are roughly in line with the timing line, which was situated so inconveniently and confusingly halfway along the pits.

Everything about the circuit was temporary, so the pits were built from steel scaffolding and wooden planks, as were the main grandstands opposite (just like Silverstone used to be, but for different reasons) and the pits and start/finish area were on the main road into Pescara. Now the normal thing was to place the timing line and the timekeepers either at the beginning of the pits or at the end, but Pescara was *different*.

The start/finish line and the timekeepers were situated halfway along the line of the pits, which would not have been much of a problem on somewhere like Brands Hatch or Goodwood, but on a 16-mile circuit it presented problems for the competitors. One lap of the Pescara circuit was equal in length to a complete race on the average British circuit, and if your pit was after the timing line you had to set off for a full lap before you could start an official timed lap. Equally, if your pit was before the timing line the watches would be started as you left and, providing you went past the timekeepers at the end of the lap, you would be all right, but it meant continuing round for another lap, which would not be timed if you stopped at your pit. So either way you had to cover two laps (each 16 miles, remember) in order to get one lap time, and even then it would include a slow start or a slow finish, unless you were ready to do a series of laps, but at 16 miles to the lap few people reeled off a series of laps in order to get one quick one, as is done today on our 80-seconds 'sprint' circuits.

I don't know who first solved the Pescara problem, whether it was *Scuderia Ferrari* when they were running Alfa Romeos, or the German teams prewar when Mercedes-Benz and Auto Union supported the *Coppa Acerbo*, but the answer was fairly simple, though today's rule-makers would have 'kittens' at the mere thought of it. If your pit was after the timing line you wheeled your car back down the pit lane to the very end and took a run out onto the circuit and across the timing-line to start your lap.

There was no dividing wall between track and pit lane in those days. If your pit was before the line and you only wanted to do one lap, you set off quite normally, but at the end of the lap you crossed the line on full-song and then anchored-up with everything and tried to stop before the end of the pits; if successful, you then pushed your car back down the pit lane to your own pit.

Prince Bira was at the first race I attended in Pescara and I was giving his mechanic a helping hand when I learnt about the 'Pescara' trick. We were wheeling his 250F Maserati backwards across the timing line when another car coming towards us on full-song crossed the line and the driver stood on the brakes and fishtailed to a stop. As he and his mechanics wheeled his car back, 'our' driver set off towards them! Our job was then to wait for him by our pit and to greet him on his return, but to be prepared for him to go by with all the brakes on and to retrieve him from the end of the pit lane, or even a bit beyond, but that meant a bit of bluffing to get the car back into the pit lane. All this added to the fun which was the Pescara Grand Prix. As I say, it was different. There were drivers who appeared to circulate all morning, and when the practice times were posted they were down as non-qualifiers, with no official laps to their credit. They had been doing single testing laps and had not known about the 'starting' or 'finishing' trick.

While all this was interesting and enjoyable, that first visit to Pescara was memorable for me personally, thanks to Stirling Moss, though neither of us realized it was important at the time. Stirling had just been taken under the works Maserati umbrella with his own 250F and they had taken an A6G sports car down with them for him to use for learning the circuit outside of official practice times. Immediately after the Saturday official practice most people went off for lunch, but not Stirling; he was all for doing some laps in the

A driver's eye view

In preparing the accompanying piece on Pescara at the end of 1995, Jenks remembered that in 1957 **Bruce Halford** *had taken part in the Grand Prix there with his Maserati 250F, which Tony Robinson had trundled down in the back of the ex-Royal Blue coach – the subject of one of the earlier stories. Jenks asked Bruce for some of his recollections, and received the following in reply:*

Pescara certainly was different! I had never been there before – or since, come to that – so that in company with most of the GP circus I didn't know it. As far as I can recall, there wasn't even a sports car race, which would have helped to get to know the circuit. My recollection is that it was the longest circuit in use for GP racing. Obviously one couldn't walk it, and there wasn't much point in going round it in the Royal Blue, with its top speed of 38mph, although Tony and I did so once – the lap time was about 50 minutes!

I had to do a compulsory three laps in the Maserati in order to qualify, and that was my practice! I just bummed a ride round with anyone who was going round, just to get some idea of the circuit. I didn't keep any records of my race results, but my recollection is that I was running about fourth when the drive let go (*Jenks thought Bruce might have been seventh at that point*).

As far as I was aware, this was the only event on the calendar at that time where Maserati took spare engines for all their cars, plus one more, so that they could change all the engines after practice because of the mileage clocked up.

We did have some spare time to see the beach, and I recall that it was so hot that one couldn't actually walk on it without shoes. It was very much a holiday resort on the Adriatic, and being in the middle of the holiday season it was very busy. I am sure Tony and I were kipping in the coach from financial necessity, but I don't think we could have found a room even if we had wanted to!

I remember having supper one night in a small restaurant when in walked Fangio and his lady. How times change: A couple of years ago I was in Monaco for the GP and saw Prost eating in a restaurant, and there must have been a couple of hundred people in there gawking at him.

Pescara was a very quick circuit. After the pit straight, parallel to the sea, it started to climb, through a couple of villages – like Gueux, on the Reims circuit – with just a few straw bales to show where one turned in the middle of the village. Climbing up, there was a big church straight ahead with apparently nowhere to go, but as one got right up to it [it became clear that] the circuit went to the right of the church. After this highest point, we went downhill, almost straight – again it was a bit like Reims, but a lot longer – then we had to brake hard for almost a hairpin, after which it was flat-out again along the pit straight.

I seem to remember that before the war the German cars were doing well over 200mph, but now a sort of chicane had been put in just before the pits. It wasn't like current chicanes, it was a sort of small meander through a housing area – first right, then left, left again and then right, back on to the straight immediately before the pits. I should think we were geared for about 175mph..... and I would have thought the fast boys would have been going even faster than that at Pescara. Yes, Jenks, it certainly was different!

sports car while everything was fresh in his mind. I had just helped wheel Bira's car into the Maserati garage when I saw Stirling climbing into the A6G. When he said he was going round the circuit I asked him if I could accompany him, and climbed in. After one exhilarating lap he stopped, expecting me to stagger out and be sick from sheer fright, instead of which I was grinning and said: "That was terrific, can we go round again?". He did not forget that little chance occasion, and the following winter, when he was planning the 1955 Mille Miglia with Mercedes-Benz, he asked me to go with him, certain in the knowledge that I would not be frightened.

By the early 1960s the world had caught up with things like the Pescara Grand Prix, and like many things it did not fit into the Brave New World, so it died an ignominious death at the hand of progress. We have to progress or we will go backwards, it is a simple law of life that you cannot stand still. But Pescara was a highlight for me, as were thousands of other things that have gone with progress, and hopefully thousands more to come.

48

ONE MAN'S MILLE MIGLIA

A long time

As I write this a vast collection of people are anticipating being part of the Mille Miglia 'retrospective' event for l995. It is exactly 40 years since Stirling Moss took me with him in a Mercedes-Benz 300SLR, when he won the 22nd Mille Miglia at record speed in 1955. It is exactly 60 years since the Mille Miglia first stirred the blood in my veins, at the tender age of 14½ years.

In the late 1920s I was mad keen on aeroplanes, especially the Schneider Trophy high-speed seaplanes. Speed was the be-all and end-all of my interests, and still is oddly enough. Mechanical things that do not race do not interest me greatly, whereas the dullest vehicle comes alive if it carries a competitive racing number. The fastest on land, sea or air are the only records that fascinate me.

Living in the big city, I soon realized that aeroplanes were not really my scene as they seemed far away up in the sky and unattainable to a 10-year-old schoolboy, so my interest turned to motor cars and motorcycles. By 1931 I had discovered motor racing, purely in newspapers and magazines, but I could relate pictures of racing cars to things one saw on the roads. By 1932 I had discovered Alfa Romeo and Maserati and Grand Prix racing, thanks to reports in *The Autocar* and *The Motor*, and the *monoposto* Alfa Romeo was my dream car; was there ever such a beautiful, functional machine as the original 2.6-litre *monoposto* Alfa Romeo?

The *Scuderia Ferrari* and their red Alfa Romeos was my 'holy grail', even though it was five years before I saw one for real. My first scrapbook of magazine cuttings started with A for Alfa Romeo. Grand Prix racing was the only sort of racing that appealed to me, though I was aware of other sorts of racing, such as the 24 Hours of Le Mans, which Alfa Romeo won, but that was about all.

In 1935, exactly 60 years ago, I read that Alfa Romeo had won the big 1,000-

mile sports car race in Italy and I thought "ho hum": another event like Le Mans, I presumed. I was more interested in the imminent appearance of the new Grand Prix 8C/35, which was due to replace the successful *Tipo* B *monopostos*.

Then photographs appeared of Carlo Pintacuda winning the 1935 Mille Miglia with his friend the Marquis Della Stufa. They were in a *Tipo* B *monoposto* Alfa Romeo! That made me sit up and take notice. A pure Grand Prix car, with mudguards, lamps, a horn, and two seats squeezed into the slightly widened cockpit. As Mr Toad would have said: "Oh, what joy. A thing of beauty to behold." From that day I widened my interests to take in this glorious Italian race in which a pure Grand Prix car was allowed to take part. The following year the Scuderia Ferrari had two-seater versions of the 85/35 Grand Prix cars, which finished 1-2-3, and Clemente Biondetti finished fourth with the 1935 *monoposto*. The seed had been sown and was to bear fruit, but little did I realize what the quality of that fruit was to be nor the enormity.

Grand Prix racing (and engineering studies) kept my mind fully occupied until 1939, when I got myself practically involved with racing cars as a very junior helper, but the important thing was that I was in the paddock with a job to do and actually on the side of the starting grid officially. No longer did I have to watch the racing cars from the public enclosures.

The Mille Miglia Alfa Romeos of 1938 left me breathless with admiration for their sheer beauty, with all-enveloping bodies by Touring of Milan, all-round independent suspension and 2.9-litre straight-eight twin-overhead-camshaft engine and two superchargers. In 1939, one of these cars, bought by Hugh Hunter, appeared on the English Club racing scene and, being in the paddock by this time, I was able to stand close to it and feel the excitement generated by this real Mille Miglia car. The photographs of Carlo Pintacuda and Clemente Biondetti came alive.

Just as the motor racing enthusiast in me was overlooking the engineer being bred into me at technical school, the war started and that put a stop to everything, and I found myself trying to behave like a responsible aeronautical research-and-development 'boffin', but I failed miserably because the seed of racing had been sown very firmly. As soon as the war was over I left the world of aeroplanes and went back to racing cars, racing

motorcycles and Grand Prix racing.

A very full life in motorcycle racing kept me busy for the immediate postwar years, but by 1952 I began to feel the lure of the Mille Miglia attracting once again and, having been a racing sidecar passenger for five years, it seemed a natural thing to do to try and get a ride as passenger in the Mille Miglia. It very nearly came off in 1952, when Leslie Johnson said he would be happy to take me with him in his Nash-Healey. It all fell through at the last minute when a well-known Fleet Street journalist said he was looking for a ride and Johnson took him. So I went on with my sidecar racing, which kept the adrenalin flowing for me.

The following year I began to wind down on motorcycle racing and develop possibilities as a race reporter for Grand Prix races and other events in Europe. Naturally I took in the Mille Miglia, but rather than try and follow the event from the press centre in Brescia I got into my old prewar Fiat 1500 and disappeared into the night. I found a long deserted straight road near Ravenna, pulled off onto the grass verge and slept in the car. I had worked it out about right for at dawn the small cars began to appear and by daylight the Ferraris, Alfa Romeos, Lancias and Maseratis began to arrive. As I watched cars coming towards me and passing at 130-140mph on this narrow country road I knew, like Mr Toad, that "this was for me".

While the competitors went on their way down the Adriatic coast to Pescara, across to Rome and then back up the mountainous spine of Italy, I drove across to Bologna to the outskirts, where the road comes down off the Raticosa pass. I already knew where my future lay, and as I watched Giannino Marzotto go by in the lead in his 4.1-litre Ferrari followed by Fangio in the *Disco-Volante* coupe Alfa Romeo, I was already in there riding with them.

During the year my eyes and ears were kept open for any chance of a ride in the 1954 event. As a race reporter I was pretty close to the HWM team during

It was very sad that the Marquis de Portago accident of 1957 should bring the 'real' Mille Miglia to an end. But it was particularly pleasing in the circumstances that the final victory should go to Piero Taruffi, who had tried in vain to win the event so many times. A popular winner indeed in his Ferrari. Here he is pictured in the Lancia D24 in which he had won both the Targa Florio and the Tour of Sicily back in 1954.

the season, and to George Abecassis and John Heath, so I pricked up my ears when I heard about the HWM-Jaguar sports car being entered for the 1954 Mille Miglia. I turned up in Brescia well before the event, hoping something would transpire. George A told me he was taking his mechanic, Frank Nagel, with him to keep him company if the car broke down. As he said: "If you are on your own and it breaks down in the middle of nowhere it can be bloody lonely down south in Italy." When I met Frank I asked him how seriously did he want to go in the HWM-Jaguar. He didn't want to go at all really, "...but the Guv'nor has asked me..." He was only too pleased to change places with me, and thought I was quite mad.

Abecassis had no objections and promptly offered to "take me up the road" on a test drive to see if I liked it. As I climbed into the passenger seat Frank leant over and said: "At 130mph you'll find you put your comic away." We were at Conte Maggi's castle, and it was straight out on to the *autostrada* and my first ride in a really quick sports-racer. It was sheer joy, straight up to 145mph without a pause, then mile after mile at very nearly 150mph. A turn round at one of the *autostrada* exits, back on to the other carriageway and flat out back to *Casa Maggi*. When we stopped I was grinning happily and all ready for the start. "See you in Brescia at 5.30 tomorrow morning," said George.

Our starting time was 6.13am on Sunday, May 2, 1954, the last car away on the minute-intervals rally-type start. By breakfast time it was all over, a rear shock absorber broke away from the axle and it was all that George could do to keep it straight at 100mph, let alone 145mph. Being the last car away meant that once we had dropped behind a reasonable schedule speed we were assumed to have retired, so the spectators got into their Fiat 500s and drove home! We were forced to retire at Ravenna, after only 188 miles (a season of modern Club racing!), but enough to make me look forward to more Mille Miglia experience.

Little did I know what was in store. With Stirling Moss in 1955 in the Mercedes-Benz, in 1956 and 1957 in Maseratis, and then it all stopped. For me it was a bit like my experience in 1939; just as I was getting into the swing of things it all came to an abrupt end, leaving only fond memories. But it was not the end of the world.

49

A TRIP TO BARI

A nice journey with asides

This is a simple story of a motoring trip in Europe before the days of an extensive motorway network as there is today. It was a remark in a book that I was reading recently, about the battle for Rome in 1944, when I read that the Italian Government, such as it was, had taken refuge in Bari. Now the name Bari, a seaport on the Adriatic coast of southern Italy, meant motor racing to me, and I recalled my first visit there in 1956. Earlier, there had been Formula One Grand Prix races there, but I never went to them, although I had read about them and seen numerous photographs which suggested it was

an interesting 'town race'. In 1956 the event was for sports cars, and as Stirling Moss was entered by the Maserati factory with a 300S I thought it would be a good excuse to go.

On Saturday, July 14, I was at the British Grand Prix at Silverstone and chatting with an American friend and fellow Porsche 356 owner, and he thought it would be a good idea to accompany me. He had been in the American forces in England, had been demobbed, and was "sort of, kinda' heading back to the USA"; the only trouble was he kept getting deflected off the direct route by more interesting things involving motor racing.

The following Tuesday I met him in London, leaving his Porsche there and

On the left, the battered wheel of the Porsche 356 after I had brought the car to rest following a busy few seconds at the steering wheel. The Porsche was quite often in the wars, and here it bears the scars of a brush with an oncoming car on a narrow Italian road.

DOING IT THE HARD WAY

Jenks asked **Mike Anthony** *to dig into his memory bank and recall the trip he made to the sports car race at Bari with his Lotus 11; the result was the following tale of derring-do which will probably stagger the typical present-day racer:*

In the 1950s Europe was much larger, not physically of course, but neither the road systems nor the vehicles were as developed or as sophisticated as today. Long journeys were not undertaken in such a cavalier manner as now.

John Eason-Gibson, then the Secretary of the BRDC, negotiated the sum of £400 for me to compete in the sports car race at Bari, which was a lot of money in those days, and even the fact that the journey to get there would be about as far as one could go without actually falling into the Mediterranean did not dampen my enthusiasm. So with high hopes I set off with Ernie Unger (a sort of travelling mechanic) in my home-made Standard Vanguard racing car transporter.

From the outset the race became almost of secondary importance; the challenge was to actually get there. When Ernie came to take his turn at driving, it proved difficult for him to come to terms with the idiosyncrasies of my transporter. To accommodate the racing car I had lengthened the basic car's wheelbase from 8ft to 13ft 6in and made an open load platform at the back. It had been inspired by Mercedes' beautiful transporter, which of course was made as one would expect. Mine, however, had not had any R&D, and apart from being difficult at times to control in a straight line, it was often prone to doing odd things in corners! I drove the rest of the way.

The descent of the Simplon pass was notable for the brakes overheating to such an extent as to boil away all the brake fluid. We progressed until just south of Rome, but then the water pump exploded. A visit was made to an Italian garage in the heart of the countryside, where all the very young and very dirty mechanics worked with almost no clothes and were barefoot. I redesigned the cooling system to work as a thermo syphon, and surprisingly it worked! We then drove sedately down to Bari and prepared both the car and ourselves for the race; the car was cleaned and we had a bath!

Practice for the race was fun. The course ran through the town and the Lotus obtained quite a good grid position. I must now explain one or two things about my Lotus 11. The year before I had had quite a successful season with a Lotus 10, which had its high Bristol engine in the normal upright position, with a bulge in the bodywork. When I came to put the Bristol engine in the Lotus 11 I decided to lay it over at 30 degrees to the horizontal. Problems arose from both the oil system and the cooling system, but on this occasion everything went well.

The Lotus front suspension was a Ford 10 solid axle cut in half and pivoted in the middle. The system used the normal fore-and-aft radius rods each side and worked quite well. In the race, however, one of these radius rods became loose where it connected to the axle (a not uncommon occurrence), which may have been caused by having to cross the tramlines that followed part of the course.

You have probably heard of bump-steer and even torque-steer; well, these in no way compare with having half an axle that can move backwards and forwards at will! Braking had to be planned, and opposite lock to wherever the car decided to go applied. Finally, common sense got the better of me and I retired.

The post-race dinner was a great success and I got an enormous cup for being the competitor who had travelled the longest distance to get to Bari!

It would be nice to say the journey home was easy, but unfortunately that was not the case. I went to Rome airport to collect a new water pump, which had been sent out by the ever-efficient AA. But the customs demanded duty, notwithstanding my having a carnet. As I didn't wish to pay this I wished them a good day and a happy life in my fluent Italian and left the pump with them! The journey continued with my most efficient thermo syphon system working well.

For a respite we came back via the south of France, then headed north until, just south of Paris, one of the front wheel bearings started to squeak; the grease must have become overheated in Italy. Unfortunately, before I could stop at a garage to replace the bearing it seized and the stub-axle turned off.

While we were sitting at the side of the road, who should come along but David Piper and Bob Hicks in their Lotus 11s; they drove these round Europe from race to race! So there we were, just south of Paris, with about 30 per cent of the Lotus 11s in the world, without an effective transporter between us! I went into central Paris by bus and metro and bought a new stub-axle assembly and then fitted it at the side of the road. I don't know if that sounds easy, but it wasn't!

During the journey my wife had been sent various postcards detailing our disasters, so she was very pleased when we finally got home!

setting off in my 356 Coupe. It was 8.30pm, but we were soon down in Kent to stop at an hotel not far from the airport at Lydd. Next morning we flew by Silver City Bristol Freighter, of fond memories, to Le Touquet and were soon on our way. A lunch stop at Reims saw us doing a couple of laps of the Grand Prix circuit, during which we met another American-in-Europe friend in his 356 Coupe, on his way from Paris to Switzerland. It was one of those chance meetings that always made European motoring interesting.

We spent the night within sight of the mountains, and next morning had a spirited crossing of the Mont Cenis pass into Italy and down into Turin. On through Alessandria we joined the *Via Emilia* and carried on down through Modena and Bologna, calling briefly at Weber Carburettors and the OSCA factory, to join the Adriatic coast at Rimini and on to Pesaro for the night.

Since Forli we had been on the 1955 Mille Miglia route, so Steve was really enjoying his 'European tour' as my passenger, and next day, Friday, July 20, we followed the route right down to Pescara. This involved two deviations, one at Senigalia and the other on the approach to Pescara, in order to do some laps of the respective open-road circuits in regular use at the time. These were the happy, carefree days when most racing circuits in Europe were on normal everyday roads, and not purpose-built facilities locked away behind walls and wire-netting.

After Pescara, civilization seemed to have stopped, towns and villages were few and far between, and traffic was almost non-existent. Farm workers all seemed to have a horse and cart, with a dog running obediently along beneath the axle. The road was fast and interesting and the little Porsche was scuttling along merrily, though the surface was anything but smooth.

Suddenly, without warning, the car swooped from one side of the road to the other and I was too busy to wonder what had happened; we were doing 65-70mph at the time, and as I brought it all to rest at the side of the road I had a feeling that both rear tyres had punctured simultaneously, but knew that this was most unlikely. We got out and our first reaction was: "Oh my gawd, the rear axle has broken", for the right rear wheel was tucked up under the mudguard. The left rear looked alright, so we jacked the car up and a very buckled wheel, tyre and hubcap fell in the road, but there was no centre to the wheel. The whole centre disc with the five bolt holes was still on the brake drum, all the nuts firmly in place.

There had obviously been some pretty horrendous graunching noises as we skated to rest, but I had been too busy to notice, and we found that the wheel jammed up under the mudguard had taken all the load. Apart from a slight crease in the bodywork there were no signs of any damage, so we took the broken wheel centre off and fitted the spare wheel.

We were still a couple of hours from Bari, so we carried on at a greatly reduced pace, conscious that the other rear wheel might break in the same way, and now having no spare wheel we'd be in real trouble! We did not dare look closely at the left-rear wheel in case it was showing signs of cracking, and the knowledge of knowing would only worry us.

We arrived safely at Bari and met Stirling, who had arrived by air, and after dinner I took him gently round the circuit to have a look at the layout, not telling him about our 'wheel escapade' as I didn't want to worry him. It was now late on Friday evening, after an interesting three days' motoring.

Fortunately, practice was late on Saturday afternoon, so we had the morning to organize a new wheel and tyre to be sent down from the Bologna Porsche agent, and to attend official scrutineering at mid-day.

On Sunday there were two races, one for sports cars up to 2,000cc, which was a Maserati benefit, with Jean Behra leading Cesare Perdisa home in a works 1-2 in Maserati 200S cars, with Giulio Cabianca third in a 1,500cc OSCA. The second race was for sports cars over 2,000cc, and the first five cars in the under-2,000cc race were invited to take part in the 'big boys' event. Stirling Moss won this event with ease in a factory 300S, Behra was second with the 2-litre car, and they were followed home by three more Maseratis, with Duncan Hamilton a poor sixth, his D-Type Jaguar not liking the rough and bumpy Bari street circuit.

The following day we inspected the Porsche wheels closely, found no further signs of cracking, so set off northwards up the mountainous central backbone of Italy, into Switzerland and across France to Le Mans for the 24-Hours race the following weekend. After that it was to the Nurburgring for the German GP the weekend afterwards, and from there Steve got a lift back to England and I went on my way north for two races in Sweden – but those are for stories some other time.

Mention the town of Bari, and my thoughts immediately turn to motor racing in the golden age of Italian racing.

50

FORTY YEARS ON

Retrospective

As the 1994 season drew to a close, Bruce Jones, the editor of the weekly magazine *Autosport*, who spends his days cramming 'a quart into a pint pot' every week to cover everything that happens in the world of sporting motoring, said: "Do you realize next year is the 40th anniversary of your great adventure with Stirling Moss when he won the Mille Miglia at record speed?" My reaction was: "Good grief! Am I really that old?" He thought *Autosport* should plan some sort of 'feature' for the occasion; a personal retro-run round the whole 1,000 miles; an analysis of how much of the original route still exists; where *autostradas* have been built on the original roads; a visit to the Mercedes-Benz Museum in Stuttgart and a re-acquaintance with the winning car in all its rebuilt glory. There were endless possibilities.

Practical and self-controlled editor that he is, he said: "There is only one problem." The event we wanted to commemorate had been held on May 1, 1955, so if we were going to plan 40 years to the day we would have to plan for May 1, 1995. These days sees the International calendar in full swing, while National events never seem to stop, so there was little hope of planning anything spectacular for the 40th anniversary of just one race.

While mulling over ideas it was announced that Mercedes-Benz were supporting the 1995 Goodwood Festival of Speed and were interested in running the 1955 Mille Miglia-winning Mercedes-Benz 300SLR "...and would Stirling Moss and Denis Jenkinson be interested in becoming involved to commemorate their victory of 40 years ago..." Our problems were solved. *Autosport* were also supporting the 1995 Festival, so it was one big happy family and the weekend of June 24/25 was there to be enjoyed to the full.

Explaining to people that May 1, 1955 was a great day, I stressed that it was the successful culmination of a project that had started three months before.

For me personally the germ of the idea was sown on Monday, September 6, 1954, the day I saw the prototype Mercedes-Benz sports-racing car on test at Monza. It was a two-seater version of the successful 1954 Grand Prix car and was intended for the Sports Car World Championship events in 1955. Little did I imagine that I was going to be part of that programme as I watched the car on test at Monza.

Watching with me at Monza was John Fitch, who was a member of the Cunningham sports car team and had driven in the Carrera-Panamericana for the Mercedes-Benz 300SL team. When he saw the sports car version of the W196 Grand Prix car he said: "That car could win the Mille Miglia. Ferrari, Alfa Romeo and Maserati couldn't beat that." This was September 1954, and drivers for 1955 were yet to be finalized. Needless to say, John was hoping to join the sports car team after his good showing for them in Mexico.

A few days later we spent an evening together and discussed John's idea for ways of overcoming the Italians' natural advantage in the Mille Miglia by it being run on their own roads. The basic idea was that the second person in the car should not be a spare driver or a mechanic, but should be a full-time 'navigator'. The idea interested me, for I had done part of the 1954 Mille Miglia with George Abecassis in an HWM-Jaguar and there were parts that I knew by previous use of the roads in my travels which were unknown to George. I soon realized there was much to be gained from a navigator who knew where he was going.

I had experienced a similar situation while passengering on a racing motorcycle and sidecar, particularly up the 21-kilometre Mont Ventoux Mountain Hill-climb and round the Solitudering, and especially round the Nurburgring. There was no easy communication between the rider and the passenger, so a thump with a clenched fist on his foot had to suffice. One thump for a left turn, two for a right turn, and a succession of thumps before the left or right indication meant: "Watch it! It's a dodgy corner." The system worked quite well.

While John waited to hear from Mercedes-Benz about their driver team for the 1955 sports car project, we went ahead on planning a 'navigational system' and spent a lot of time pouring over large-scale road maps, as well as planning reconnaissance runs in his 1,100cc Fiat, as he was living it Italy at the time.

So if I was going to look for a 40th anniversary of the Mille Miglia project it had to be September 6, 1994, and that date was long past. It was at the New Year, 1955 when Mercedes-Benz settled their programme, and all they could promise John Fitch was a works reserve drive and an entry in a 300SL Gullwing to win the GT class. Then Stirling Moss telephoned me to ask if I would like to join him for the Mille Miglia now that the Stuttgart firm had confirmed that not only would he be in the W196 Grand Prix team, but also in the sports car team, along with Fangio, Karl Kling and Hans Herrmann.

When I talked to John Fitch about the situation he said: "Even using our system we could not hope to win outright with a 300SL, but Stirling in an SLR could win. Go and join him and take our system with you, and good luck to both of you." I met Stirling at *The Steering Wheel Club* of fond memory, and we shook hands on the deal.

He was already thinking along the same lines of using a 'navigator' and had asked me because he was certain that I was 'mad' and 'fearless'. As he said: "I've seen you riding with Eric Oliver, the sidecar World Champion, so what more could I ask?" By the time we had finished lunch we were 'all systems GO' on the project, so February 4, 1995 was another real 40th anniversary, but only from the aspect of talking about the project. It was Friday, February

4, at 7.30am when the real work began when we left Brescia in a prototype 300SLR on our first test run round the 1,000-mile lap.

Autosport really entered into the spirit of this '40 years on' and gave us a four-page feature entitled 'Four eyes are better than two' in their issue of February 9, 1995, 40 years to the day from when we had set off for Italy together for the first time. With planning for the Goodwood Festival of Speed in full swing and the promise of four demonstration runs up the course of the hill-climb, life really was 'beginning again at 40'.

That dyed-in-the-wool enthusiast Alain de Cadenet could not stand by and see the 40th anniversary on May 1 go by unheralded, and he proposed a small private luncheon for Stirling and me, with a few friends. It was held at a small Italian family restaurant in London, and the menu was one that Enzo Ferrari had offered BRDC Members Earl Howe and Sir Henry Birkin when they passed through Modena in the winter of 1933 on a reconnaissance run for the Mille Miglia of that year in a prototype K3 MG Magnette.

The Goodwood Festival was glorious and a fitting finale to a lot of activity in this '40 years on'. The 300SLR was as exciting to ride in as it had been 40 years ago, especially as I was being driven by the same Stirling Moss, exuding the same enthusiasm at 65 as he had at 25.

This is the menu for the celebratory luncheon that Alain de Cadanet so kindly put on for Stirling and me on May Day 1995, 40th anniversary of Mercedes' Mille Miglia win. A generous act, which we appreciated very much.

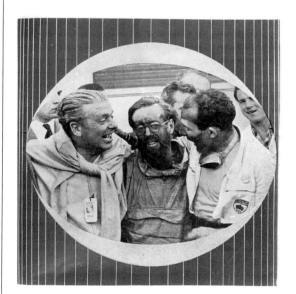

1st May 1995

In Celebration of the 40th Anniversary of the Moss/Jenkinson Victory in the 1955 Mille Miglia, A Luncheon in their honour.

Antipasto all'Brescia
Secundo piatto di Pesci
Frutta   Formaggio
Chianti Ruffino
Caffe

51

From *Motor Sport*, April 1955

CONTINENTAL NOTES

With the European racing season getting under way towards the end of March, there was much to get organized and quite a bit of motoring to do before one could be ready to set off to cover the 1955 racing events in Europe. In addition to this there was an offer to be passenger to Stirling Moss in the Mille Miglia, an offer, needless to say, which was accepted quicker than these words can be written.

Unlike some people who enter the Mille Miglia, the Mercedes-Benz team are out to do their utmost to win, fielding four cars, to be driven by Fangio, Kling, Moss and Herrmann, and as early as February we made a quick flight out to Brescia to begin practice. As is well known, the Mille Miglia covers 1,000 miles of Italian roads, from Brescia in the north, down the Adriatic coast as far as Pescara, over the mountains around Popoli and Aquila to Rome, then north up the Appenine Chain, crossing the Radicofani, Futa and Raticosa passes to Bologna and back across the plains of Lombardy to Brescia. On race day the whole of this 1,000 miles of normal roadway is virtually closed to the public, but it is quite impossible to close any of it for practice, so that any laps done before the race must be on open roads amid the hurly-burly of Italian motoring life. Arriving at Brescia we were shown the 'practice car', which was a 300SLR Mercedes-Benz, and at 7am we set off on a practice lap, there being no intention of going fast, for the object of the operation was to see how the chassis and its components stood up to 1,000 miles of rough Italian roads.

It might be worthwhile here to clarify the various types of 300 Mercedes-Benz cars being built. The 300 as such is the single-ohc six-cylinder touring limousine, built on conventional lines, having coil-spring and wishbone ifs and swing-axle rear suspension. A shorter version of this is made in two-seater form, with fixed or drop-head coupe body, and this is known as the 300S. Then there is the much-coveted 300SL, almost identical with the cars raced at Le Mans in 1952, but now having fuel injection. This model has a multi-tube spaceframe, a tuned 300 engine tilted over to the left, similar suspension to the other two models, and the pretty coupe two-seater body with the gullwing doors. Now Mercedes-Benz have made the 300SLR, which bears no relation to the above cars apart from being of 3 litres capacity. The 300SLR is mechanically the same as the Type W196 Formula One car, with the eight-cylinder engine enlarged to 3 litres and running on normal fuel. The driver has been moved to the left, astride the propshaft, the gear-change positioned centrally in the cockpit and a passenger seat fitted on the right. As the driving position is similar to the Grand Prix cars, with the pedals very wide apart, it is a good thing if the passenger has small feet and short legs.

It was the prototype 300SLR which was given to us in the early hours with the instructions not to exceed 170mph in fifth gear, always fill the tank with Agip Supercortemaggiore petrol, not to hurry, to take two days over completing the first lap, and not to drive in the dark. Following us were Kling and Herrmann in a 220 Mercedes-Benz and another similar car full of technicians and mechanics.

After a preliminary plug-check we got into our stride, our personal object being to make notes about the road conditions as we went along. Moss soon found that this *rennsportwagen*, as the Germans so aptly name this type of machine, was quite happy cruising between 145 and 155mph amid the general run of Italian traffic. The acceleration from 50 to 150mph gave the feeling of being absolutely constant, there was no kick in the back, no sudden surge forward, but a constant increase in speed, while the suspension was so comfortable and the roadholding such that the rev-counter reading and gear-lever position were the only guides to mph. Quite literally, anything under 100mph was a pace at which to make notes and regard the scenery, while waiting for the road to clear so that we could go on into fourth and fifth gears. The noise, both of the engine and gearbox, was identical to that of the Grand Prix car, while the exhaust note from the two short pipes just in front of my right ear was only a few decibels down on last year's Grand Prix racers. It was interesting that the volume of noise hardly seemed to vary with the rpm of the engine; once the throttle was open the noise came in with a decided bang, whether we were doing 2,500 or 7,500rpm. The brakes retarded the car with a deceleration that was as deceptive as the acceleration, accompanied by the most vile smell of burning brake-linings, for with inboard brakes all the heat and smells waft up into the cockpit. On two occasions Moss had to make rapid stops and then the cockpit filled with blue smoke from the linings and hot drums.

While we were not going at racing Mille Miglia speeds, for Moss refused to take any chances, at no time using more than his own half of the road and never squeezing through gaps, we were still averaging over 90mph, including obeying traffic lights and going round all the islands. Having reached Pescara by lunch time, the average still being well in the eighties, we stopped to eat, the car not protesting at all at being driven round the town in search of a reasonable restaurant, and then being parked outside between an Aprilia and a Fiat 1900. It was a fully equipped sports car with starter, dynamo and lights.

By this time, of course, the populace were delirious, and Luigis, Giovannis and Vittorios were appearing from all directions. We were forced to lunch in semi-darkness as the windows of the restaurant were blacked out by inquisitive faces eager to see the *"Inglese, Sterlinee Morss."*

Soon on our way again, we wound up into the mountains around Popoli and on the way to Aquila we cruised for many kilometres across a plateau at just over 160mph. It was a most fascinating experience to look sideways at the driver at this speed, to see his youthful face looking as relaxed as most people's do when sitting in front of the fire after a good meal; but behind the goggles the eyes had a comforting look of complete concentration and confidence. There was nothing for me to do except give a quick look at the instruments, do some sums to convince myself we were doing more than 160mph, and then watch the scenery go by. Naturally, over the mountains the average speed was forced down, for even Moss in a Mercedes-Benz cannot average much more than 60mph, but down into Rome the roads improved, as they did out again, northwards to Viterbo. At that town the light was beginning to fade so we packed up and once more motored about relatively quietly looking for the pre-arranged hotel, for the 220 Mercedes-Benz cars were now about three hours behind us.

Next morning we were off again to an early start, and that day provided for me one of my most memorable motoring experiences. It is not difficult to find someone to drive you along a straight road at 150mph, or for that matter to do it yourself, providing the conditions are favourable, but to be driven over three really arduous mountain passes in a car of the potential of the 300SLR by a driver whom I can only describe as an 'artist', is something to which mere words cannot do full justice.

The Mercedes-Benz' handling calls for sharp corners to be taken with the power on, which provokes rear-end breakaway, and this is counteracted with the steering wheel. A left-hand corner, for example, means that you arrive on a normal line, lock over to the left and open the throttle, and then immediately put on right lock, but only to an amount to counteract the tail-swing caused by opening the throttle. If done correctly the car leaves the corner under full power with the driver feeding-off the right lock back to a straight position as the car accelerates. To do this the car must have three vital things: a tendency to oversteer, sufficient power to be able to provoke breakaway on the rear wheels at will, and a steering ratio that allows the driver to go from lock to lock without moving his hands on the rim, for there would not be time. To say that Moss has mastered this technique, which can only be applied on sharp corners, would be an understatement. He threw the SLR round the hairpins and through the multitude of S-bends in a series of controlled flicks and slides, and on the dry roads the car skated about as a Morris Minor would on snow at 20mph driven by a rally driver. We crossed the mountains in this manner, the car being whisked round the bends and corners, with the driver complete master of the machine. Up the pass it was nearly all done on accelerator pedal and steering wheel, second gear being ideal for the whole climb, while down the other side only occasional dabs on the brake pedal were required.

In no time at all it seemed this living with the gods was over and we were in Bologna, though actually it had taken nearly two hours, and all at an average of over 60mph. From Bologna back to Brescia was normal fast Italian motoring, mostly around 120-130mph, as the traffic was pretty heavy, and arriving back at the garage well before dark we left the car by the bench as there were no mechanics in sight, and returned to the hotel for a much-needed bath.

Our overall running average had been nearly 75mph, and some idea of the safety limit to which Moss drove when traffic was about can be gained by the fact that never once did I press my feet on the bulkhead or clutch wildly at the scuttle. In less than an hour we went back to the garage and found the car on four axle-stands, the wheels off, the tyre wear measured, the front brakes dismantled completely, the lining wear measured, the undertray off, the engine checked over for oil leaks, etc, the transmission and clutch dismantled and checked, and the two engineers and six mechanics waiting for Mr Moss to return from his bath and tell them if the car was to his liking – and every nut on a Mercedes-Benz is split-pinned!

Next morning the car was ready for its second lap and we got off to a fine start, but after averaging 95mph for the first hour and a half, fate stepped in and it is best that a veil is drawn over the details of that second lap. First the rain came, then a stone punctured the radiator, and after the mechanics had rushed another one to us and fitted it, the snow started. We struggled on for another 200 miles in weather conditions which ranged from hail to three inches of slush on the roads, with ice forming on the windscreen and goggles faster than we could rub it off. Nearing Rome the weather cleared up and conditions were perfect once again, but shortly after Rome we were passing a flock of sheep at 70mph when the attendant shepherd struck one of them with a hefty stick and it leapt sideways into our left-hand headlamp. While the dead mutton flew up into the air we spun and, in going into the ditch, a rear wheel struck a low concrete bollard and that was that.

Shortly after, Kling and Herrmann arrived in their 220 and we continued the second lap in the rear seats. Next day the snow covered the whole of central Italy, which put paid to any further practice or testing... – D.S.J.

52

From *Motor Sport*, June 1955

WITH MOSS IN THE MILLE MIGLIA

On May 1 motor-racing history was made, for Stirling Moss won the 1,000-mile Mille Miglia, the first time in 22 years that this has been achieved by a British driver, and I had the very great privilege of sitting beside him throughout this epic drive.

But let us go back to the beginning, for this win was not a fluke on the spur of the moment, it was the result of weeks, even months, of preparation and planning. My enthusiasm for the Mille Miglia race goes back many years, among the reasons being the fact that it is permissible to carry a passenger, for this event is for all types of road-going cars, from family saloons to Grand Prix-type racing/sports cars, and when I had my first taste of the lure of the Mille Miglia as a competitor last year, with Abecassis in the HWM, I soon set about making plans for the 1955 event.

Regular *Motor Sport* readers will remember that last year I enthused over a little private dice that Moss gave me in a Maserati, and at the time I mentioned to him my desire to run in the Mille Miglia again. Then in September, whilst in discussion with the American driver John Fitch, we came to the decision that the only way a non-Italian could win the Mille

Miglia was by applying science. At the time he was hoping to be in the official Mercedes-Benz team for the event, and we had long talks about ways in which the driver could use a passenger as a mechanical brain, to remove the responsibility of learning the circuit. When it is realized that the race is over 1,000 miles of ordinary, unprepared Italian road, the only concession to racing being that all traffic is removed from the roads for the duration of the race, and the way through towns is lined with straw bales, it will be appreciated that the task of one man learning every corner, every swerve, gradient, hummock, brow and level-crossing, is nigh impossible. Even the top Italian drivers, such as Taruffi, Maglioli, Castellotti, etc, only know sections of the route perfectly, and all the time they must concentrate on remembering what lies round the next corner, or over the next brow.

During the last winter, as is well known, Moss joined the Mercedes-Benz team and the firm decided that it would not be possible for Fitch to drive for them in the Mille Miglia, though he would be in the team for Le Mans, so all our plans looked like being of no avail. Then, just before Christmas, a telephone call from Moss invited me to be his passenger in the Mille Miglia in a Mercedes-Benz 300SLR, an invitation which I promptly accepted, John Fitch having sportingly agreed that it would be a good thing for me to try out our plans for beating the Italians with Moss as driver.

When I met Moss early in the new year to discuss the event I already had some definite plan of action. Over lunch it transpired that he had very similar plans, of using the passenger as a second brain to look after navigation, and when we pooled our accumulated knowledge and ideas a great deal of ground work was covered quickly. From four previous Mille Miglia races with Jaguars Moss had gathered together a good quantity of notes, about bumpy level-crossings, blind hill-brows, dangerous corners and so on, and as I knew certain sections of the course intimately, all this knowledge put down on paper amounted to about 25 per cent of the circuit.

Early in February Mercedes-Benz were ready to start practising, the first outing being in the nature of a test for the prototype 300SLR, and a description of the two laps we completed, including having an accident in which the car was smashed, appeared in the April *Motor Sport*. While doing

The Radicofani was just one of the interesting passes on the Mille Miglia route, but unfortunately there was no time to enjoy the scenery, although in this case we had paused for a breather during practice and note-making.

The 300SLR laid bare. It was that huge fuel tank behind the cockpit that gave me my most anxious moments during the race when it started to spray me with petrol shortly after one of our refuelling stops.

this testing I made copious notes, some of them rather like Chinese due to trying to write at 150mph, but when we stopped for lunch, or for the night, we spent the whole time discussing the roads we had covered and transcribing my notes. The things we concentrated on were places where we might break the car, such as very bumpy level-crossings, sudden dips in the road, bad surfaces, tramlines and so on. Then we logged all the difficult corners, grading them as 'saucy ones', 'dodgy ones' and 'very dangerous ones', having a hand sign to indicate each type. Then we logged slippery surfaces, using another hand sign, and as we went along Moss indicated his interpretation of the conditions, while I pin-pointed the place by a kilometre stone, plus or minus. Our task was eased greatly by the fact that there is a stone at every kilometre on Italian roads, and they are numbered in huge black figures, facing oncoming traffic.

In addition to all the points round the course where a mistake might mean an accident, and there are hundreds of them, we also logged all the long straights and everywhere that we could travel at maximum speed even though visibility was restricted, and again there were dozens of such points. Throughout all this preliminary work Moss impressed upon me at every possible moment the importance of not making any mistakes, such as indicating a brow to be flat-out when in reality it was followed by a tight left-hand bend. I told him he need not worry, as any accident he might have was going to involve me as well, as I was going to be by his side until the race was finished. After our first practice session we sorted out all our notes and had them typed out into some semblance of order, and before leaving England again I spent hours with a friend, checking and cross-checking, going over the whole list many times, finally being 100 per cent certain that there were no mistakes.

On our second visit to Italy for more laps of the circuit, we got down to fine details, grading some corners as less severe and others as much more so, especially as now we knew the way on paper it meant that we arrived at many points much faster than previously when reconnoitring the route. On another lap I went the whole way picking out really detailed landmarks that I would be able to see no matter what the conditions, whether we had the sun in our eyes or it was pouring with rain, and for this work we found Moss' Mercedes-Benz 220a saloon most useful as it would cruise at an easy 85mph and at the same time we could discuss any details.

Our whole plan was now nearing completion, we had 17 pages of notes, and Moss had sufficient confidence in me to take blind brows at 90-100mph,

believing me when I said the road went straight on; though he freely admitted that he was not sure whether he would do the same thing at 170mph, no matter how confident I was. He said he'd probably ease it back to 160mph for, though that 10mph would make no difference to the resulting crash if I had made a mistake, it comforted him psychologically! Throughout all this training we carefully kept a log of our running time and average speeds, and some of them were positively indecent, and certainly not for publication, but the object was to find out which parts of the 1,000 miles dropped the overall average and where we could make up time, and our various averages in the 220a, the 300SL and the 300SLR gave us an extremely interesting working knowledge of how the Mille Miglia might be won or lost. Our second practice period ended in another accident and this time a smashed 300SL coupe, for Italian army lorries turn across your bows without warning just as English ones do. Rather crestfallen, we anticipated the rage of team-chief Neubauer when we reported this second crash, but his only worry was that we were not personally damaged; the crashed car was of no importance, these things happened to everyone and anyway their only interest was to win the Mille Miglia, regardless of cost.

Leaving Italy for another brief respite, we both worried-out every detail we could think about, from every aspect, the car, the route, our hand signals – for we could not converse in the 300SLR – any emergencies that might arise, anywhere we could save seconds, details of our own personal comfort which would avoid fatigue, and so on. We lived and breathed Mille Miglia day in and day out, leaving no idea untried. The joy of all this was that Daimler-Benz were doing exactly the same things on the mechanical side, supervised by engineers Uhlenhaut, Kosteletsky and Werner, while the racing department were working unceasingly and Neubauer was worrying-out every detail of the race-organization in Italy. We were putting all our efforts into this race, knowing that they were negligible in comparison with those of the factory.

After Easter we went out to Brescia for our third and final practising session, the technical department, with Kling and Herrmann, having already made an extra one. During their practice period they had thrashed the prototype car up and down the section from Rome to Florence, for this part of the route was the hardest. There are few straights, but all the time the car is averaging nearly 100mph, the chassis being subjected to strains from every possible angle, and as the 58-gallon petrol tank would be full when leaving Rome, this part of the route would be the most likely on which a breakdown would occur.

By now our details of the route were perfected and I now wrote them all down on a special sheet of paper 18 feet in length. Moss had had an alloy case made, on the map-roller system, and for our final practice I employed this machine, winding the paper from the lower roller to the upper one, the notes being read through a Perspex window, sealed with Sellotape in the event of the race being run in rain. A complete lap in a 300SL was done as a sort of dress rehearsal, this car being ideal as it had a maximum of nearly 140mph, good acceleration, and was a very good approach to racing conditions, while at the same time we could speak to each other if the need arose, though normally all our conversation was done by hand signals, there being about 15 altogether, to cover every aspect of conversation. During this dress rehearsal we employed an amusing technique in the more deserted parts of the route, especially in the mountains, where I kept an eye on the approaching road out of the side windows, and even out of the rear one on mountain hairpins and, by continually shouting "Yes" while the road was clear, Moss could have a real go at 'nine-tenths' on the section of road just in front of him, certain in the knowledge that no traffic was approaching, for it must be remembered that all our practice was being done on normal Italian roads, open to the public. This technique, while being amusing to us, was also useful to Moss as it meant he could get the feel of the road surface conditions at racing speeds.

By now the Mille Miglia date was approaching and all round the 1,000 miles we saw more and more signs of growing enthusiasm, occasionally seeing other competitors practising parts of the route, while the police were beginning to leap off the pavement, stop the traffic and wave us on over crossroads with excited cries of "*Mille Miglia – via*" and, of course, the Italian

Alfred Neubauer, wearing his favourite hat, makes sure that everything is in order as Stirling and I settle into the cockpit and prepare for battle. He brought team management to a high level with his thoroughness and dedication to detail, but in many ways he was Mercedes' front man to divert media attention from the engineers doing the real work.

165

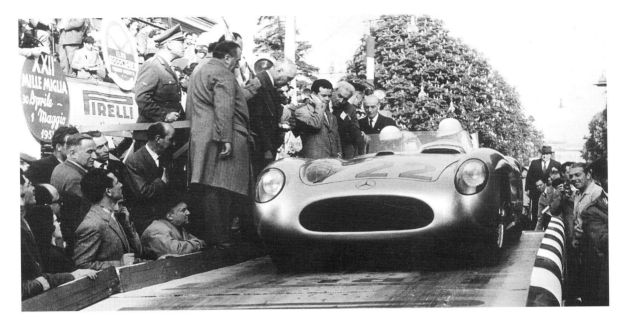

populace were leaping straight up into the air with joy as Moss fought the sliding SL through many of the corners. It was interesting that the average English enthusiast would turn his head and look if he saw a 300SL being really motored, whereas the Italians, from errand boys to bank managers, will spontaneously leave the ground and spin completely round, with excited waves, at the same sight, and then rush to another point in the hope of getting a further glimpse of the speeding car. We completed our third practice period without any crashes, though the 'hack' SLR decided to give up the ghost while we were having a final run in it, but we were entirely blameless; old age creeps on the best vehicles, and this one had done the equivalent of at least six Mille Miglias in the hands of Moss, Fangio, Kling and Herrmann, the four drivers for the race.

A week before the event we went to Stuttgart to try out the actual car we were using in the race, and several laps of the fast Hockenheim circuit convinced us that we had a truly magnificent 3-litre sports car under us, the eight-cylinder fuel-injection engine giving well over 290bhp on normal pump petrol, and the car geared to give a maximum of 170mph at the peak revolutions of 7,500rpm, though we were given no ultimate limit, should the car wind itself over this downhill. On this SLR the seats were made to measure for us, being cut-and-shut just like a tailor would make a suit, while every detail in the cockpit received our personal attention, and anything was altered to our desire without question. When we finally left the racing department at 5pm on Tuesday, April 26, we had the pleasant feeling that we had just left an organization that knew no limit to the trouble they would go to in order that we might start the Mille Miglia with everything on our side.

Next day we flew to Brescia and when we went round to the garage in the evening the cars were already there, having been driven down in the fast racing lorries overnight. We were now satisfied with almost everything we could think about; we had practised wheel-changing over and over again, in case we had tyre trouble, and I would add that we impressed the Mercedes-Benz mechanics by changing a rear wheel in 1min 25sec from stopping the car to starting off again, including getting the tools and spare wheel out of

This is the moment we had all worked so hard for. Stirling fires up the eight-cylinder engine for the first time, the Mercedes mechanics having pushed the car silently on to the starting ramp at Brescia in order to prevent strain on the clutch.

the boot and putting everything back again. We had practised fitting the temporary aluminium aero-screens that went in front of the Perspex screen should it be broken by a stone – Mercedes-Benz engineers remembering how Hermann Lang was nearly suffocated at 170mph at Donington Park in 1938 when his windscreen was broken. We had tried changing plugs; we had studied the details of the pipes of the fuel-injection, the petrol pumps, various important parts of the wiring system, how the bonnet catches functioned; we were given spare ignition keys, shown where numerous small spares were stowed should we stop by the roadside with minor trouble; and by the end of the week we felt extremely confident that we could give of our best in this toughest of motor races, lasting for more than 10 hours over every known road condition, over mountains and through cities, for 1,000 miles.

On the Friday before the race we did a final test on the nearby *autostrada* to try out some windscreen modifications to improve the airflow along the cockpit sides. Also Moss tried out a new mechanism fitted to the gear-change that would prevent him from changing from second gear to fifth gear. The gear-gate is exposed, with first left-forward, second centre-rear, third centre-forward, fourth right-rear, and fifth right-forward. Being used to four-speed boxes Moss was occasionally going across the gate from second to fifth, and when he told the engineers about this the racing department set to and designed, drew and made an entirely foolproof link-mechanism that fitted on the top of the gate that would prevent this. He mentioned this on Tuesday afternoon and on Friday morning the new parts arrived in Brescia and he was trying the mechanism out before lunch – at such speed does a true racing department work.

For the week before the race I had been going to bed extremely early, a complete reversal of my normal life, for to suddenly get up at 6am gives me a feeling of desolation until well past mid-morning. Moss had been employing similar tactics, so that when we went down to the start at 6.30am on the morning of May 1 we were both feeling ready for anything.

All the previous week a truly Italian sun had blazed out of the sky every day and reports assured us that race-day would be perfectly dry and hot, so we anticipated race speeds being very high. I had a list of the numbers of all our more serious rivals, as well as many of our friends in slower cars, and also the existing record times to every control point round the course, so that we would have an idea of how we were doing. We had privately calculated on an average of 90mph – 2mph over the record of Marzotto – providing the car went well and the roads were dry. Mercedes-Benz gave us no orders, leaving the running of the race entirely to each driver, but insisting that the car was brought back to Brescia if humanly possible. Moss and I had made a pact that we would keep the car going as long as was practicable having decided in practice at which point we could have the engine blow-up and still coast in to the finish, and how many kilometres we were prepared to push it to the finish, or to a control. At Ravenna, Pescara, Rome, Florence and Bologna there were Mercedes-Benz pits, complete with all spares, changes of tyres should it start to rain, food, drink and assistance of every sort, for in this race there are no complicated rules about work done on the car or outside assistance; it is a free-for-all event.

The enormous entry had started to leave Brescia the previous evening at 9pm, while we were sleeping peacefully, the cars leaving at 1-min intervals, and it was not until 6.55am on Sunday morning that the first of the over-2,000cc sports cars left. It was this group that held the greatest interest, for among the 34 entries lay the outright winner of this race, though many of the 2-litre Maseratis and smaller Oscas and Porsches could not be overlooked.

Starting positions were arranged by ballot beforehand and the more important to us were: Fangio 658, Kling 701, Collins (Aston Martin) 702, Herrmann 704, Maglioli (Ferrari) 705; then there went off a group of slower cars, and Carini (Ferrari) 714, Scotti (Ferrari) 718, Pinzero (Ferrari) 720, and then us at 7.22am. There was no hope of seeing our team-mates, for they left too long before us, as did Maglioli, but we were hoping to catch Carini before the end. Our big worry was not so much those in front, but those behind, for there followed Castellotti (Ferrari 4.4-litre) 723, Sighinolfi (Ferrari 3.7-litre) 724, Paulo Marzotto (Ferrari 3.7-litre) 725, Bordoni (Gordini 3-litre) 726, Perdisa (Maserati 3-litre) 727 and, finally, the most dangerous rival of them all, that master tactician, Taruffi (Ferrari 3.7-litre) 728. With all these works Ferraris behind us we could not hang about in the opening stages, for Castellotti was liable to catch us, and Sighinolfi would probably scrabble past us using the grass banks, he being that sort of driver, and Marzotto would stop at nothing to beat the German cars, so if we didn't press-on straight away there was a good chance of the dice becoming a little exciting, not to say dangerous, in the opening 200 miles.

Neubauer was ever present at the start, warning Moss to give the car plenty of throttle as he left the starting ramp, for Herrmann had nearly fluffed his take-off; he also assured us that we could take the dip at the bottom of the ramp without worrying about grounding. The mechanics had warmed the engine and they pushed it up onto the starting platform to avoid unnecessary strain on the single-plate clutch, one of the weak points of the 300SLR. The route-card which we had to get stamped at the various controls round the course was securely attached to a board and already fitted in its special holder, the board being attached by a cord to one of my grab-rails, to avoid losing it in the excitement of any emergency. We both settled down in our seats, Moss put his goggles on, I showed him a note at the top of my roller device, warning him not to apply the brakes fiercely on the first corner, for the bi-metal drums needed a gentle application to warm them after standing for two days.

We are on our way, the crowds are thinning and we settle down to 10 hours of concentrated work. Even with dark goggles, visibility was something of a strain for Stirling during the first leg as we headed south-east straight into the sun.

Thirty seconds before 7.22am he started the engine, the side exhaust pipes blowing a cloud of smoke over the starter and Sig Castegnato and Count Maggi, the two men behind this great event, and then as the flag fell we were off with a surge of acceleration and up to peak revs in first, second and third gears, weaving our way through the vast crowds lining the sides of the road. Had we not been along this same road three times already in an SLR amid the hurly-burly of morning traffic, I should have been thoroughly frightened, but now, with the roads clear ahead of us, I thought Moss could really get down to some uninterrupted motoring. We had the sun shining full in our eyes, which made navigating difficult, but I had written the notes over and over again, and gone over the route in my imagination so many times that I almost knew it by heart, and one of the first signals was to take a gentle S-bend through a village on full throttle in fourth gear, and as Moss did this, being quite unable to see the road for more than 100 yards ahead, I settled down to the job, confident that our scientific method of equalling the Italians' ability at open-road racing was going to work.

At no time before the race did we ever contemplate getting into the lead, for we fully expected Fangio to set the pace, with Kling determined to win at all costs, so we were out for a third place, and to beat all the Ferraris. Barely 10 miles after the start we saw a red speck in front of us and had soon nipped by on a left-hand curve. It was 720, Pinzero, number 721 being a non-starter. By my right hand was a small grab-rail and a horn button (the steering was on the left of the cockpit, by the way) and this button not only blew the horn, but also flashed the lights, so that while I played a fanfare on this, Moss placed the car for overtaking other competitors. My direction indications I was giving with my left hand, so what with turning the map roller and feeding Moss with sucking sweets there was never a dull moment. The car was really going well now, and on the straights to Verona we were getting 7,500 in top gear, a speed of 274kph, or as close to 170mph as one could wish to travel. On some of these long straights our navigation system was paying handsomely, for we could keep at 170mph over blind brows, even when overtaking slower cars, Moss sure in the knowledge that all he had to do was to concentrate on keeping the car on the road and travelling as fast as possible. This in itself was more than enough, but he was sitting back in his usual relaxed position, making no apparent effort, until some corners were reached when the speed at which he controlled slides, winding the wheel from right to left and back again, showed that his superb reflexes and judgment were on top of their form.

Cruising at maximum speed, we seemed to spend most of the time between Verona and Vincenza passing Austin-Healeys that could not have been doing much more than 115mph and, with flashing lights, horn blowing and a wave of the hand, we went by as though they were touring. Approaching Padova Moss pointed behind and I looked round to see a Ferrari gaining on us rapidly, and with a grimace of disgust at one another we realized it was Castellotti. The Mercedes-Benz was giving all it had, and Moss was driving hard but taking no risks, letting the car slide just so far on the corners and no more. Entering the main street of Padova at 150mph, we braked for the right-angle bend at the end, and suddenly I realized that Moss was beginning to work furiously on the steering wheel, for we were arriving at the corner much too fast and it seemed doubtful whether we could stop in time. I sat fascinated, watching Moss working away to keep control, and I was so intrigued to follow his every action and live every inch of the way with him, that I completely forgot to be scared. With the wheels almost on locking-point he kept the car straight to the last possible fraction of a second, making no attempt to get round the corner, for that would have meant a complete spin and then anything could happen. Just when it seemed we must go head-on into the straw bales Moss got the speed low enough to risk letting go the brakes and try taking the corner, and as the front of the car slid over the dry road we went *bump!* into the bales with our left-hand front corner, bouncing off into the middle of the road and, as the car was then pointing in the right direction, Moss selected bottom gear and opened out again.

All this time Castellotti was right behind us, and as we bounced off the bales he nipped by us, grinning over his shoulder. As we set off after him, I gave Moss a little hand-clap of appreciation for showing me just how a really great driver acts in a difficult situation.

Through Padova we followed the 4.4-litre Ferrari and on acceleration we could not hold it, but the Italian was driving like a maniac, sliding all the corners, using the pavements and the loose edges of the road. Round a particularly dodgy left-hand bend on the outskirts of the town I warned Moss and then watched Castellotti sorting out his Ferrari, the front wheels on full understeer, with the inside one off the ground, and rubber pouring off the rear tyres, leaving great wide marks on the road. This was indeed motor racing from the best possible position, and beside me was a quiet, calm young man who was following the Ferrari at a discreet distance, ready for any emergency. Out of the town we joined an incredibly fast stretch of road, straight for many miles, and we started alongside the Ferrari in bottom gear, but try as the Mercedes-Benz did the red car just drew away from us, and once more Moss and I exchanged very puzzled looks. By the time we had reached our maximum speed the Ferrari was over 200 yards ahead, but then it remained there, the gap being unaltered along the whole length of the straight. At the cut-off point at the end we gained considerably, both from the fact that we knew exactly when the following left-hand corner was approaching and also from slightly superior brakes. More full-throttle running saw us keeping the Ferrari in sight, and then as we approached a small town we saw Castellotti nip past another Ferrari, and we realized we were going to have to follow through the streets until there was room to pass. It was number 714, Carini, so soon, and this encouraged Moss to run right round the outside of the Ferrari on a right-hand curve, confident from my signals that the road would not suddenly turn left. This very brief delay had let Castellotti get away from us but he was not completely out of sight, and after waving to Peter Collins, who had broken down at the roadside before Rovigo, we went into that town at terrific speed. Straight across the square we went, where in practice we had had to go round the island; broadside we left the last right turn of the town, with the front wheels on full opposite lock and the throttle pedal hard down. Castellotti was in sight once more but out on the open roads he was driving so near the limit that on every corner he was using the gravel and rough stuff on the edges of the road. This sent up a huge cloud of dust, and we could never be sure whether or not we were going to enter it to find the Ferrari sideways across the road, or bouncing off the banks and trees, for this sort of hazard a scientific route-navigating method could not cope with. Wisely, Moss eased back a little and the Ferrari got ahead of us sufficiently to let the dust clouds settle.

Along the new road by the side of the River Po we overtook Lance Macklin in his Austin-Healey, and he gave us a cheery wave, and then we went through Ferrara, under the railway bridge, over the traffic lights and down the main streets and out onto the road to Ravenna. All the way along there were signs of people having the most almighty incidents, black marks from locked wheels making the weirdest patterns on the road, and many times on

170

corners we had signalled as dangerous or dodgy we came across cars in the touring categories lying battered and bent by the roadside, sure indication that our grading of the corner was not far wrong.

To Ravenna the road winds a great deal and now I could admire the Moss artistry as he put in some very steady 'nine-tenths' motoring, especially on open bends round which he could see and on those that he knew, and the way he would control the car with throttle and steering wheel long after all four tyres had reached the breakaway point was a sheer joy, and most difficult to do justice to with a mere pen and paper. Approaching the Ravenna control I took the route-card board from its holder, held it up for Moss to see, to indicate that we had to stop here to receive the official stamp, and then as we braked towards the 'CONTROLLO' banner across the road, and the black and white chequered line on the road itself, amid waving flags and numerous officials, I held my right arm well out of the car to indicate to them which side we wanted the official with the rubber stamp to be. Holding the board on the side of the cockpit we crossed the control line, bang went the rubber stamp, and we were off without actually coming to rest. Just beyond the control were a row of pits and there was 723, Castellotti's Ferrari, having some tyre changes, which was not surprising in view of the way he had been driving.

With a scream of "Castellotti!" Moss accelerated hard round the next corner and we twisted our way through the streets of Ravenna, nearly collecting an archway in the process, and then out on the fast winding road to Forli. Our time to Ravenna had been well above the old record but Castellotti had got there before us and we had no idea how Taruffi and the others behind us were doing. Now Moss continued the pace with renewed vigour and we went through Forli, waving to the garage that had salvaged the SL we crashed in practice, down the fast winding road to Rimini, with another wave to the Alfa Romeo service station that had looked after the SLR that broke its engine. I couldn't help thinking that we had certainly left our mark round the course during practice.

Ever since leaving the start we had had the rising sun shining in our eyes and, now, with the continual effects of sideways 'g' on my body, my poor stomach was beginning to suffer and, together with the heat from the gearbox by my left buttock, the engine fumes, and the nauseating brake-lining smells from the inboard-mounted brakes, it cried "enough" and what little breakfast I had eaten went overboard, together with my spectacles, for I made the fatal mistake of turning my head sideways at 150mph with my goggles lowered. Fortunately, I had a spare pair, and there was no time to worry about a protesting stomach, for we were approaching Pesaro, where there was a sharp right corner.

Now the calm, blue Adriatic sea appeared on our left and we were on the long coastal straights, taking blind brows and equally blind bridges at our full 170mph, and I chuckled to myself as I realized that Moss was not lifting his foot as he had threatened. We were beginning to pass earlier numbers very frequently now, among them some 2-litre Maseratis being driven terribly slowly, a couple of TR2 Triumphs running in convoy, and various saloons, with still numerous signs of the telling pace, a wrecked Giulietta on the right, an 1,100cc Fiat on the left, a Ferrari coupe almost battered beyond recognition and a Renault that had been rolled up into a ball. Through Ancona the crowds were beautifully controlled, barriers keeping them back on the pavements, and we were able to use the full width of the road everywhere, and up the steep hill leaving the town we stormed past more touring-car competitors who had left in the small hours of the morning while we were still asleep. All this time there had been no signs of any of our close rivals. We had passed the last of the Austin-Healeys, driven by Abecassis, a long way back, and no Ferraris had appeared in our rear-view mirror.

It was a long way down to the next control point, Pescara, and we settled down to cruising at our maximum speed, the car giving no impression at all of how fast it was travelling, until we overtook another competitor, who I knew must be doing 110mph, or when I looked sideways at the trees and hedges flashing past. It was now mid-morning and the sun was well above us but still shining down onto our faces and making the cockpit exceedingly hot, in spite of having all the air vents fully open.

Through the dusty, dirty Adriatic villages we went and all the time I gave Moss the invaluable hand signals that were taking from him the mental strain of trying to remember the route, though he still will not admit to how much mental strain he suffered convincing himself that I was not making any mistakes in my 170mph navigation. On one straight, lined with trees, we had marked down a hump in the road as being 'flat-out' only if the road was dry. It was, so I gave the appropriate signal and with 7,500rpm in fifth gear on the tachometer we took off, for we had made an error in our estimation of the severity of the hump. For a measurable amount of time the vibro-massage that you get sitting in a 300SLR at that speed suddenly ceased, and there was time for us to look at each other with raised eyebrows before we landed again. Even had we been in the air for only one second we should have travelled some 200 feet through the air, and I estimated the 'duration of flight' at something more than one second. The road was dead straight and the Mercedes-Benz made a perfect four-point landing and I thankfully praised the driver that he didn't move the steering wheel a fraction of an inch, for that would have been our end. With the heat of the sun and the long straights we had been getting into a complacent stupor, but this little 'moment' brought us back to reality and we were fully on the job when we approached Pescara. Over the level-crossing we went, far faster than we had ever done in practice, and the car skated right across the road, with all four wheels sliding, and I was sure we were going to write-off some petrol pumps by the roadside, but somehow 'the boy' got control again and we merely brushed some straw bales and then braked heavily to a stop for the second control stamp.

Approaching this point I not only held the route-card for the driver to see, but also pointed to the fuel filler, for here we were due to make our first refuelling. However, I was too late, Moss was already pointing backwards at the tank himself to tell me the same thing. Just beyond the control line we saw engineer Werner holding a blue flag bearing the Mercedes-Benz star, and as we stopped everything happened at once. Some 18 gallons of fuel went in from a gravity tank, just sufficient to get us to our main stop at Rome, the windscreen was cleaned for it was thick with dead flies, a hand gave me a slice of orange and a peeled banana, while another was holding a small sheet of paper, someone else was looking at the tyres and Moss still had the engine running. On the paper was written 'Taruffi, Moss 15 seconds, Herrmann, Kling, Fangio,' and their times; I had just yelled "second, 15 seconds behind Taruffi" when I saw a uniformed arm trying to switch off the ignition. I recognized an interfering police arm and gave it a thump, and as I did so, Moss crunched in bottom gear and we accelerated away as hard as we could go. What had seemed like an age was actually only 28 seconds!

Over the bridge we went, sharp right and then up one of the side turnings of Pescara towards the station, where we were to turn right again. There was a blue Gordini just going round the corner and then I saw that we were overshooting and with locked wheels we slid straight on, bang into the straw bales. I just had time to hope there was nothing solid behind the wall of bales when the air was full of flying straw and we were on the pavement. Moss quickly selected bottom gear and without stopping he drove along the pavement, behind the bales, until he could bounce down off the kerb and continue on his way, passing the Gordini in the process. As we went up through the gears on the long straight out of Pescara, I kept an eye on the water temperature gauge, for that clonk certainly creased the front of the car, and may have damaged the radiator, or filled the intake with straw, but all seemed well, the temperature was still remaining constant.

There followed three completely blind brows in quick succession and we took these at full speed, the effect being rather like a switchback at a fair, and then we wound and twisted our way along the barren valley between the rocky mountain sides to Popoli, where a Bailey Bridge still serves to cross a river. Along this valley I saw the strange sight of about 50 robed monks, with shining bald pates, standing on a high mound and waving to us as we went by with a noise sufficient to wake the devil himself. Up into the mountains we climbed, sliding round the hairpins with that beautiful Moss technique I described two months ago in *Motor Sport*, and then along the peculiar deserted plateau high up in the mountains we held our maximum speed for many kilometres, to be followed by a winding twisting road into Aquila, where up the main street the control was dealt with while still on the move. We certainly were not wasting any seconds anywhere and Moss was driving absolutely magnificently, right on the limit of adhesion all the time, and more often than not over the limit, driving in that awe-inspiring narrow margin that you enter just before you have a crash if you have not the Moss skill, or those few yards of momentary terror you have on ice just before you go in the ditch. This masterly handling was no fluke, he was doing it deliberately, his extra special senses and reflexes allowing him to go that much closer to the absolute limit than the average racing driver and way beyond the possibilities of normal mortals like you or me.

On the way to Rome we hit a level-crossing that had been just 'bumpy' in the SL and 'smooth' in the 220a; the resultant thud threw us high out of our seats into the airstream, and with a crash we landed back again, nearly breaking our spines, but the Mercedes-Benz suspension absorbed it all without protest and there was no feeling that anything had 'bottomed' unduly severely. This sort of thing had happened three or four times already, for our route-noting was not infallible, and it seemed unbelievable that nothing broke on the car each time. Although we occasionally saw a train steaming along in the distance we never came across any closed level-crossings, though if we had we had a remedy. In practice we had tried lifting the barrier, Italian gates being two long poles that lower across the road, and found that the slack on the operating cables was just sufficient to allow the car to be driven under the pole, much to the annoyance of the crossing-keeper. However, this did not arise and down into the Rome control we had a pretty clear run, being highly delighted to overtake Maglioli soon after Rieti, he suffering from an arm injury received in practice and a car that was not going well. With a grin at each other we realized that one of our unseen rivals was now disposed of, but we still had Taruffi behind us on the road, and no doubt well ahead of us on time, for all this ground was local colour to him. Coming down off the mountains we had overtaken Musso driving a 2-litre Maserati and as we had calculated that we were unlikely ever to catch him if we averaged 90mph for the whole race, we realized we must be setting a fantastic record speed, but as Taruffi had been leading at Pescara, his average must be even higher.

The last six miles into the Rome control were an absolute nightmare; there were no corners that needed signals, and we would normally have done 150-160mph, but the crowds of spectators were so think that we just could not see the road and the surface being bumpy Moss dared not drive much over 130mph for there was barely room for two cars abreast. It seemed that the whole of Rome was out to watch the race, and all oblivious of the danger of a high-speed racing car. While I blew the horn and flashed the lights Moss swerved the car from side to side and this had the effect of making those on the very edge leap hastily backwards, thus giving us a little more room. The last mile into the control was better organized and I was able to show Moss the control card, point backwards at the fuel tank and also at the fibre disc wired to the steering column which had to be punched at this control. *Bang* went the stamp and we then drew into the Mercedes-Benz pit and switched off the engine; this was our first real stop since leaving Brescia nearly 3½ hours ago, and our average speed to this point was 107mph, the average to Pescara having been 118mph, the mountain section causing it to drop from there to Rome.

As we stopped Moss leapt out to relieve himself, I felt the car rise up on the jacks and heard the rear hub nuts being beaten off, the windscreen was cleaned and a welcome shower of water sprinkled over me, for I was very hot, very tired, very dirty, oily and sweaty and must have looked a horrible sight to spectators. The fuel tank was being filled, someone handed me a drink of mineral water and an orange, and offered a tray of sandwiches and cakes, but I felt incapable of eating anything firmer than a slice of orange. A hand appeared in front of me holding a sheet of paper and I snatched it and read: 'Moss, Taruffi, Herrmann, Kling, Fangio' and the times showed we had a lead of nearly two minutes. Bump went the car as it was dropped down off the jacks, and with a lithe bound Moss was into the driving seat again and as we took the hairpin after the control I managed to yell in his ear: "First by more than one minute from Taruffi" and then the noise of the exhaust and wind prevented any further words.

On the next bend we saw a silver Mercedes-Benz, number 701, well off the road among the trees and badly wrecked. We knew it was Kling and exchanged long faces with each other, wondering how badly hurt he was, but this had no effect on Moss and he now began to put everything he knew into his driving, on this most difficult section, while I had to concentrate hard in order to give him warnings and signals of the approaching road conditions, for this was indeed a difficult section for both of us. Past Monterosi we waved to the Agip service station where we had a sheep-killing incident in practice, and then we sped on our way through Viterbo, sliding this way and that, leaving the ground on more occasions than I can remember, yet all the while feeling completely at ease, for such is the confidence that Moss gave me, and round the corners I never ceased to marvel at the superb judgment with which he weighed up the maximum possible speed at which he could go, and just how far he could let the car slide without going into the ditch or hitting a wall or rock face. Now there was the continual hazard of passing slower cars, though it must be recorded that most of them gave way splendidly, keeping one eye on the mirror.

Just after Acquapendente I made my first and only mistake in navigating, that it was not serious is why you are reading these words now; having just given warning of a very dodgy right-hand bend I received a shower of petrol down my neck and looking round to see what had happened we arrived at another similar corner and I missed the signal. Fortunately Moss had recognized the corner, for he knew many parts of the course extremely well, and after seeing that the petrol was coming from the filler due to surge, I looked back to see an irate Moss face saying very rude things at me and shaking his fist, all the while cornering at a fantastic speed. How serious the fuel surge was I did not know, and as the exhaust pipes were on the side of the car I decided it would be all right and said nothing to Moss, as he appeared not to have received any of the spray. For the next 10 or 15 miles I received this gentle spray of cold fuel, cooling in the enormous heat of the cockpit, but a little worrying in case it got worse.

Mission accomplished! Alfred Neubauer and Rudolf Uhlenhaut look as pleased as we were as they join in the victory celebrations. Bearing in mind that we thought we had probably finished second as we crossed the finishing line, to learn that we had not only won, but had broken just about every record there was to break, was very, very satisfying.

Up the Radicofani pass we stormed and the way the car leapt and slithered about would have really frightened me had I not already had a lot of experience of its capabilities and of the skill of Stirling Moss; as it was I sat there and revelled in the glorious feeling of really fast motoring. Over the top of the pass we swept past a saloon car competitor, into a downhill right-hand bend followed by a sharp left-hander. Now previous to this Moss had been pointing to the front of the car and indicating that a brake was beginning to grab on occasions, and this was one of them. Without any warning the car spun and there was just time to think what a desolated part of Italy in which to crash, when I realized that we had almost stopped in our own length and were sliding gently into the ditch to land with a crunch that dented the tail. "This is all right," I thought, "we can probably push it out of this one," and I was about to start getting out when Moss selected bottom gear and we drove out – lucky indeed! Before we could point the car in the right direction we had to make two reverses and as we accelerated away down the mountainside I fiddled about putting the safety catch back on the reverse position of the gear-gate, while we poked our tongues out at each other in mutual derision.

At the Siena control we had no idea of whether we were still leading or not, but Moss was quite certain that Taruffi would have had to have worked extremely hard to catch him, for he had put all he knew into that last part of the course, he told me afterwards. Never relaxing for an instant he continued to drive the most superb race of his career, twirling the steering wheel this way and that, controlling slides with a delicateness of throttle that was fairy-like, or alternatively provoking slides with the full power of the engine in order to make the car change direction bodily, the now dirty, oily and battered collection of machinery that had left Brescia gleaming like new still answering superbly to his every demand, the engine always being taken to 7,500rpm in the gears, and on one occasion to 8,200rpm, the excitement at that particular instant not allowing time for a gear-change or an easing of the throttle, for the way Moss steered the car round the sharp corners with the back wheels was sheer joy to experience.

On the winding road from Siena to Florence physical strain began to tell on me, for with no steering wheel to give me a feeling of what the car was going to do, my body was being continually subjected to terrific centrifugal forces as the car changed direction. The heat, fumes and noise were becoming almost unbearable, but I gave myself renewed energy by looking at Stirling Moss, who was sitting beside me, completely relaxed, working away at the steering as if we had only just left Brescia, instead of having been driving for nearly 700 miles under a blazing sun. Had I not known the route I would happily have got out there and then, having enjoyed every mile, but ahead lay some interesting roads over which we had practised hard, and the anticipation of watching Moss really try over these stretches, with the roads closed to other traffic, made me forget all about the physical discomforts. I was reminded a little of the conditions when we approached one corner and some women got up and fled with looks of terror on their faces, for the battered Mercedes-Benz, dirty and oil-stained and making as much noise as a Grand Prix car, with two sweaty, dirty, oil-stained figures behind the windscreen, must have looked terrifying to peaceful peasants as it entered the corner in a full four-wheel slide.

The approaches to Florence were back-breaking as we bounced and leapt over the badly maintained roads and across the tramlines, and my heart went out to the driver of an orange Porsche who was hugging the crown of the steeply cambered road. He must have been shaken as we shot past with the left-hand wheels right down in the gutter. Down a steep hill in second gear we went, into third at peak revs, and I thought: "It's a brave man who can unleash nearly 300bhp down a hill this steep and then change into a higher gear." At speeds up to 120-130mph we went through the streets of Florence, over the great river bridge, broadside across a square, across more tramlines and into the control point.

Now Moss had really got the bit between his teeth, nothing was going to stop him winning this race, I felt; he had a rather special look of concentration on his face and I knew that one of his greatest ambitions was to do the section Florence-Bologna in under one hour. This road crosses the heart of the Appenines, by way of the Futa pass and the Raticosa pass, and though only just over 60 miles in length it is like a Prescott hill-climb all the way. As we got the route-card stamped, again without coming to rest, I grabbed the sheet of paper from the Mercedes-Benz man at the control, but before I could read more than that we were still leading, it was torn from my grasp as we accelerated away among the officials. I indicated that we were still leading the race, and by the way Moss left Florence, as though at the start of a Grand Prix, I knew he was out to crack one hour to Bologna, especially as he also looked at his wrist-watch as we left the control. "This is going to be fantastic," I thought, as we screamed up the hills out of Florence, "he is really going to do some 'nine-tenths-plus' motoring," and I took a firm grip of the 'struggling bar' between giving him direction signals, keeping the left side of my body as far out of Moss' way as possible, for he was going to need all the room possible for his whirling arms and for stirring the gear-lever about. Up into the mountains we screamed, occasionally passing other cars, such as 1900 Alfa Romeos, 1100 Fiats and some small sports cars. Little did we know that we had the race in our pocket, for Taruffi had retired by this time with a broken oil pump and Fangio was stopped in Florence repairing an injection pipe, but though we had overtaken him on the road, we had not seen him, as the car had been hidden by mechanics and officials.

All the time I had found it very difficult to take my eyes off the road. I could easily have looked around me, for there was time, but somehow the whole while that Moss was really dicing I felt a hypnotic sensation forcing me to live every inch of the way with him. It was probably this factor that prevented me ever being frightened, for nothing arrived unexpectedly, I was keeping up with him mentally all the way, which I had to do if I wasn't to miss any of our route marking, though physically I had fallen way behind him and I marvelled that anyone could drive so furiously for such a long time, for it was now well into the Sunday afternoon.

At the top of the Futa pass there were enormous crowds all waving excitedly and on numerous occasions Moss nearly lost the car completely as we hit patches of melted tar, coated with oil and rubber from all the other competitors in front of us, and for nearly a mile he had to ease off and drive at a bare 'eight-tenths', the road was so tricky. Just over the top of the Futa we saw a Mercedes-Benz by the roadside amid a crowd of people; it was 704, young Hans Herrmann, and though we could not see him, we waved. The car looked undamaged so we assumed he was all right.

Now we simply had to get to Brescia first, I thought, we mustn't let Taruffi beat us, still having no idea he had retired. On we went, up and over the Raticosa pass, plunging down the other side in one long series of slides that to me felt completely uncontrolled but to Moss were obviously intentional. However, there was one particular one which was not intentional and by sheer good fortune the stone parapet on the outside stepped back just in time, and caused us to make rude faces at each other. On a wall someone had painted 'Viva Perdisa, viva Maserati' and as we went past in a long controlled

slide we spontaneously both gave it the victory sign and had a quiet chuckle between ourselves in the cramped and confined space of our travelling hothouse and bath of filth and perspiration. On another part of the Raticosa amid great crowds of people we saw an enormous fat man in the road, leaping up and down with delight; it was the happy body-builder of the Maserati racing department, a good friend of Stirling's, and we waved back at him.

Down off the mountains we raced, into the broiling heat of the afternoon, into Bologna, along the dusty tramlined road, with hordes of spectators on both sides, but here beautifully controlled, so that we went into Bologna at close on 150mph and down to the control point, Moss doing a superb bit of braking judgment even at this late stage in the race, and in spite of brakes that were beginning to show signs of the terrific thrashing they had been receiving. Here we had the steering column disc punched again and the card stamped, and with another Grand Prix start we were away through the streets of Bologna so quickly that I didn't get the vital news sheet from our depot. Now we had no idea where we lay in the race, or what had happened to our rivals, but we knew we had crossed the mountains in 1hr 1min and were so far ahead of Marzotto's record that it seemed impossible.

The hard part was now over, but Moss did not relax, for it had now occurred to him that it was possible to get back to Brescia in the round 10 hours, which would make the race average 100mph. Up the long fast straights through Modena, Reggio Emilia and Parma we went, not wasting a second anywhere, cruising at a continuous 170mph, cutting off only where I indicated corners or bumpy hill-brows. Looking up I suddenly realized that we were overtaking an aeroplane, and then I knew I was living in the realms of fantasy, and when we caught and passed a second one my brain began to boggle at the sustained speed. They were flying at about 300 feet filming our progress and it must have looked most impressive, especially as we dropped back by going round the Fidenza bypass, only to catch up again on the main road. This really was pure speed, the car was going perfectly and reaching 7,600rpm in fifth gear in places, which was as honest a 170mph-plus as I'd care to argue about. Going into Piacenza, where the road doubles back towards Mantova, we passed a 2CV Citroen bowling along merrily, having left Brescia the night before, and then we saw a 2-litre Maserati ahead, which shook us perceptibly, for we thought we had passed them all long ago. It was number 621, Francesco Giardini, and appreciating just how fast he must have driven to reach this point before us, we gave him a salutary wave as we roared past, leaving Piacenza behind us. More important was the fact that we were leaving the sun behind us, for nice though it was to have dry roads to race on, the blazing sun had made visibility for both of us very tiring.

Through Cremona we went without relaxing and now we were on the last leg of the course, there being a special prize and the Nuvolari Cup for the fastest speed from Cremona to Brescia. Although the road lay straight for most of the way, there were more than six villages to traverse, as well as the final route card stamp to get in the town of Mantova. In one village, less than 50 miles from the finish, we had an enormous slide on some melted tar and for a moment I thought we would hit a concrete wall, but with that absurdly calm manner of his, Moss tweaked the wheel this way and that and caught the car just in time, and with his foot hard down we went on our way as if nothing had happened. The final miles into Brescia were sheer joy, the engine was singing round on full power, and after we had passed our final direction indication I put my roller-map away and thought: "If it blows to pieces now, we can carry it the rest of the way." The last corner into the finishing area was taken in a long slide with the power and noise full on and we crossed the finishing line at well over 100mph, still not knowing that we had made motor-racing history, but happy and contented at having completed the whole race and done our best.

From the finishing line we drove round to the official garage, where the car had to be parked, and Stirling asked: "Do you think we have won?" to which I replied: "We must wait for Taruffi to arrive, and we don't know when Fangio got in." At the garage it was finally impressed upon us that Taruffi was out, Fangio was behind us and we had won. Yes, won the Mille Miglia, achieved the impossible, broken all the records, ruined all the Mille Miglia legends, made history. We clasped each other in delirious joy, and would have wept, but we were too overcome and still finding it hard to believe that we had won. Then we were swept away amid a horde of police and officials, and the ensuing crush amid the wildly enthusiastic crowds was harder to bear than the whole of the 1,000-mile grind we had just completed.

Our total time for the course was 10hr 07min 48sec, an average of more than 157kph (nearly 98mph) and our average for the 85 miles from Cremona to Brescia had been 123mph. As we were driven back to our hotel, tired, filthy, oily and covered in dust and dirt, we grinned happily at each other's black face and Stirling said: "I'm so happy that we've proved that a Britisher can win the Mille Miglia, and that the legend 'he who leads at Rome never leads at Brescia' is untrue – also, I feel we have made up for the two cars we wrote off in practice." Then he gave a chuckle and said: "We've rather made a mess of the record, haven't we – sort of spoilt it for anyone else, for there probably won't be another completely dry Mille Miglia for 20 years."

It was with a justified feeling of elation that I lay in a hot bath, for I had had the unique experience of being with Stirling Moss throughout his epic drive, sitting beside him while he worked as I have never seen anyone work before in my life, and harder and longer that I ever thought it possible for a human being to do. It was indeed a unique experience, the greatest experience in the whole of the 22 years during which I have been interested in motor-racing, an experience that was beyond my wildest imagination, with a result that even now I find it extremely hard to believe. After previous Mille Miglias I have said: "He who wins the Mille Miglia is some driver, and the car he uses is some sports car." I now say it again with the certain knowledge that I know what I'm talking and writing about this time. – D.S.J.

53

From *Motor Sport*, June 1956

ANOTHER MILLE MIGLIA WITH MOSS

A Tale of Woe

Some years ago there was a popular ballad entitled *Trees* and the last line ran: '... but only God can make a tree.' By the grace of God and one of His trees I am able to write the story of my 1956 Mille Miglia.

But let us go back to the beginning, which for me was shortly after the 1955 Mille Miglia when Moss asked me if I would go with him again, and naturally I said I would. This year we had not got the finance and organization of Daimler-Benz behind us, in fact we had the complete opposite, provided by Maserati, and a week before the race it was difficult to believe that we were competing. Moss was racing at Aintree, so on the way back from Sicily I did a little reconnoitring of the course and called in at Modena to pick up a practice car and have a look at our 'racer', which was to be a new 3½-litre. The practice car was in use by Giardini, who was somewhere round the 1,000-mile course and was due back on Saturday, April 21, while there was no sign at all of our 3½-litre. However, there was one new car nearing completion, it being destined for Taruffi, and mechanically this new design of chassis, engine and transmission looked pretty good. In every corner of the works were sports Maseratis in various stages of repair and disrepair; there were 2-litre A6G models, 1½-litre 150S, 3-litre 300S and 2-litre four-cylinder 200S models, varying from a bare chassis-frame to a complete car. Rows of engines were being assembled, others were on the test-beds being run-in or power-tested, and the activity was obviously going to go on day and night, as it had for some time previously.

Giardini returned with the practice car, a once-pretty coupe A6G with body by Zagato, but now a very weary and dirty-looking motor car, having completed seven laps of the Mille Miglia course in various hands, it being the only available practice car.

By Sunday morning it had been dusted over and was ready for another lap with Moss and myself, and before taking delivery I went out to the Modena Autodrome, actually the perimeter track of the Modena aerodrome, with the chief mechanic Bertocchi, and he proceeded to put in four very fast laps in the pouring rain to see if all was in order. Everything was, so I set off for Milan airport, the weather still coming down vertically, and I had strict instructions not to exceed 5,500rpm as the engine was getting tired, and to keep an eye on the oil level, this production engine being wet-sump. On the way to Milan airport, where I was to meet Moss direct from his lucky win at Aintree, the weather cleared up and I had the opportunity to enjoy this rather pleasant Maserati coupe.

Everything about it was pure 'racing car', the steering being light and positive, the short gear-lever, operating in an open gate, being a joy to use, though first and second gears were so far apart that it needed a dull pause while changing. However, the other ratios were lovely and the gear-changing was great fun, while for normal road motoring the roadholding was such that it was difficult to reach anywhere near the limit. Although a very low coupe, the visibility was without criticism and the driving position, even for my dwarf-like stature, was ideal. The brakes were good, but tended to judder badly, though this wore off in time, and the engine was so lively that an eye had to be kept on the rev-counter all the time to avoid going over the limit, and 5,500rpm in top came up all too easily, equal to 98mph. When new these engines can go to 6,000rpm, which would give an easy 107mph on the rear-axle ratio we had in. There was quite a lot of exhaust noise, but little from the engine and virtually no wind noise from the body, while the smoothness of the six-cylinder engine impressed me enormously.

Rather reluctantly I handed the car over to Moss, the only consolation being that I would now be able to see how well it could go, and we returned to Brescia for an early night. On the Monday morning we left Brescia at 5.54am, our starting time in the race, in order to get some appreciation of the sun conditions at that hour. We rather optimistically assumed the sun would be shining, in spite of rain showers throughout the previous week. Without exceeding 5,500rpm (98mph), we soon discovered that we were averaging a higher speed round the course than we had done in practice last year with a 300SL Mercedes-Benz when using a maximum of 130mph, the reason being that the little Maserati was so much more manageable. It could be flicked from side to side of the road with the minimum of effort, and in and out of the traffic with very little space required, while the gearbox would keep the revs up.

Stopping for lunch after nearly 400 miles, we met Bellucci and Perrella surveying the course in a 1900 Alfa Romeo, both having Maserati entries in the race. Bellucci was to drive a new 2-litre four-cylinder in the 150S chassis and his friend a normal 150S. Pressing on again we came to a road block and a long line of traffic, and discovered that we had caught up with the Tour of Italy motorcycle race, a sort of six-day Mille Miglia for small motorcycles. Also waiting were two more Italians practising in an Alfa Romeo and the German driver Erwin Bauer, who was in a special Mercedes-Benz 220a. This was outwardly a normal car devoid of bumpers and unnecessary weight, but it was fitted with the new twin-carburettor 220a engine. We arrived at the tail of the motorcycle race, so that all we saw were a few stragglers going along at a bare 30mph, and when we suggested to the police who were guarding the barrier that they let us through, their reply was unanswerable. They said that the road was closed until 3.30pm and that next Sunday, when we were driving in the Mille Miglia, it would also be closed until 3.30pm. We would not like it if they let motorcycles on to our course, and equally the motorcyclists would not like it if they let cars on today. We went back and sat in the Maserati.

As the time for opening the roads approached the crowd began to get restive, for clearly the last competitor had gone, and there was much shouting that Moss should be let through, but the police were adamant. We got the Maserati up past the queue of traffic, to the head of the line, and there was a bit of 'undergound' movement by some of the enthusiastic lorry drivers, during which they urged us to make a break for it and motor off, but the police were not fooled and we had to wait until 3.30pm. Then off we went and for the next 50 miles or so the roads were very clear so we had a good dice, but were rather piqued to find that the 220a Mercedes-Benz was sitting on our tail, and it took a lot of work to shake it off. The rest of the day's run was uneventful and we got as far as Siena by the time darkness fell, having by now developed a very great regard for the 2-litre Maserati coupe, which at first we thought was rather a rough old lot.

Next morning we were off again at 7am, up to Florence and over the mountains to Bologna, the little coupe going really well and crossing the Futa and Raticosa with never a single hesitation. Some idea of how it was going can be gained from the fact that our running time since leaving Brescia would have put us third in the 2-litre *Gran Turismo* category had we been in last year's race with the car, and this was on open roads, in and out of traffic.

We arrived back at Modena and went to the Maserati factory, where Taruffi had just finished testing the first new 3½-litre car, so off we went to the Autodrome and Moss put in a few laps with the car, but was not very impressed as it understeered rather violently. We wanted to do another lap of the course, and it now being Tuesday we wanted to get off at once, so another car was produced, as the 2-litre coupe had to be got ready for the race. It was due to have a new engine, gearbox and rear axle, and some happy Italian was going to race it on Sunday.

Bertocchi produced a special two-seater sports car for us, which was an experimental car built in 1954. They had taken a normal 2-litre A6G two-seater, chopped off the rear of the chassis and fitted the back end of a GP car to it, de Dion, side-mounted gearbox and all. The steering had been changed to right-hand and a de-tuned 2½-litre GP engine fitted. Except for the right-hand drive it looked like a normal 2-litre sports outwardly, and in 1954 it had been driven by Fangio and Marimon in the Supercortemaggiore race at Monza. With this 'weapon', for it really was rather a potent piece of machinery, we set off on our second lap, stopping for lunch after Brescia and making good time down to the Adriatic, using a maximum of 115mph in view of the traffic. In the late afternoon the rain started and we discovered that the Maserati was anything but waterproof, and though the showers were intermittent it rather put a stop to us learning very much and we stopped for the night at Pesaro.

Next morning saw us ready to leave at 7am but the Maserati became truculent and wetted all its plugs, subsequently needing a tow all round Pesaro before it would run on six cylinders. This was accomplished by an old man in a Fiat *Topolino*, who was press-ganged into the job by the happy locals who followed us on bicycles, scooters and in cars. By 8am we were well under way and singing down the Adriatic coast, but our song was soon cut short, for the heavens opened and we were soaked to the skin, and it rained nearly all the way to Rome. Apart from appreciating just how slippery Italian roads can get in the wet, which we knew already anyway, we learnt little on this second lap. By the time we reached Rome we had water in the brakes and also in the kingpins, so that the steering was almost solid and Moss was doing most of the steering with the throttle and the rear wheels. By the time we reached Siena the sun was out, but it was not much help and during the afternoon we struggled on our way over the mountains once more, amid streams of traffic,

Another year, another car. This time we are back on the Brescia starting ramp, but sitting in a Maserati 350S, and unlike the previous year, Stirling is on my right. The car had only been completed hours before the start, so it was far from fully sorted, and it would give us some anxious moments in the difficult driving conditions ahead.

for it was a national holiday in celebration of some victory or defeat somewhere in the distant past. With the Maserati being so low and right-hand drive, Moss discovered a novel way of making 'mimsers' move over. He drew up alongside and thumped on the side of their bodies with his fist, the resulting 'dong' being audible above the Maserati exhaust, so it must have been devastating inside a travelling tin-box. We got back to Modena rather damp, very dirty and not a little tired, having done 2,000 miles round Italian roads in 2½ days. At least we thought we would be able to try the new 3½-litre for size, but there was not a hope, for it was still in the body-builders and there was clearly more than a day's work to do.

As the race was getting precariously near we suggested that perhaps we ought to take a 3-litre, which was well-proven, and not wait for the new 3½-litre. At that the technical faces at Maserati fell, for this 3½-litre was their new baby. It was not a rehash of the 3-litre, it was all a new design, chassis-frame, de Dion rear end, engine, clutch, gearbox, transmission, everything was new, but we felt forced to suggest that perhaps it was a bit too new for the Mille Miglia. Then we learnt that Taruffi was not happy with his 3½-litre and was going to race with one of the old 3-litres, and the Maserati people agreed to prepare another 3-litre for us, just in case.

On Thursday we left for Brescia to attend the prize-giving of the 1955 race, it being a tradition of the Mille Miglia that the prizes are given one year after the event. We were up again at 6am on Friday morning, having agreed to a bed-early-up-early routine for the whole week before the race, and went back to Modena, once more hoping to try our 3½-litre. It was still in the body-builders and had 22 mechanics working on and around it, so we could not say they were not trying, but it was nowhere near completed. All day was spent wandering aimlessly round the factory, our spirits sinking lower and lower, and trying to decide whether to take a 3-litre, or wait for the 3½-litre. The technical 'bods' kept encouraging us with information about how good the car would be, and by showing us plans for the future both in sports and Grand Prix racing, but we were beginning to wonder. At 11am we were told it would be ready at 2pm, then 5pm, then 7pm, and when the sun went down we gave up and said we would be back at 5.30am next morning. When we left the car was still on axle stands, unpainted and not yet run in, while four mechanics were working on a 3-litre for us.

Next morning, soon after dawn, we were back and there was our new 3½-litre, painted, trimmed and tested, everyone having been up all night, and Bertocchi having taken it round the Autodrome at 3.30am. On the bottom of the radiator air intake a protruding 'lip' had been built and there were vague mentions of the front of the car lifting at over 130mph, but that this would cure it. In order to learn something we had demanded that we took the 3½-litre and the 3-litre out to the Raticosa mountain and try them in turn over the same piece of the course, and in the early hours of the morning before the race we set off from Modena to Bologna and the mountains, with Bertocchi following in the 3-litre.

We decided to do a timed climb for 10 kilometres up the mountain, and a timed descent over the same stretch, thus taking in every possible type of corner and gradient. On the way to the mountains we had managed a quick 5,200rpm in fifth gear, equal to 145mph, and had found that the front of the car wandered about rather disconcertingly. After three goes up and down the Raticosa we eventually made the best time with the new 3½-litre and settled on it for the race, much to the relief of engineers Alfieri and Colotti. Although quicker from A to B the new car was far from right, having far too much understeer and not responding to anything the driver did to induce oversteer,

The nose-heavy Maserati was certainly quick, but its wayward behaviour on the streaming wet roads meant that rarely could its full performance be used. Also, life was not made any easier by the fact that we were soon soaked to the skin and getting colder with every mile.

should he enter a corner too fast. Most cars can be made to break adhesion on the rear wheels, either by using the power, the brakes, the steering, or letting the clutch in sharply in a lower gear, but this 3½-litre refused to respond to any such treatment. The real fault lay in the fact that the new de Dion rear end had made such a vast improvement to the adhesion of the rear tyres under all conditions that the front was now lacking. An understeering car is alright providing you do not overdo things in a corner; if you do then you must provoke rear-wheel breakaway in order to counteract the lost adhesion of the front tyres. Although we agreed to take the new car we were very conscious of the fact that, though its overall cornering power was higher than the 3-litre it did not allow any margin of error, and in the Mille Miglia the margin of error must be quite high.

Leaving the car at the factory for attention to minor details and the fitting of a few home comforts in the cockpit, we set out once more for Brescia, a steady two-hour run from Modena, for it was now well into the morning and we aimed to be in bed by 6pm. Maseratis were fully appreciative of the shortcomings of the new chassis, but it was too late to alter the geometry of the suspension and reduce the understeer at this late hour. During the afternoon the whole team of cars, 2-litres, 3-litres and the 3½-litre, arrived at Brescia for scrutineering, and we were greeted with the unhappy news that our car was making a funny smell at over 120mph. At 6pm, when we had been hoping to retire to bed, we had to take the car out on the autostrada for a further test. Sure enough, at 120mph there was a smell of scorching rubber, but by the time we stopped it had disappeared and nothing could be found amiss, so in a rather unhappy frame of mind we retired to bed. The car was geared to do 165mph and so far we had not gone over 145mph, so we had not only the scorching rubber smell but also the weaving to think about, and in addition it suddenly occurred to both of us that the 'protruding lip' had been removed without explanation.

Next morning, Sunday, we were up at 5am and a friend took us out to the start, where the mechanics had the 3½-litre waiting and warm, and though the weather was fine, team manager Ugolini told us to expect rain within an hour of the start. At 5.54am we rolled down off the ramp and were away, our number being 554, while Taruffi had 553, Collins 551, Castellotti 548 and Perdisa 547. Though we had tried to cheer each other up by suggesting where we were going to pass them all, we both knew that in reality it was a question of where Musso and Fangio were going to pass us, for Musso was starting two minutes behind us, number 556, and Fangio was number 600, the last away. Before very long I could sense that Moss was far from happy with the car, for he was driving with great caution even on wide open bends, and over some of the humps which I signalled as 'flat out' he was easing the throttle. Understeer is a quality that a passenger cannot feel, and only by watching how far the driver turns the steering wheel for a given corner can one appreciate just how much understeer is being applied. On the limit the initial loss of adhesion is felt instantaneously by the driver, but not until the front of the car fails to change direction is the passenger aware of it. With an oversteering car the passenger can feel every degree of slip-angle that the rear wheels develop and can live with the driver through every corner and situation. Occasionally Moss would give me long glances and it was obvious that the handling was far from pleasant, while on the straights he was working it up to 5,600rpm in fifth gear (nearly 160mph) and the front was wandering in a horrid manner, so I began to realize why he was easing off for some of the flat-out humps. In spite of the faults of the chassis, the engine was running well, and we were making reasonable time, but nothing like record time, and we got to Padova in a little over an hour, but, just as Ugolini had warned us, the rain started.

Up to now we thought we had been having trouble, but with the rain it really started, for water poured in from under the car and rose between the seats in a heavy spray, so that in addition to the rain beating on us from over the windscreen we had more rain beating upwards from the rear of the seats. In a matter of minutes we were soaked to the skin and under the driving seat there was a good two inches of water. Not content with being that depth it was turbulent, as though being beaten by an egg whisk, and as fast as I tried to dry spare goggles for Moss, those he was wearing became useless. Even a car which will run straight at high speed can be trying in the wet, so just how he was coping with this Maserati I could not imagine, yet I occasionally saw as much as 5,200rpm on the rev-counter with the gear-lever in fifth.

By this time we had passed some of the slower competitors, but naturally had seen no sign of the other works drivers. On a long straight before Ferrara we were groping our way along at about 130mph when Musso went by in his 3½-litre four-cylinder Ferrari and how he could see we could not imagine, for rain was really coming down now. A bit later, on a winding section, the rain eased off a little and we saw Musso just ahead of us, and this spurred Moss on and he caught and passed the Ferrari, forcing the nose of the Maserati alongside Musso as we approached a corner in a village so that the Ferrari gave way. On another long straight nearing Ravenna we caught up with a 2-litre Ferrari travelling at about 120mph, and the spray and general derision flying out the back was fantastic. Nothing we could do attracted the driver's attention, for the road was only wide enough for two cars and he was having to concentrate to stay in the centre. For two or more kilometres we sat in the

This is where our 1956 Mille Miglia ended after we had understeered into a kerb with the right front wheel, ridden along a high bank, flown back across the road at the next corner, broken through a barrier and parked against a convenient solitary tree, which saved us from a perilous journey into a rock filled river bed 300ft below.

wake of this car, at times the water even obliterating its red tail, which was only about two feet in front of our car. In a do-or-die effort Moss forced his way alongside, the concrete posts on my side of the road being uncomfortably close, and then we were past and, by comparison, the mere rain seemed like a dry day. The only encouraging thought was that Musso was going to have to go through the same performance, for the road was still straight for miles; not that we wished him any harm. Just before Ravenna we overtook John Heath going very carefully in the HWM, though we were not to know it would be the last time we should ever see him.

The Ravenna control came and went without a hitch, our card was stamped while we were still on the move, and then away we went again. The roads were like ice-rinks in places, and in some of the towns the cobblestones were so slippery we had to cross them on a trailing throttle, for to accelerate would have spelt disaster. Down to the Adriatic coast we went, the rain never ceasing, and we were now so wet that cold was beginning to set in, in spite of the heat from the engine coming through the bulkhead. Our nice neat tin of biscuits and fruit was full of water and the food was a messy pulp, while I looked at our drinking bottles of orange juice and smiled to myself, for we must have drunk a gallon of rainwater already and I felt sure it was beginning to seep through the pores of my skin. We were wearing waterproof clothing, but we might just as well have been sitting naked, and had we been on a stripped chassis we could not have been wetter.

I looked at Moss as he peered into the rain and wondered what it is that makes a driver carry on under such circumstances, for apart from all the physical discomforts there was the added mental strain of knowing that he had little or no safety limit with the car should he overdo a corner, while over some of the humps it gave some really horrible wavers on the front end. But still he battled on and, when I realized that all the other drivers were suffering from much the same problems, I saw the Mille Miglia in its true light and began to get a glimmering of why people race in it and why they were refusing to give up. All along the road we were seeing wrecked cars, some in ditches, others upside down, another with its nose through a wall, one so far off the road in a field it was difficult to see how it would ever get out again.

I began to realize that this was not a motor race, this was something far greater, far tougher – it was a battle between the human race and all those things its agile brain had schemed up. Here was Man trying to prove to himself that the machines he made, the roads he built, the houses, the walls, the bridges, everything he had constructed, were for his use and that he was master of them all, but Nature was putting up her best opposition and everything that Man had made with his own brain and hands was now conspiring to kill him. If we gave up now it would be admitting defeat by our own devices. I could see that we must go on, we must fight our way through; this was not a battle of one man against another, it was an impossible fight of Man against himself, and if he gave up now the human race was going to lose some of its reason for existence.

It was only under such terrific pressure that the human being could satisfy itself that it was master of the earth. This was more than a motor race, we were not racing against Musso or Castellotti or Fangio; it seemed that we were fighting for the mere right to go on living. Maybe we were not good enough to win this battle, but others would be, and I felt that whoever was leading this greatest of all battles must go on to the bitter end, no matter how many fell by the wayside. Knowing racing drivers as I do, I was sure that some of them would fight their way through, and I could see clearly, perhaps for the first time, just why a man drives a racing car in competition.

Shortly before Fano, on another long straight, Musso came by again, and we just could not hold on to him, but later on, after Senigallia, we saw him by the roadside, and our first thought was that he had broken the car. However, we saw that he was relieving his bladder, for to race with it full is to risk serious internal injury in the case of a slight bump. As we neared Pescara, the rain stopped and a feeble sun tried hard to break through the clouds, and for the last 20 minutes before reaching Pescara the roads were almost dry, but we were still sodden. In front we saw a 3-litre Maserati and, though we were doing 5,600rpm in top gear, we were gaining nothing on it along the straights. After a few corners we got close enough to recognize the yellow helmet of Perdisa, but in spite of our extra ½ litre we could not overtake him on the straight. After some more villages we closed on him and sat in his slip-stream right into Pescara, out-braking him for the S-bend over the level-crossing, and arriving at the control and our first refuelling stop just in front of him. In spite of both Maserati cars arriving together the mechanics did an excellent job of work and both tanks on our car were filled quickly and we were away again. The pit had told us that we were fourth in our class, but only sixth overall, the fantastic von Trips being second in his 300SL and Castellotti leading all the way.

Barely five minutes out of Pescara, heading for the Abruzzi mountains, the rain started again, and once more there was some goggle changing and cleaning to do for the driver, and now we had Perdisa on our tail. All the way to Popoli we passed and repassed, but as we soared up into the mountains on our way to Aquila Moss began to throw the Maserati about a bit more and we shook Perdisa off, though it was obvious that the 3-litre was proving far more easy to handle on the wet and slippery road. On one bend we had seen the 300SL of von Trips, off the road and facing us, with all the front smashed in, and we hoped he was not hurt, while up in the mountains we came across a 1900 Alfa Romeo well and truly jammed into the retaining wall.

By Aquila, the rain had stopped once more, but for only a few minutes, for as we started the descent down towards Rieti it began again, and this time in real earnest, with clouds almost down to road level. Just before Rieti is reached the road descends down the mountainside, in a series of quite fast bends, to the village of Antrodoco, which lies at the very foot of the mountains. On our way down this descent we had one really big slide, during which it was pretty obvious that Moss had lost complete control, but by sheer luck the car stopped sliding before we had used up the width of the road. With only four kilometres to go to the foot of this mountain descent we entered a right/left gentle S before rounding a sharp right-hand bend, all downhill. Everything was going fine, apart from the torrential rain, and as Moss entered the S-bend on a straight line across the apex he braked, ready for the sharp right-hander. The next few moments were some of the fullest I have ever spent.

For a fleeting moment the front wheels locked on the slippery road, and that was that, all adhesion on the tyres was lost and the car slid helplessly across the road towards the right-hand bank. With a resounding crash we hit a small stone wall, bounded over it and began to mount the earth bank on the right of the road. By good fortune the car was still going straight and we tore down a barbed-wire fence, and then I realized we were some 15 feet above the road, at 45 degrees to the horizontal, and I was convinced the car would now roll over sideways, for I could see Moss way above my right shoulder. Instinct, or motorcycle training, made me curl up and keep my arms tucked out of the way, and then I felt the car retain the horizontal once more and I remember

thinking with relief that it was not going to roll over after all. I looked up just in time to see that we were now plunging down the end of the bank, then there was a fleeting glimpse of the road and in front of us was a black-and-white concrete retaining wall of post and rails, on the outside of the sharp right-hand bend. I ducked, there was a loud bang, a jolt, and the car had stopped. All was silent, except for the horn, which was blowing loudly. With some relief I realized that at least we were not on fire, for I was very conscious of the large petrol tank alongside my seat. As we came to rest I heard Moss yelling "Get out, quick," and saw him leap from the car. I got out quickly and fell flat on my face among shrubs and grass, and together we scrambled away from the wreckage, all the while the only sound being the long single note of the electric horn and steady beat of the pouring rain.

We made sure that neither of us was hurt and then cautiously went back to the poor battered Maserati and switched off the main electric circuit, which stopped the noise of the horn and left only the noise of the rain. The car had come to rest nose first against a tree about 15 feet from the road, but down a 60-degree grass slope. As we climbed back onto the road we heard cars approaching and saw Musso and Perdisa go by, and waved to them that we were all right. Then we walked back and surveyed the path of our uncontrollable flight, from the moment we lost adhesion on the front wheels.

We found the first wall we had hit was about 12 inches high, and it was on that impact that I realized that our Mille Miglia was over. Then we looked at the tracks along the 45-degree bank and realized that had we been going slower we would never have travelled the whole length and would have certainly finished upside down in the road. At the end of the bank we had flown off a 3ft wall and made contact with the retaining wall on the outside of the bend without touching the road, for neither of us remembered feeling a bump as we landed. Then Moss felt that he had a scratch on his right cheek, and we found that the barbed wire had made a tiny line just below his right eye. When we found the windscreen scratched, the glass of the watch he wears on his right wrist, and the glass of his goggles and his helmet also scratched, we realized how very close to a nasty injury he had been. Then we looked over the edge of the road and immediately at each other, both thinking the same thoughts. The Maserati was resting nose first against the only tree for many yards around, and beyond the tree the 60-degree slope went on down for 300 feet to a boulder-strewn river bed at the bottom, with nothing stronger than small bushes in the way.

It was at that moment that I remembered the ballad *Trees*.

The whole incident had started at about 70mph and had taken some 200 yards to exhaust itself, and the fact that neither of us had anything broken or bruised was just one of those lucky breaks that keep some people alive.

There was nothing we could do about the car so, salvaging spare goggles, our route book and a solitary banana, we set off to walk to Antrodoco, some 3½ kilometres farther down the mountainside. Just then we heard a Ferrari approaching, and it could only be Fangio, so we stood on the side of the road and gave him a 'thumbs-up' sign and, bless his dear old Argentinian heart, he stopped to ask if we were all right and then offered us a lift in his passenger seat to the next town. We waved him on, indicating that he was supposed to be racing, but he smiled and shrugged, and indicated that he was in no hurry and was 'touring' to finish. Fangio is too old and wise to hurry in impossible conditions – he obviously had no intention of doing himself any damage. 'The Master' knows when and where to go fast. We continued to splash our way down the road and after a time we met some of the locals coming up, they having seen the car appear over the edge of the bank from below.

Our return to Brescia was a long and tedious process and, but for keeping a sense of proportion and humour, it would have been a misery. A competitor in a 1900 Alfa Romeo stopped and gave us a lift to the outskirts of Rome, where a spectator took us in a Fiat 1400 to a hotel. We were both looking very bedraggled and shivering with cold and wet, and the hotel manager was rather taken aback at our demand for a room and a bath at lunch time. Eventually we got our circulation going again, had a meal and rang the Maserati agent in Rome. In quite a short time he arrived with some dry clothes and, packing our sodden racing gear into brown-paper parcels, we took a taxi to the station. There were five minutes to spare before an express left for Bologna and as I watched Stirling Moss standing at the ticket office, buying two singles to Bologna, wearing a borrowed suit and raincoat, with a brown-paper parcel tied with string under one arm and his crash-hat and goggles under the other, I roared with laughter, for this really was the funniest way to finish a Mille Miglia, especially remembering how we had finished last year's race. On the train we heard that Castellotti had won the race, and we paid tribute to outstanding courage and skill.

By 9pm we were at Bologna and telephoning Moss' mechanic, Alf Francis, who was staying at Modena, and he came out in the Vanguard to collect us. Our troubles were not over yet, for the continuous rain had swollen the rivers and the main road was flooded. The police sent us off on a 20-mile detour which ended at a bridge that had been washed away, so we returned to the main road, and after lots of yelling and shouting we splashed our way through the floods. Taking turns at driving we arrived back at Brescia at 2.30am, and we crept into the hotel and to bed feeling happy to be alive but so tired it was hard to believe. – D.S.J.

54

From *Motor Sport*, July 1993

HARMLESS FUN

Dear Reader,

The heading for this letter was sparked off when I unexpectedly came across a group of sporting cars gathering in a lay-by near my home. They were on their way to the West Country to take part in the recent Norwich Union Classic Car Run, and had used my part of the world to assemble from various directions, "just to make sure we were all together and under control". Team leader was my old friend Duncan Rabagliatti, and he was in his sports Kieft, while the rest were in a variety of cars such as a sports Connaught, a small de Tomaso coupe, Allard, MGA, Triumph TR2, Lea Francis, Swallow Doretti and probably something else which I have forgotten.

When they were "all present and correct" they set off towards Castle Combe, from where they were starting the rally, and as I watched them go I thought "What a happy bunch of motoring enthusiasts, thoroughly enjoying themselves, causing nobody any anguish (except jealousy, perhaps) and having a lot of harmless fun."

Thinking around this matter I wondered if any of them had aspirations of getting deeper into the game of rallying, and if so, would the point come when it changed from "harmless fun" into "a serious matter", then into "a serious business" and ultimately into "a profession". At the beginning the activity was "a nice day out", while the end of the logical path upwards becomes "a matter of life and death" with a World Championship and fame and fortune at the pinnacle. At some point along the path the "harmless" part would disappear and then the question would be "when did the fun disappear?". Probably those points depend on the individual, but sadly they seem to come no matter what branch of the sport you are involved in.

You can view the whole gamut of motor sport as being built on a vast pyramid, a structure with sloping sides meeting at a point. What we call the grass-roots of the sport form the base, and the pinnacle is whatever form of competition you happen to like. For me the pinnacle is Grand Prix (or Formula One) racing, and if you are a racing driver then your aim should be to eventually win Grand Prix races. If your activity is car designing, or engine development and building, then your pinnacle is for your designs to win those races. Anyone joining the pyramid of the sport, from the base, or even part way up one of the sides, must surely be looking up. I cannot really believe that anyone joins our sport looking down. On the way up some may look back, not in anger (like John Osborne), but in sadness, when they realize that great changes are taking place on the way up that were not visible when ambition made them start the climb to the top.

In Great Britain I think we have one of the best motor sporting pyramids in the world, built on one of the widest bases imaginable, which means that the slope up to the top on any side is not as steep as in other countries. This does not mean that it is easier to get to the top, for on any pyramid there is precious little room on the point, but there are lots more starting points, and getting a foot on the pyramid base-line has never been so easy. On our particular pyramid the immediate way up is very crowded, almost overcrowded I would say, and if you are not prepared to become "professional" at a very early stage in your climb upwards you will soon become swamped by the opposition unless you possess vast reserves of hidden talent.

Not everyone has the burning desire to climb upwards, and many are very happy to "just mess about with motors" around the base of the British pyramid and not get in anybody's way. It is a vast sea of "harmless fun", and long may it stay that way. But because of this strength in the base of our pyramid, the pyramid itself is much more secure than in some less fortunate countries.

What worries me is that now and then I meet someone who is not content with our solid pyramid, and wants to alter things "to make it better". When I look deeply into these people I usually find that all their efforts are directed at making it better for them, not for the pyramid itself. If I suggest that they have got it all wrong, and that the pyramid they are building is upside down, they go away muttering "He just doesn't understand". Maybe I don't understand them, but I do know that building a pyramid with the point on the ground instead of up in the air is a misguided activity.

Nearly as bad are those who want to build their pyramid on a base-line of infinity. All our pyramids are of the same height and all the points are very small, so the shallower the slope the easier it will be for everyone to reach the pinnacle, and that is a geometric impossibility. Similarly, a pyramid with a base-line that is too small will mean the slopes are too steep and no-one will get to the pinnacle.

As with everything in life, a compromise has to be found, and as far as the sport is concerned in Great Britain we seem to have a well-structured pyramid built on good compromise, and long may it stay that way. The sight of my friends setting off on a day of simple pleasure with their old cars, as were hundreds of others all converging on Silverstone for the final big gathering at the end of the day, made me very appreciative of the work being done behind the scenes to organize a gathering like the Norwich Union Run, and to keep the base of our pyramid solid and sound, with no flaws spreading upwards.....

Yours, D.S.J.

Jenks scatters the markers as he tries a spin-turn during a slalom in front of the Nurburgring grandstand with his Porsche 356. Another spot of harmless fun.

"From infancy, Jenks had simply wanted to be different..."

– Doug Nye

Denis Sargent Jenkinson - DSJ, or most commonly just Jenks – sprawled full-length on the Watsonian racing sidecar, nose inches from its cowl's tiny window, watching the 1949 Sidecar Italian Grand Prix develop – first-hand – at Monza. It was bedlam there. To his right rode the Fangio of his form of racing. His name was Eric Oliver – the multiple World Champion. As Jenks used to recall: "When Eric slipstreamed a rival he really let him know who was there!"

Reaching well above 100mph along the Monza straights, he had their Norton's front wheel jammed in between Ercole Frigerio's leading works Gilera '4' and its sidecar. And all Jenks could see, just inches ahead of his scarred, fly-spattered Perspex screen, were the soles of the plimsoles of his Italian counterpart, Lorenzo Dobelli. What an introduction to the racing world...

He followed it, and lived it, and loved it, for the rest of his busy life. For *Motor Sport* magazine's 150,000-plus monthly readers during the 1950s and 1960s, Jenks' lifestyle seemed entirely enviable. He was actually being paid – we assumed – to follow the circus in his Lancia Aprilia, or Porsche 356, or E-Type Jaguar company cars. He was universally admired and respected – he occasionally got his publishers sued, which seemed like particularly good fun – and in an era which saw the media commonly pulling punches and kow-towing to advertisers, *Motor Sport*'s fearless outspokenness was a breath of fresh air. It was a periodical with tremendous personality and great authority, and it had been shaped entirely in this form by 'WB' – Editor Bill Boddy – and, postwar, by 'DSJ' – *our* Continental Correspondent, *our alter ego* on the scene.

From infancy, Jenks had simply wanted to be different, and to run his own life in his own way. He succeeded partly because he was then, and he remained ever after, a tough little nut.

He had grown up utterly obsessed by motor cars and by motor racing. He was the youngest of four children, born on December 11, 1920, in Honor Oak Park, south London. His father was a foreign exchange manager for Thomas Cook, the travel agency, an upright, hard-working and respectable gentleman, although his office-bound occupation left his youngest son deeply disinterested. There were two daughters, the elder Joyce, or JJ, the younger Monica, to whom DSJ felt the closest affinity. His elder brother Harold was respected, and after *our* Jenks left home to join the motor sporting world, Harold, too, became a 'Jenks' in his career in the commodities market.

Joyce remembers losing her kid brother on a trip round the shops when he was only three. After an anguished search he was found staring transfixed at cars in a dealer's window...there was to be no turning back.

When Jenks was 12 he discovered *Motor Sport*, and from 1933 he religiously saved tuppence a week to buy the latest issue at the end of each month. He had a flair for drawing, and his first thoughts for a possible job were "technical illustration – nuts and bolts and that sort of thing...". His surviving school books are full of doodles and sketches of racing and sports cars, but he soon found he couldn't relate to the end products of art school...

As soon as he could afford a bicycle he would pedal away from the family home in Devonshire Road, Forest Hill, and ride for miles out into the countryside, regardless of wind, rain and distances involved, if the destination could be something as rewarding to him as the motor race meetings at Crystal Palace, the Lewes hill-climb or the Brighton Speed Trials. Brooklands races at Weybridge were not yet in favour – "...too expensive by far...".

He joined what was then The Polytechnic Craft Schools in London for the autumn term of 1936. His boyhood pal Bob Newton recalled: "We spent the first year in the Preliminary School of Architecture and Engineering in Little Titchfield Street before moving to the main School of Engineering at 309 Regent Street – only about five minutes' walk away. There we studied – well, some of us did – until the end of the summer term of 1941.

"The Little Titchfield Street building contained a well-equipped gymnasium in which we had hour-long sessions twice weekly. Jenks was an excellent gymnast, with such superb balance he was frequently selected to show the rest of us how the apparatus should be used." Brother Harold also used the Poly's gym "to keep fit before I entered the Navy...".

DSJ's cycling exploits had packed muscle onto his small frame; he had a tremendous power-to-weight ratio, and he cycled everywhere and anywhere, at one point recording in his diary a total of 220 miles "...this week".

Father had been a keen games player, and his youngest son was naturally competitive, a high attainer. Harold remembered him suddenly taking up swimming: "He borrowed my trunks – said he was going up to the local swimming baths – and he simply taught himself. He became better than proficient within a few weeks – which was typical – then promptly won a highboard diving competition. That was perhaps the first rather daredevil thing he attempted."

At 'The Poly', Bob Newton and Jenks spent lunch hours listening to jazz or swing records in the Assembly Hall, or wandering around the car dealerships lining Great Portland Street and Warren Street "...and sometimes the major engineering tool shop, Buck & Ryan, in Euston Road.

Training to be an engineer. Jenks, in short sleeves and glasses, alongside his pal Bob Newton during a practical test at the School of Engineering in Regent Street, London, circa 1940.

"During one such jaunt, after Rosemeyer had won in the Auto Union at Donington Park in 1937, we discovered his winning car exhibited in the Auto Union showroom in Great Portland Street. It stayed for two weeks and we drooled over it practically every day – until Jenks had us thrown out by an officious young salesman after I had commented that Rosemeyer was a fair size and it couldn't have been easy for him to get in and out; Jenks simply pressed the two catches which released the steering wheel and pulled it off...Mayhem!"

Jenks and Harold spectated at Donington Park in 1938 when Auto Union won again, this time with Nuvolari driving, but even then DSJ was growing apart from his family – seeking more the company of any who would share his increasingly consuming enthusiasms.

Most weekends were spent with Newton, usually at his home in Barnet, where Bob's father ran a garage: "Jenks would cycle from his home in Forest Hill – on the opposite side of London – and we would spend the day at my father's premises, messing about with cars and motorcycles. I taught him to ride my elderly flat-twin Douglas motorcycle there.

"Come late afternoon, he'd set off to cycle all the way back home again. Distance was no object to Jenks – yet he'd fitted his bike with an enormously high fixed-wheel gear which most people wouldn't even look at!

"We also spent a good deal of time on the 'phone in the evenings, ostensibly discussing homework, but the conversation usually drifted onto motor racing or jazz records, which – much to my parents' annoyance – I used to play to him over the 'phone... Throughout the 60 years of our friendship he rarely spoke of his family, and even during lunches on those Saturdays with my parents, when naturally they inquired about his, he would clam up almost to the point of giving offence – my mother found this quite disturbing and never understood him..."

Even then, in adolescence, Jenks had a quirky sense of fun: "When he rang he'd never announce himself as 'Denis' or 'Jenks' – he always said merely 'Oh to be in England...', to which I was expected to respond with the next line..."

They saved the admission price to Brooklands meetings, then Jenks answered a letter in *Motor Sport* asking for help to run a racing car. It was from Bob Cowell, in Croydon, and Easter 1939 found him on the competitors' side of the fencing at 'The Track' as a very junior mechanic, polishing the Cowell Alta 'EOY 8', changing its plugs and being towed to-and-fro behind its wheel, although he would not actually drive such a car "up the road and back" until 1946.

One activity which extended into the early war years, and which Jenks and Bob occasionally attended on Sunday afternoons, was model car racing: "These sessions were held on the long stretches of the multi-storey car park at Olympia, where petrol-engined cars about 12 inches long would reach speeds of 50-60mph – sometimes with dire results at the end of the course. We even decided to build a model of the Whitney Straight 2.9 Maserati, but I'm afraid it didn't get beyond the manufacture (by me) of the chassis side-members!"

Jenks regarded World War Two as merely a pestiferous squabble between governments, which spoiled his fun by calling a frustrating halt to racing just as he had been getting into it. He began to keep highly detailed diaries in which he honed the simple and direct reportage which later earned him his living. In common with probably millions of other teenagers, he was living in London in dangerous times, but few others would have observed and recorded them so acutely.

Cycling to Poly one morning: "...when I got to Peckham Rye the sirens went. I carried on, and when I got just past Walworth Road, guns opened fire and bombs began to whistle down and planes roared above, so much so I stopped under a railway bridge for a bit. Things really were warm and no mistake, and about five minutes later I carried on and hadn't gone more than half a mile when I ran into a thick cloud of dust…from the bombs which had just fallen… Just before lunch, Newton and I went round to Cavendish Square and had a close-up of John Lewis', and boy, what a mess. There was a girder there about 30 inches depth, just twisted all over the place. We had a look at a wrecked pub in Foley Street. A rather interesting thing about this wreckage was that on one of the walls still standing was a mantlepiece, and on the mantlepiece was a vase, still standing there!"

Evenings and nights were spent largely in the cellar at home: "Not long after we'd been in the cellar we heard a swishing sound, which really gave me 'the willies', I don't mind admitting, and the odd thing was that there was no bang afterwards! Harold came in later and said he'd heard it and said a balloon had been shot down, so we reckon that noise was the cable following. I went to sleep on the mattress about 11pm and didn't wake until 5.45am, and then went to bed…"

On September 15, 1940 – later commemorated as 'Battle of Britain Day', which Jenks would have detested as a glorification – he recorded how: "After breakfast we had a warning and saw about 50 planes and a number of dogfights, and an oil bomb fell in a garden opposite Devon House and smothered everywhere with oil and paraffin. I went out to West Wickham and saw plenty of wreckage about on the way… I went down Corkscrew (Hill) and along Addington Road and happened to look over towards Biggin Hill and saw a vertical black streak in the sky. I didn't take much notice, but when I looked again I saw that it was falling rapidly and watched it drop behind the hills, then there was a pause and 'Crump', then great clouds of black smoke came up. I reckon it was an aeroplane up by Biggin Hill aerodrome…"

He rode up to the fighter base to 'rubberneck' over the fence, then "had a marvellous dice" down towards Keston and on to the Bromley road, where "…just before the ponds I heard terrific gunfire, so I drew up onto the common under the trees. Then two German bombers came across and there were two fighters chasing the second one, and I could see the twinkling light of the Browning guns firing. When they got over the common the fighters sheared off and the AA guns opened up, and then all of a sudden a whole stream of balls of fire streaked upwards and burst around the planes; presumably they were the famous 'flaming onions'… About 8pm I came home and Harold and I fluctuated between the cellar and kitchen, coming up each time there was a lull…" The undeniably adrenalized immaturity in some of these entries converted into the clarity of his postwar race reports.

But Jenks' extremely strong character also emerged in 1940 as he refused absolutely to inflict harm on another human being "just because some politician says so," and as brother Harold prepared to enter Naval training, beginning a distinguished three years of active service in the destroyer HMS *Intrepid*, DSJ registered as a conscientious objector.

He completed his Regent Street engineering studies at the end of the summer term of 1941 and, along with Bob Newton, was directed to join the Royal Aircraft Establishment at Farnborough. He cycled from Forest Hill down to the RAE for his first interview, and thereafter became a fixture on the Surrey/Hampshire border. Working at the RAE, he lived in digs in Park Road, where in his spare time he would earn extra pennies drawing car plans for Percival Marshall, which sold as model-makers' blueprints.

It was at the RAE that he really got to know 'WB' – Bill Boddy – who was then working at Air Technical Publications while editing *Motor Sport* in his spare time. Bill, though shy, could be very entertaining. Also in this RAE motoring circle were Charles Bulmer, later Editor of *The Motor*, and Joe Lowrey, who would become its Technical Editor. Trained first as engineers, and motoring and motor racing enthusiasts at heart, they all became motoring journalists who *really* knew their stuff.

Another wartime chum in this RAE period was Holland (Holly) Birkett, the vet in nearby Fleet, a luminary of the 750 Motor Club who ran an Austin Ulster, owned a Bugatti and who (vitally) had a wartime essential-service petrol allowance. If perhaps they had been sitting up far into the night, discussing the excitements of the prewar Land's End Trial, they might suddenly decide to go and see dramatic Porlock Hill for themselves, and they'd drive off to do just that on Holly's petrol – returning with the dawn.

Joe Lowrey recalled how Jenks was always 'up' for any ride at all in an interesting car: "I was posted down to Cornwall and drove down in my HRG, and Jenks insisted upon coming along as passenger, even though I told him I wouldn't be coming back for some weeks – he caught the train back...and even then he'd actually slept all the way down, curled up in the back of the car. When I remarked what a waste that must have been, because he'd missed it all, he wouldn't hear a word of it...'No, no, no, it was a great experience not to be missed' – he really was...different."

When RAF pilot Mike Oliver boomed past the RAE one day in his blown 1750 Alfa, Jenks actually chased him down at the traffic lights, begged a lift, and again caught the bus home. Mike was a great friend of Rodney Clarke, the founder postwar of Continental Automobiles at Send, Surrey, who was another *Bugattiste* and wartime motoring man at the RAE to whom Jenks enthusiastically latched on. When Rodney and Mike developed their Connaught marque into the 1950s, Jenks became a great supporter, and so as a journalist was uniquely well connected not only to tell their tale, but also to respect confidences when it was right to do so. Such involvement might be regarded as anathema by the modern mass-media, a betrayal of journalistic independence – but Jenks was never 'a journalist' in anything other than his passport or tax return; he was more 'our man on the inside'.

Typical Jenks traits really developed at the RAE. Bob Newton: "We'd all accepted that racing had to be set aside while we got on with sorting out the Germans, but not Jenks. Although I didn't know he was formally a conscientious objector, he was just totally apolitical and loudly disagreed with the need for all this conflict..."

Vintage motorcycling pal Mick Wilkins met Jenks at the RAE and recalls vividly: "...we all first knew him as the little feller with the big hat and no socks – he'd worked out that he could swop the saved clothing coupons for petrol coupons..."

He certainly lived cheaply. But in 1944 he bought a Frazer Nash for £250 – £150 of it postponed for a year! – and in 1947 he actually drove it in the first postwar British motor race meeting at Gransden Lodge. But motor racing was plainly beyond his pocket. He sold the 'Nash and bought a racing 350cc Norton International for £100. Renting a lock-up was cheaper than digs, so home became a sleeping bag beneath a workbench in a lock-up at North Camp, then another by the mainline station in nearby Farnborough. Jon Derisley, later to become a Lotus racer, was a schoolboy nearby. "We heard that there's an old man in a lock-up round the back who's got a *racing* motorbike!" – fantastically exciting intelligence in those days – so one lunchtime a party of inquisitive schoolboys ventured round to take a peek. And there he was – long ginger beard, hence the 'old man' tag (Jenks was

barely 26). "And you know how open he was with interested youngsters? Well, when he spotted us he roared '.... off!' – and we all fled..." Jenks would have loved that story, the unexpected inversion in the payoff.

With perhaps just one exception, he never liked small children. He nicknamed one friend's year-old daughter '159' because, when she bawled, she made exactly the same noise, and her mouth was exactly the same shape as the grille on a Formula 1 *Alfetta* 159...

He loved jazz – traditional, of course – but liked good classical concerts too. He also tried to play the clarinet, but had more success learning to race the Norton. In 1947 he finished last in the Hutchinson 100 at Dunholme Lodge aerodrome, and also ran at tracks like Oliver's Mount and Cadwell Park. He had got to know a rider with experience of the prewar Continental touring motorcycle 'circus', David Whitworth, who encouraged him to join the revived British road-racing group which would be going back into Europe in the new year, 1948.

So, astride the Norton – with just a shoulder pack and a soft bag strapped across its tank – Jenks went off to compete in three springtime Belgian race meetings which were being run on successive weekends – only for his engine to seize in practice for his very first, at Mettet.

He had only a pound in his pocket, and unless he could mend the Norton he'd be stuck, not only with no means of earning any more, but also without any means of transport. The race meeting was organized by a local *garagiste* named Jules Tacheny, "who was very understanding and said that if I could get it to run for a lap or two he would pay me my starting money. The important thing was to be on the grid for the start."

Jenks got the Norton running after a fashion and he was "...putting the finishing touches to the Norton and whistling contentedly when at about 1am Jules came into the garage to lock up". Next day the big-end failed after a couple of laps and Jenks quietly retired unnoticed, but "dear old Jules Tacheny paid me in full...he explained that when he had heard this whistling he was very moved by the sheer enthusiasm of '*Les Anglais*'. Consequently, he was very happy to pay me for my efforts. I didn't try to explain that it wasn't English enthusiasm, it was English desperation!"

198

At the prize-giving, Manx GP winner Eric Briggs – whom Jenks had met racing at Cadwell Park – offered to take him and the broken Norton on to Brussels in his big van, whence he could catch the train to Ostend and home. During the drive to the capital, Briggsy suggested that perhaps Jenks might like to stay on and help for the next two races, fettling Eric's bikes, running the pit and signalling, in return for board and lodging in the van. Delightedly, he agreed; all he wanted to do was to stay with this travelling circus, with which he had become entranced.

At the prize-giving after that Brussels meeting, Jenks found himself sitting at the same table as Eric Oliver, who was also in his first season of Continental touring, but already regarded as the absolute master of motorcycle sidecar racing. Eric used two regular passengers, but both had full-time jobs and could only compete by taking holiday leave. He was looking for 'new ballast' after the third Belgian race, at Floreffe. Jenks said he'd like to try – just to stay on this intoxicating tour – so Eric invited him to report at Floreffe a day early "...and I'll give you a try-out before practice". After a few brisk laps there on open roads, Eric said: "You'll be all right – you don't rock the boat." Minimum regulation weight for a sidecar passenger was 60kg – Jenks in his kit scaled 59.9kg; he was 'In'.

He soon discovered Oliver's uncompromising racing standards. "I learned at close quarters why real World Champions are naturals and not manufactured," he would write. "On a starting grid he was there for one reason only – to win..." Eric's favourite remark after a twitchy moment was "I think we were sharing control there for a bit!", by which he meant ESO/DSJ versus their "lethal device" – the 596cc Norton/Watsonian combination. They won in the Dutch GP meeting at Zandvoort and began a great partnership which actually only survived for 18 months, though they would remain on very good terms for life.

A dapper Jenks with Eric Oliver receiving their rewards and congratulations at a Parisian presentation ceremony honouring their FIM Sidecar World Championship with Oliver's Norton/Watsonian outfit.

They built a new combination for 1949, when the FIM launched its Sidecar World Championship, and that year they were only beaten twice – on grass by a methanol-burning 1,000cc JAP, and in the Italian GP when the spark plug dropped out because Eric hadn't pinched it up tight. That morning at Monza, Jenks had gone through his normal routine of checking every nut, bolt, adjustment and clearance, and his final task before the start, after warming-up the single-cylinder engine, would be to change the soft start-up plug for its hard racing counterpart.

"On the big square-head alloy double-knocker Norton engine, space under the tank was a bit limited. You had to use a special, short-handled plug spanner. It wasn't a difficult job, but it called for care or you could snag the spanner on a fin and crack the alloy, or pull for tightness with the spanner fouling a fin and think the plug was tight on its solid copper washer. It was the sort of job you didn't do while talking to someone, and while Eric was happy to chat to people on the grid I was content to go on quietly with the plug changing.

"For some reason which escapes me, Eric decided to put the hard plug in on the Monza starting grid himself. Similarly, for some unknown reason, I didn't check the job..."

For several laps they passed Frigerio's Gilera and were repassed by it until, on one lap, leading out of the Porfido corners before the pits straight, "...the engine suddenly cut out and we coasted to a stop on the side of the track. Long before we stopped I could see what the trouble was; there was no sparking plug in the hole, nor was there a plug hanging on the plug lead!"

Jenk whipped out the plug spanner tucked into Eric's left boot and wound-in the spare plug from his pocket. They restarted and finished fifth, then were hustled onto the podium in the concrete grandstand to celebrate their World title. "While everyone was waving and cheering, we did not feel very proud of ourselves as we had made a team cock-up..."

For decades after, long after Eric Oliver had died, Jenks kept the truth of that race to himself. Also, for decades afterwards, he covered races from that same grandstand, but never reminisced about his day upon that podium. No question of "During the 1940s..." and much less "When I was World Champion..." There was no trace of that in Jenks' psyche, he was too interested in what was happening now – and how he could tell us about it now – for him to go off on what he would regard as a vain ego trip down memory lane. That kind of behaviour was for those he would dismiss as 'bullshit merchants'.

And he had really absorbed the fine grain of racing lore. For example, Oliver was an absolute master at gearing for a circuit, and he also tested with Jenks not leaning out to the maximum through every corner, to minimize frontal area. When they did this at Spa, through some left-handers, "I could feel the chair lifting through the bends, but when we straightened up Eric would give me a quick thumbs-up – on some circuits this meant we could raise our top-gear sprocket half a tooth, and if a tail-wind got up we could go up a whole notch..." – tiny advantages which could destroy the opposition.

Another time, they tested their standard works Norton bottom end and internals against their own highly polished set, to reduce oil drag. They set a baseline time, then pulled off the back of the course to their garage, stripped the standard engine, rebuilt it with the still-warm head and barrel on the polished parts, and then went out for the second session. Down the straight there was 'the unfair advantage' – an extra 200rpm. Before the race they regeared to take an even 'unfairer' advantage, and another win was almost guaranteed.

200

Perhaps their finest joint race was at Spa in 1949. A carburettor feed banjo broke on lap 1 and DSJ found the only way to keep the engine running cleanly was to plug the leak with his thumb! Whenever he had to take his thumb off the leak the engine would starve. He was wrestling with this dilemma into another fast curve when he felt Eric's big boot pressing on his back – "stay flat on the chair". They two-wheeled round that corner, then the next... For 50 minutes Jenks remained a flat little Dutch boy with his thumb against the bawling, buzzing Norton's carburettor and another GP win was their's, although "...my right arm was numb to well beyond the elbow, and it was quite a few days before things returned to normal".

When Jenks wrote his classic analysis *The Racing Driver* in 1958, he enlarged upon the vital characteristic of 'tiger' in a real racer – the added ingredient which in certain circumstances will elevate performance above that of mere mortals, and as an example he recalled Eric Oliver's ride in the 1949 Sidecar Swiss Grand Prix, on the man-eating Bremgarten circuit at Berne, which of course he had witnessed from the modern on-board TV camera position,.

They had minimized the Norton outfit's fuel tankage to save weight, but practice at Berne indicated they had overdone it and would run out before the finish. They were tempted to chance it, but then realized that fuel surge at low level during the last couple of laps would almost certainly starve their engine away from corners. They fitted a sealed half-gallon can in the nose of the sidecar, the idea being that late in the race Jenks would pressurize it by blowing into one rubber tube, driving the reserve fuel up into the main tank through another tube. True to conscientious form, they tested this 'Heath Robinson' arrangement on race morning and proved it would work, only for one of the judges to ban the idea outright.

"After 10 minutes' heated argument with the Swiss judges, who obviously didn't want to see Oliver win, Eric and I were in a pretty excitable and highly-strung state. The five-minute signal had been given before we found a solution... Rex McCandless, of the Norton works team, came over and said: 'Leave it all to me, lads; you come into the pits on lap 12 and I'll have a gallon of fuel and a funnel ready for you'.

"We had no alternative, for by now there were less than three minutes to the start, so we wheeled our machine onto the grid, without our extra tank and with insufficient fuel to last the race. At no time during the racing season had we ever been able to gain enough time to allow for a pit-stop, for the opposition was exceedingly powerful, so the situation looked hopeless. As we waited for the final two minutes before the start we agreed that 'no bloody Swiss is going to stop us winning this race'. We estimated a lead of 50 seconds would be needed to allow for our stop, always assuming that Rex had the precious gallon ready to slosh into the tank. That meant gaining five seconds a lap over our rivals, and practice had shown us to be only just over one second faster than the next man...but at that moment nothing was impossible...

"While waiting for the last few seconds before we pushed-off we decided on a drill for the stop. While Eric looked after the filler cap, I would retard the ignition and select first gear ready for the restart, for we would have to stop the engine.

"Up went the flag; five-four-three-two-one – take the strain – off, and into the lead we shot. The first five laps are but a hazy memory, but I recall that Eric was at close on ten-tenths all the way round the circuit and I was determined to keep pace with his every move. His inspired riding gave me inspiration, so that as fast as he threw the outfit into a slide I leapt into position to keep it balanced. We strained every nerve and muscle we had; the Norton was made to give every ounce of power it possessed, the brakes were used until they were smoking. Our passage during those opening laps was sheer madness; we slid through bends, we brushed banks, we cut the grass edges, every trick that Eric knew to save fractions of seconds was brought into play. We were 'tigering' in a way I had never experienced before, or since for that matter, and I marvelled that Oliver could keep up this pace without a single mistake.

"Our pit signalled a steadily increasing lead of four or five seconds a lap; we were doing it – the impossible. By lap 12 we had 48 seconds' lead over the second team. As we approached the pits bend, normally taken at 85-90mph, Eric cut the engine, sat up and opened the tank filler, and in a silence you could almost feel we shot into the pit area. There was Rex, just as he'd promised, and our planned routine went just like clockwork.

"In went the precious petrol and off we went again, having been stationary for exactly 12 seconds, during which time I had heard the gasp of wonderment from the grandstand as the thousands of spectators realized why we had stopped.

"As we accelerated away Eric looked down at me for the first time since the start of the race and stuck his tongue out. Looking back I could see the second, third, fourth, fifth and sixth outfits coming into sight 'but you're too late, my friends', I thought. 'We've done it, we've beaten the almost impossible odds', and Eric continued at a mere nine-tenths for the remaining four laps, knowing that all was now secure, and we won the Swiss Grand Prix by over a minute from the Swiss Champion. The relief at the end of the race had us almost in tears..."

Oliver and Jenks took their combination and solo Nortons around Europe in their Austin 'three-way' truck, Eric with his ladyfriend and Jenks with various companions encountered *en route*, although even then he was still notably shy with females and, as one friend recalls, "...could go completely soft over any who gave him a second look".

They happily lived under canvas at the race meetings, much to their rivals'

Jenks concentrating hard in the wet aboard his Norton. Often, his 350cc machine would be competing against 500s, but he would always set himself a realistic target. This usually meant improving on his previous best performance amongst the 350s, and if in the process he beat a 500 or two, that would be a bonus.

disgust, who said "You're letting the side down" – but they preferred to pocket the cash they saved. The bonus was that major motorcycle meetings were being combined with motor races, so Jenks began to report on both for *Motor Sport*, *The News Chronicle* and *Motor Cycling*. He also wrote for *Iota* as 'Barbarossa' – red beard. He called it "The cushiest job I know".

Eric Oliver always regarded his European travelling as "a trip away from home" and he liked to nip back to Britain as often as possible to look after business affairs and for fresh clothes, but Jenks had no home ties whatsoever. He hankered after a more European lifestyle, so from 1950-52 he left Oliver and joined forces with the Belgian *garagiste* and racer Marcel Masuy ('Mazz-wee'), who went racing in style and stayed in hotels... Jenks lived in Brussels, polished his languages, prepared Masuy's bikes and cars and was paid £14 a week by him, plus expenses. They ran a 600cc BMW *Rennsport* with Vanderschrick Precision sidecar through 1950, followed by a 'Garden Gate' Norton/Watsonian in '51 and a 'Featherbed' Norton in '52.

Jenks had planned to race bikes until 1956-57, when he hoped to switch full-time to *Motor Sport*. But on March 11, 1953, the magazine's owner, W J Tee, offered him a full-time appointment. "That kind of door opens only once, so I took it" – and his serious riding career was over.

The rest of his motoring life has been well recorded, but meanwhile, the private Jenks was to remain very private indeed. At around his time in Belgium, 'home' was a cottage room adjoining *The Phoenix* pub in Hartley Wintney; from November '53 he rented Stratford Lodge, near Odiham. Then, for nearly 35 years from November '61, home became a saggy-roofed single-storey lodge house hidden behind a dense wood deep amongst Hampshire farmland. He bought it, he said, "to enjoy my own trials course right by the back door".

It offered peace and seclusion at the cost of no mains electricity or 'modern' drainage and a water supply hosed-in from a farm barely in sight across the fields. What should have been the living room became a methodically arranged but choc-a-bloc workshop. The other four cramped rooms bulged with books, magazines, car and 'bike parts and filed race data. An open fireplace in one of them was topped by a chimney flue so open that heavy rain could actually douse the fire.

The tiny kitchen was dominated by a big, black Aga solid-fuel range, which Jenks alone knew how to drive. It would light for nobody else, but he could massage it into pulsating life. With the wintertime kitchen temperature up around 80 degrees he'd sit within Aga-glow at a tiny table by the window over the sink, and tell us what was really going on in the racing world...

In his later years, I might call by the lodge "to see how the gnome is", and he'd be "beavering away", as he would say, on an article or a book manuscript, or in the workshop "fettling", and his thick derry boots would always be parked by the sizzling Aga, while the rail along its front would sport an array of foot-warmers – "you gotta have an endless supply of hot socks", he would advise, so perhaps the economies of 50 years earlier had finally caught up.

Upon his death, the local *Farnham Herald* ran a major story on someone who, to them, was a freshly discovered and hitherto unsuspected local celebrity, for Jenks had always kept a low profile "in the parish", as he would

Photographer Bob Light captured one of Jenks' favourite moments on two wheels. The date is August 12, 1990, and DSJ, riding his beloved 650cc Tribsa towards the Esses, is on course for a time of 39.75 seconds, his fastest ever climb of Shelsley Walsh.

put it. Yet amongst local motoring and motorcycling men, and to his farming neighbours, he was such a special friend, because when he was around, things were never dull – there was invariably something to puzzle over, to analyze, or to trigger gales of laughter. And in his younger days, his little lodge house had plainly been very happy for him, and for his latest girlfriends – one of whom, over many years, meant the world to him. He loved her deeply.

Yet, despite being so overtly non-materialistic, Jenks was always intensely possessive, of property and people alike. He cultivated separate interest-groups of close friends, yet discouraged independent contact between each group. Many of us have only met for the first time since his stroke in January 1996, and to maintain such separation over 30-40 years is incredible, particularly since we now find we all get on famously. So how did he do it? *Why* did he do it? Search me... possessiveness is surely the only answer.

Throughout his life he admired people with inquisitive, inquiring minds, and to those he befriended he remained intensely loyal. One such was Sandy Burnett, another old friend from the RAE days, who would often accompany Jenks on his high-speed road tests of exotic cars in the free-and-easy '50s, when the 70mph blanket limit was not even a bad dream.

In March 1956, Mercedes-Benz GB loaned him a 300SL for a *Motor Sport* road test and he invited Sandy along for the ride, which was to take place at night on the otherwise empty roads of his favourite public road circuit.

They blasted off from Camberley at 3am, saw 128mph across Hartford Bridge Flats on the A30, and averaged 72.8mph to Andover before entering a right-hander between Stockbridge and Romsey, where the tail slid wide and, as Sandy vividly recalls, "Jenks just failed to correct it... the car spun through 180 degrees, losing most of its energy, leaving just sufficient for the wheels to dig into the grass verge and topple us slowly onto our left side. It all went

Many of the vehicles which passed through Jenks' hands ended up looking very different from how the manufacturer intended. This bike transporter and general-purpose pick-up began life as a Rover P4 saloon. It may have scored 10/10 for practicality, but it was unlikely to win any prizes in a coachwork contest!

quiet, and I asked Jenks, below me, if he was all right, and he said 'I think so'. So I opened the gullwing door through a very peculiar geometry, clambered up and out, and we both dropped down onto the road. We pushed the car back onto its wheels, and nothing seemed too bad, it hadn't even leaked any fluids. It was just first light when we heard this padding sound, and looking up we saw a chap jogging towards us – in his pyjamas! We knew this would all be too complicated to explain, so we jumped in, restarted, and off we shot... although we tacitly agreed that a few mph less might be prudent..."

And after 3hr 11min 20sec – all carefully logged by DSJ, of course – they completed the rest of the chosen course back to Camberley, having averaged 61mph; *Time allowance for righting car and inspecting allowed. Rather slow from then on!* reads his 'Circuit Dicing' log, which is typical Jenks. Somehow, in his company there was never a dull moment... neither was he ever slow...

One final vignette: Towards the end of his competitive life, Jenks was very proud of his homebuilt TriBSA spring 'bike, which in 1991 took him below 40 seconds for the first time at Shelsley Walsh. And in 1993, at the Colerne sprint, he ripped across the line ever-faster on each of his three runs with it. Ending that lovely day, our little gnome, in his baggy black racing leathers, removed his crash helmet, stroked his beard straight and told Mick Wilkins cheerfully: "If I die tonight, I'll die a happy man."

That alone should tell you all you need to know about Jenks, the man...

Jenks doubting – quite justifiably – Doug Nye's ability as a photographer at Easter Thruxton, 1976.

"Jenks just lived for speed, preferably from car or bike, but from anything with a blast to it."

– Bill Boddy, MBE

Denis Jenkinson, DSJ – or just Jenks to you and me. What can I say...? Firstly, that we were such very close friends. Our first meeting was at the Royal Aircraft Establishment in Farnborough during the war, where he engineered aeroplane parts and I wrote handbooks for the RAF. It was there that I recognized how enthusiastic and knowledgeable Jenks was about all things associated with motor racing, and so was able to persuade him – though not without some initial difficulty – that when peace broke out he must write for *Motor Sport*, which at the time I was running by remote control with the help of equally keen folk whom hostilities had parted from their cars.

It duly came about, Jenks becoming *Motor Sport*'s valued and inimitable Continental Correspondent and Grand Prix reporter. Yet as his fame spread worldwide and he enjoyed four Mille Miglias from the cockpit – one with George Abecassis in an HWM and three with Stirling Moss, including that record win in the Mercedes-Benz 300SLR – he never changed from being the dedicated all-round enthusiast. He still mended my disreputable vintage cars and suffered all-night runs in them, knowing that when they broke down he would have to mend them, and he accompanied me on many happy expeditions looking at the more unusual cars listed in *Motor Sport*'s classified ad columns.

When we moved to Wales, the idea was that Jenks would live in the cottage and we would play with cars kept in the barn, but it was not to be. Returning from one of those GP visits, he was on the deck of the boat, enjoying a rough passage, when he met a girl who was doing likewise. She had something I hadn't – apart from a 3-litre and a Le Mans 4½-litre Lagonda and an Amilcar (not to mention an MGB, although DSJ would have scorned that!). So he preferred to make visits to London rather than to faraway Wales...and perhaps it was just as well as he had planned to store bikes upstairs in the house and engines on the ground floor!

So Jenks continued to reside in his Hampshire lodge, lit by 6-volt car bulbs hanging from the ceiling, fed from a Fiat 500 engine and dynamo – and woe-betide anyone who had a car with 6-volt electrics if the lodge lights went dim during a party; his or her battery would be quickly substituted and might well have become flat by leaving-time!

Memories of our long friendship could fill this book on their own. So I will conclude by saying that Jenks just lived for speed, preferably from car or bike, but from anything with a blast to it. I am reminded that he went off quietly to Heathrow one day to see Concorde take off on one of its early flights, and he did likewise to see the new British 120mph trains thunder past along a suitably straight stretch of track. In cars, his first experience of 'the ton' was with Bob Cowell in an Alta; next, there was an easy 125mph in Marcel Masuy's Veritas-BMW sportscar on the Nurburgring; then came 150mph in the HWM-Jaguar; 175mph with Moss in the Mercedes and 180mph in the big Maserati; but 200mph he only experienced flying alongside Jim Clark in his Comanche.

And now it is all over. But Jenks' articles and books will stand for all time as a fitting memorial to this quite remarkable character, this 'one-off' among motoring writers. That this book contains new material from the unique little bearded arch-believer in all kinds of motoring sport is indeed good news. Splendid, too, that the BRDC first saw fit to encourage Jenks to pen the 50 cameos that now form the centrepiece around which the remainder of this volume has been built. We should all be grateful for that.

In 1938 Jenks attended the Donington Grand Prix with his brother, Harold, and 40 years later he was back at the track again, this time to examine the Mercedes-Benz W154/39, which had just arrived from Czechoslovakia.

"I owe him more than I can say."
– Nigel Roebuck

Jenks' standards were always exacting. At Silverstone, years ago, a bunch of us were given a ride in a factory Porsche 935, and at the wheel was a man who had won a Grand Prix. Jenks – of course – was first to go. Afterwards, we asked how it had been, and his expression told its own tale. "Fantastic!" he said. Pause. "Just think what it would have been like with a proper driver..."

He was overdoing it, of course, and knew it, but then everything was relative in Jenks' world. "I've never been interested in who won a race," he said to me once, "until I know who was behind him."

Like anyone involved in racing journalism, Jenks well knew that to admire the driver was not necessarily to like the man. He had his villains, as well as his heroes, and once you were into either file, there you stayed for ever. That said, though, there remained a fundamental esteem for anyone who raced, be it in cars or on motorcycles.

He came from a hard school – this, after all, was one who hung out of a sidecar through Burnenville and Malmedy – and while he would grieve when a driver died, so he accepted it as a natural, if unwelcome, adjunct to a sport which could never be safe, in any workaday sense of the word.

Significantly, it was the loss of Mike Hailwood which affected him most of all: for one of his greatness to die on a track, running at 'full-noise', would have been one thing; but to perish in a road accident, through the fault of another, was unacceptable.

Jenks took so much simple joy in motor racing. He might be crotchety as hell, for whatever reason, in the traffic on the way to a circuit, but once into the paddock – around racing cars – his mood would be transformed, and he never lost that. After Gilles Villeneuve had won the 1981 Monaco Grand Prix, I walked down the hill to Ste Devote, and there encountered DSJ, literally dancing a jig of delight. Drenched through, glasses misted up, he was the same way, too, when Ayrton Senna won in the rains of Estoril four years later.

Although his chief interest in the sport always lay with machinery – in engines, above all – Jenks was always fascinated by the genus racing driver in all its forms, and if Grand Prix racing was obviously his first love, he was never one to denigrate other areas of the sport. One time, over breakfast in Long Beach, he saw someone coming into the room and urgently asked who he was. "He's a racing driver, isn't he?" It was Cale Yarborough. "Knew it!" said Jenks, triumphantly. "Didn't know who he was, but I could tell he was a racing driver. Something about his walk, the look in his eyes..."

I tried for years to get him to come to Daytona or Indianapolis with me, for Jenks, above all things, loved raw speed. "Don't think I could stand the excitement," he would say. "It would all be too much." He never did go to either 500, but eventually visited Indy, and babbled about it like a schoolboy afterwards.

During dinner at the *Autosport* Awards, only a couple of days after Jenks' death, Stirling Moss called for a moment's quiet, then asked us to raise our glasses to the little man. "He was," Stirling said, affectionately, "a wonderful bloke, and without doubt one of the true eccentrics."

No argument there, as anyone can attest who ever visited his home. Jenks' domestic arrangements were...unorthodox. You got used, for example, to the lack of electricity: power, such as it was, came from a small generator, and was insufficient to provide illumination for two rooms at once, so that if anyone needed to use the loo, everyone else was in total darkness until his or her return.

This Jenks saw as nothing out of the ordinary. "Blackout time," he would cheerfully announce, and there was the same insouciance when once I questioned the siting of a Daimler V8 engine at the foot of his bed. "Nowhere else to put it," he said, as if that explained everything. "No space in the sitting room." Indeed there wasn't; that was given over to a selection of motorbikes, in various stages of repair.

That really was the whole thing about Jenks. His great charm – and a source of endless amusement to his friends – was that he truly believed that his was the logical way, that the rest of the world was curiously out of step. Bliss was fettling one of his cars or bikes, to the accompaniment of Sidney Bechet.

Although the absence of electricity never bothered him, he would have been lost without his telephone, which was used with abandon, and around the clock. Countless times I would be on the point of sitting down to eat and the 'phone would ring: "I've been thinking about that lap of Senna's on Saturday..." the quiet voice would say, and you knew that supper was a lost cause.

Other than cars and bikes, and memorabilia associated with them, Jenks

Jenks giving a demonstration of balance and co-ordination. Always one for the unconventional, here he has forsaken the paddock road at Nivelles, Belgium, in favour of the line of half-buried tyres as he rushes to his next port of call.

cared absolutely nothing for material possessions, but he loved good food and wine, and would sleep like a child after a hearty dinner: the great storm of October '87 may have devastated southern England, but it failed to awaken the guest in Stirling Moss' spare bedroom that night...

His favourite period of racing, certainly in recent times, was the height of the turbo era, when boost was unlimited and such as Renault and BMW laid around 1,400 horsepower at their drivers' backs for qualifying. That, combined with 'one lap' tyres and the ability of a Senna, made for drama as distilled as Grand Prix racing has known, and Jenks revelled in it, particularly at what he considered a 'proper' circuit, like the Osterreichring or Spa-Francorchamps.

Ayrton was one of his great heroes, a man whose artistry could, and occasionally did, move him to tears. It pleased him enormously to receive a Christmas card each year: 'To friend Jenkinson, from Ayrton Senna.' And although he would probably have denied it, I don't believe he ever felt quite the same about racing after Imola in 1994. It was good he wasn't there that day.

"May the 1st," he murmured sadly on the 'phone the following week. "We won the Mille Miglia on May the 1st, and I always associated it with such pleasure. Now this..." His diary entry reads simply: 'Absolute bloody disaster.'

Gaining entry to Jenks' personal hall of fame was not the work of a moment: "In my teens," he said, "my hero was Bernd Rosemeyer, and everybody's hero was Nuvolari." And since the war? "It's a waste of time comparing different eras; you can only go for drivers supreme in their own time. There are just five in my top bracket: Ascari, Moss, Clark, (Gilles) Villeneuve and Senna."

Arguing with Jenks – on this or any other subject – was like trying to fold a paper in a high wind. In a certain mood, black was white, and that was the end of it. He took a special delight in playing devil's advocate. "Hang on a minute," you'd splutter, "how can you criticize Prost for doing no more than necessary to win a race, and then praise Fangio for always trying to win at the slowest possible speed?" "Different," he would reply, studying the menu. "Well, how is it different?" "Just is..."

A minute or two later, once he had got you to the point of apoplexy, there would come a sly grin, and you would realize once again that you'd been had. He could, on occasion, be maddening, and none of his friends would claim otherwise, but neither would they suggest that, at heart, he was other than the kindest of men, who liked nothing better than to share his enthusiasm for motor racing, his experience in the sport.

"Jenkinson!" you would hear all the time if you were in his company in Italy. Even 40 years after that Mille Miglia victory with Moss, he was widely recognized in this country he adored. And sometimes, at the end of a day, Alan Henry and I would drive with him into the hills near Imola, where the road signs read 'Futa' and 'Raticosa', and the spirits abide of Nuvolari and Varzi, Castellotti and Taruffi.

When I was a kid, I would read Jenks' writings in *Motor Sport* and, even more than his race reports, I relished 'Continental Notes', in which he would discuss anything that touched his world. Quite often there would be a detailed description of a journey on open and uncluttered roads, by Porsche 356 or E-Type Jaguar, to a race somewhere, and I would think to myself that life could scarcely be better than this.

If anyone fired in me the desire to write about motor racing, it was this little fellow with the beard. When a piece had those initials DSJ at its foot, you knew it was the real thing. I am proud to have been among Jenks' friends; like so many of my contemporaries, I owe him more than I can say.

"Motor racing is full to the brim of contrived eccentrics, but Jenks was the genuine article." – **Alan Henry**

Looking back on it, I suppose the two most memorable episodes I enjoyed with Jenks both involved high-speed motoring trips to the Continent. The first was in the summer of 1974 – my first full season of F1 reporting for *Motoring News* – when he invited me to join him in the passenger seat of his white 4.2 Jaguar E-Type Roadster for the journey to the Austrian GP at Osterreichring. It was quite an experience. We drove the entire distance with the hood down – no namby-pamby seat belts you understand – and blasted all the way from Liege to Judenberg in a comfortable day's motoring.

Two things struck me. Firstly, just how easily the E-Type breezed along at 110mph, and how gently Jenks teased the controls. He clearly regarded the car, then four years old, like a comfortable, well-used pair of slippers. He was 53 years old then – three years older than I am as I write these words – yet I still rather regarded him as Old Father Time, albeit respectfully.

The second trip came the following spring, when we retraced the Mille Miglia route in a Mercedes 450SE 'limo' driven by *Motor Sport*'s Managing Editor Michael Tee. We flew to Stuttgart with Stirling Moss, visited the test track and, while Moss flew back to London, Michael, Jenks and myself climbed aboard a 450SE loaned by the factory and headed off for Brescia.

In the next three days we covered the entire route to produce a five-page feature which was carried the following month within the pages of the magazine. To be honest, it was a great 'jolly', but one on which I learned an enormous amount about the Mille Miglia in particular and motor racing in general.

On reflection, I think that trip was why Jenks seemed to be a little lukewarm over the rash of retrospective events which have sprung up over the last decade or so. When people asked him if he was coming on the Mille Miglia revival, he would simply reply "done all that – and done the real one!". And, of course, he had. Apart from being respected for more than 40 years as *Motor Sport* magazine's Continental Correspondent, he gained lifelong celebrity status for navigating Stirling Moss' Mercedes 300SLR sports-racing car to that record-breaking victory in the 1955 Mille Miglia.

The great thing about Jenks was that he was a genuine eccentric. Motor racing is full to the brim of contrived eccentrics, but Jenks was the genuine article. About three years ago, I arrived at his cottage in the Hampshire woods to find an ageing 1977 Mercedes 280SE standing outside. Bemused, I asked him where on earth it had come from.

"Well, it's rather difficult to explain," he replied. "I needed a new runabout, so I went out intending to spend about £1,100 on a Citroen 2CV and I saw the Merc on a garage forecourt. It seemed too good an opportunity to miss!" Jenks drove the Merc for a few months – despite the fact that it had a rattley camshaft – and then had a minor collision in a supermarket car park. It was,

The height of ingenuity. Jenks finds a trolley jack useful for having an eye-to-eye with his pal Alan Henry.

he reflected, a little too big for his requirements after all. So it was pushed into the undergrowth in the grounds of his home and allowed to take its chances with the foliage.

Such offbeat tales about Jenks are many and varied. In 1978 he decided that he knew me well enough for me to collect him from his home when we were off on one of our *Motor Sport* jaunts together. "Come for breakfast," he said breezily. I arrived at about 8 o'clock. "Poached egg?" he inquired. I accepted the invitation enthusiastically. "You can have the plate," he added. So I did. And Jenks, once he'd cooked his own, turned the poacher out onto the gently angled draining board and, with admirable precision, he just finished the last mouthful of egg before it was poised to slide into the sink!

Afterwards, I recounted the tale to Stirling. "Poached egg on draining board, a real Hampshire delicacy," I said. Much later I discovered that Stirl had incorporated my anecdote into many of his after-dinner speeches; my brother-in-law even heard him recount it on Radio 4. I walked in fear and trembling for months, worried that Jenks would be annoyed that his bid for Delia Smith's crown had been leaked to a wider audience!

In the immediate postwar years he spent every penny on a racing Norton to embrace a gypsy-like existence in Europe, earning a bob or two racing in predominantly minor league events. By 1949 he had paired up with Eric Oliver to ride 'in the chair' and help him win the Sidecar World Championship.

In 1954 he partnered John Heath in an HWM-Jaguar on the Mille Miglia, then of course came that epic victory with Stirling in the Mercedes 300SLR in 1955, using Jenks' unique pace-notes – a 17ft long sheet of paper encased in a little metal box which he scrolled past a Perspex window and augmented by a series of pre-arranged hand signals – an idea he had originally dreamed up in discussion with the American driver John Fitch, who had been hoping to share a 300SL with him in the event.

It was only the second time in history that this classic event had been won by a non-Italian, but although Jenks partnered Moss again in 1956 and 1957, now with the Maserati team, they were out of luck, an unscheduled trip down the side of a mountain halting them in 1956 and a broken brake pedal in 1957, after which the race was banned following the fatal accident to the Ferrari driver, the Marquis de Portago, his navigator and several spectators.

After their 1955 win, Jenkinson wrote: "I think that Stirling Moss is the greatest driver, and a genius." The two men remained lifelong friends. For his part, to this day Moss remains full of admiration for Jenks' contribution to their historic victory. "No amount of money, nothing, would persuade me to sit for 10 hours in a car that somebody else was driving at 170mph over blind brows," he said later in tribute.

Yet to characterize Jenks as someone obsessed by misty-eyed nostalgia would be totally wrong. He was absolutely intrigued by all sorts of contemporary motor racing machinery. The sight of a Williams-Honda turbo roaring past at full-song, or the latest Ferrari V12 screaming its head off at over 16,000rpm, was music to his ears.

He was also fascinated by what made Grand Prix drivers tick. His book *The Racing Driver* – published almost 40 years ago – still stands as the most complete and definitive work of analysis on this subject. He was full of admiration for the late Ayrton Senna, a man he ranked right up in the panoply of all-time F1 Gods. Poignantly, Ayrton was killed on May 1, 1994 – the day which Jenks had always associated with so much joy, for it was on May 1 39 years earlier that he and Moss had rolled off the starting ramp at Brescia, the gleaming Mercedes 300SLR belching smoke from its side exhausts, to speed a path into the motor racing history books. Those of us who were close to him believed that his interest in F1 never fully recovered in the wake of Senna's passing.

For many years, Jenks was amongst a small group of us who stayed for the San Marino Grand Prix weekend in a small hotel at Fontenalice, not far from the Mille Miglia route. Some evenings we would 'bunk off' early from the frenzy of the F1 paddock and take a nostalgic tour up into the mountains. If this well-travelled little man loved anywhere, then he loved Italy. For its people, its passion for motor racing and, perhaps most of all, for its pace of life.

Jenks' last public appearance was at Goodwood for the 1995 Festival of Speed. My son Nick and I acted as his 'minders', chauffeuring him down to sunlit Sussex in a Mercedes S280 and generally fussing around to make sure he was comfortable. It was the 40th anniversary of his epic Mille Miglia victory with Stirling, and Mercedes brought along the very 300SLR which they had used on that spring day in 1955. The emotion of the occasion was almost too much for him to take.

On the Monday morning after the Goodwood extravaganza, many national newspapers carried photographs of Moss and Jenks climbing the hill in the 300SLR. It was as if the years had fallen away and they were storming the Raticosa and Radicofani passes, deep in the heart of Italy, four decades earlier. And that is how I shall remember Jenks. He could be argumentative, insufferably pompous and downright infuriating at times – even to his pals – but his friendship was steadfast and, to a generation of younger motor racing writers, he was a remarkable mentor and a wonderful inspiration.

This is a sight of Jenks which very few were ever to see. So convinced was he that Jochen Rindt would never win a Grand Prix that he bet his beard he never would. True to his word, out came the scissors after Jochen had won the 1969 US GP, but Jenks stayed close to home that winter while the whiskers grew again before the 1970 season.

"I have always remembered a different kind of Jenks classic." – **Eoin Young**

Ask any schoolboy under the age of about 75 which was Jenks' greatest piece of motor racing writing and to a man they will say his report on the 1955 Mille Miglia. I agree that it was a classic that only he could have written, someone with the sheer guts and determination and fearlessness, the only man who could make so much of the opportunity presented to him. Hemingway on wheels. He took us all with him for those thousand miles round Italy and we have revered him for it to this day.

I have also always remembered a different kind of Jenks classic. Recently, I could recall *what* it was, but I couldn't remember exactly *when* it was, but Doug Nye and Alan Henry came to my rescue and I found the *Motor Sport* for July 1968 – not so far from 30 years ago – when he covered the Belgian Grand Prix on the old Spa circuit as though he was sitting beside you at the edge of the track and just whittering on, the way he used to. It was almost as though he had set out to be mischievous.

He wrote the first half of the report covering practice as a 'straight' piece. If you remember, this was the race when Ferrari and Brabham first fitted a wing – as opposed to tentative fins – during practice, and although every other constructor would hurriedly copy the idea, Jenks was skeptical:

Eoin Young and Jenks pose for Sue Lord's camera at Goodwood in 1994 before DSJ swaps his cap for a helmet and goes off for another blast up the hill.

"Ferrari came out with an elaborate aerofoil mounted high above the gearbox like a miniature Chaparral. Whether any of these devices had any real effect is debatable, for the results depended entirely on the psychological effect on the drivers. Like contented cows, contented drivers drive well, and a driver convinced of the improved stability of his car would take the fast corners just that bit faster."

The Friday session had been dry on the long Spa-Francorchamps road course, and on Saturday it rained. Most drivers lost their enthusiasm and the grid was settled on Friday's times, with Amon's Ferrari a clear polesitter, 3.7sec faster than Jackie Stewart in the Matra-Ford, who was 2sec faster than Jacky Ickx in the other Ferrari on the three-car front row. Surtees (Honda) and Hulme (McLaren-Ford) shared the second row.

It was agreed that if it was still raining by the time of the 3.30pm Sunday start it would be delayed for an hour, and if it was still raining then, the cars would start at 10sec intervals and the race would be run on a time basis, like the Targa Florio or the motorcycle TT.

Jenks noted after the warm-up that Ickx had asked for all his Ferrari fins and rear wing to be removed, but that Amon kept his on. Then he devoted 27 lines to a formal if brief description of how Amon led, then Surtees took over with the Honda, Ickx lost a cylinder, Hulme and Stewart swopped the lead until Hulme broke a driveshaft, and then on the last lap Stewart ran out of fuel. McLaren crossed the line, ecstatic at finishing second, only to be told that he had won the race; once convinced that this was the case, he became even more ecstatic!

Jenks then set out to write what he called his Francorchamps Monologue. It was all first-person in quotes. I'll cherry-pick for you, and bring you the typically Jenks observations that always reflected his enthusiasms and his

216

prejudices, those little written digs that so appealed to his reader and so infuriated the person to whom the dig referred.

"There's the 1min board; what a magnificent noise all those engines make; no wonder I'm going deaf after 20 years of Grand Prix racing. They are all rolling down the hill nicely; must be tricky on this downhill start to keep everything on the boil with only two feet to operate clutch, brake and accelerator. I suppose they are all doing a heel-and-toe act on the brake and accelerator...

"Here we go; stop creeping, Ickx, even if this is Belgium; wow!, the revs the Ferraris are using, how fascinating to see the throttle slides jiggling in and out like that...

"To see those two Ferraris going up the hill in first and second place is quite like old times. That was the Honda in third place. Talk about red rags to a Honda. This should make Surtees cast off a lot of worries and inhibitions and show us the great racing driver that he really is. He will not settle for following *two* Ferraris for long. Bonnier was going slowly, wasn't he; wonder if he will make it back to the pits to collect his starting money?...

"It must be wonderful to be leading the pack round the long Stavelot bend, knowing you have a completely clear run ahead of you up the long incline to La Source and through those super-fast corners; 170mph, 175, 180mph, who knows? Revs, tyres, gear ratios are all very well, but only an accurate beam would ever record the truth...

"This is Grand Prix racing, and it's not for the faint of heart. Imagine taking that long downhill sweep of the Burnenville, the car all twitchy and all four tyres sliding; they must be doing 130mph past the little cafe. Wish I was there, but I can't be everywhere. There's only one place from which you can really see a motor race, that's alongside the driver. Pity we can't have two-seater Grand Prix cars...

"Oh ho! The Honda has nipped by Amon. How about that? Surtees really leading a Grand Prix in the opening phase, that's more like it. Pity he's only got Amon and Ickx to race against. He should have Gurney, Hill, Brabham and Stewart all around him. That would make a Grand Prix, and I suppose poor Clark would have been in front of all of them. Hill is not really getting into his stride, he ought to be past McLaren by now, and Redman is holding off Brabham. I suppose 'Black Jack' cannot see any prize money in view, so he's not going to strain himself. There's Rindt coming into the pits; the Repco 4-cammer still needs a lot of development. Rindt is not exactly being the Ace of Aces that he thinks he is...

"Here they come again, Surtees still leading; Amon is making it very obvious that he'd like to get by, but he'll never do it. Nobody goes past Surtees when 'Big John' is really having a go, not even Brabham...

"That's the end of Rindt's 4-cam Repco engine. Wonder if he's ever seen the mess that a loose valve seat makes inside an engine when the bits fall into the cylinder at 9,000rpm?...

"Oh dear, the ambulance is going off, wonder who has pranged? Redman, Oliver and Bianchi have yet to appear on this lap. The loudspeakers say it is Redman. Hope it's not serious. Nice lad, Redman. Been having a good season, too. Unlike him to crash. Wonder if something broke?...

"Looks like oil coming out of the Ferrari nose. Poor Amon, last year Brabham threw stones at him at Silverstone and Nurburgring, now Surtees has done it, right through the oil radiator, and there is a wire mesh guard in front of it, too. I wonder sometimes whether drivers like Surtees and Brabham carry a pocket-full of stones, just in case!...

"Hulme is now first. Doubt whether he and Stewart will really race and get nasty; too docile and friendly these chaps and, anyway, Stewart said after practice he could not take any chances with his right forearm in that plastic corset device...

"Stewart leading! Surprising that Hulme let him by, he must have forgotten all the old Brabham elbows-out training...

"PUMP OIL is written on Tyler Alexander's signal-board and it's for Hulme. That will be the Bendix pump that returns the oil from the catch-tank to the main tank. I thought it was switched on all the time. Those Cosworth engines aren't right, they shouldn't breathe that much oil. Bet that surprised Alexander, Hulme leading again; surprised me...

"McLaren leading his bunch again, that's the orange cars second and third. Where's Hulme? I spoke too soon. He's missing. McLaren and his bunch are now racing for second place...

"Twenty-five laps gone. Stewart's dropped 10sec. He's all right. I expect he's looking across the fields at Stavelot to keep an eye on them, and McLaren's orange car must be easy to pick out. With the keen eyesight these chaps have got he can probably see the McLaren at the hairpin in the mirror from the top of Eau Rouge...

"After this lap, one more lap for Stewart. Matra will be so pleased with their victory, it's been on the cards since South Africa. On Dunlop tyres, too. Long time since Dunlop have won a Grand Prix, and at one time they had a monopoly. Always felt they got over-confident and complacent in those days! Too easy to do. We'll hear Stewart coming out of Blanchimont soon and through Virage Seaman. Wonder how many people pause to pay respects to that small stone by the Clubhouse that marks where Dick Seaman crashed. Was it 1938 or 1939? Remember actually weeping when I heard he was dead. Have got hardened to racing drivers being killed nowadays. Perhaps I haven't. Wept genuine tears at Brands Hatch when I heard Clark was dead. Only two months ago. Seems like a different age altogether...

Here comes Stewart, one more lap to go. Good grief! He's in trouble. Coasting down into the pits. Oh my goodness, what a panic. There go McLaren and Rodriguez, racing to win now. Like Monza last year. They are putting petrol into the Matra. It won't restart. Another battery. The starter motor must be cooked. And here's Oliver, the Lotus is out of fuel. This is ridiculous, they've all miscalculated. Oh Tyrrell, you've thrown the race away. That really is too bad. It's restarted. He'll finish, but in fourth place...

"Here's a jubilant McLaren, the lucky devil, to win like that. It's justice, really, for Hulme should have won...

"There's McLaren. Good for him to win, and with his own car; must feel marvellous. Well done, congratulations. You really didn't know you'd won? Not until Phil Kerr greeted you in the paddick? But you waved your arm in jubilation as you crossed the line? Pleased to finish second! It was some race. Always is at Spa..."

He had literally been thinking out loud, painting word pictures with his pen, for he wrote everything longhand. I thought it was a marvellously evocative piece of writing, nearly as good as being out there and doing it. I was sure he would switch his style to this direct form of communicating his enthusiasm to the reader, but he said he wasn't going to do it again. Ever. I asked why. A reader – *one* reader – had written in and said he didn't like it, so Jenks wasn't going to do it again. He said he wrote for *all* his readers. That was Jenks.

The piece was signed DSJ as usual. Generations of motorsporting enthusiasts mourn the loss of those three initials they regarded as a friend, someone who told it the way they thought it must be. And it was.

218

"He was my teacher when it came to driving on the Continent." – Jesse Alexander

I first met Jenks at Pau, in south-west France, in 1955. I had been to the Mille Miglia that year and managed to capture him on film as he and Stirling rounded the summit of the Raticosa at full chat in the 300SLR. Our friendship did not develop, however, until a chance meeting in the paddock at Pau a month later. He had spied my new Porsche and it turned out that we both had just recently taken delivery of Porsche 356 automobiles at the Stuttgart factory, his a Continental coupe, mine a cabriolet. This sparked a relationship that spanned many years while I photographed racing in Europe for Amercian magazines and he covered the sport as Continental Correspondent for *Motor Sport*.

Jesse Alexander sent Jenks this photograph of himself and his family at their newly built home in Switzerland in 1958, inviting him over for an 'official inspection'.

The photograph of Jenks I have on my darkroom wall is a reminder of the great times we shared together during those wonderful years of the 1950s and 1960s on the European circuits. Several occasions we drove to Sicily and back in our Porsches, using his one year and mine the next, to cover the Targa Florio. During those pre-*autoroute* days we often travelled in tandem from my home in Switzerland to Reims in France or to Monza in Italy over the Alpine passes and on the secondary roads of Europe. He was my teacher when it came to driving on the Continent; I learned that it is more difficult to lead than to follow! Jenks drove quickly but safely, savouring every minute behind the wheel, including the inevitable lunch stop at a favourite restaurant. His sense of humour, his inability to suffer fools, these were the hallmarks of his personality. Jenks was always talking about "keeping one's sense of proportion".

His enthusiasm for all kinds of motorsport was well-known. When I returned home to the USA, I and his many other American friends looked forward to his annual visit to the Long Beach Grand Prix. He was not crazy about travelling long distances on a jumbo jet, but once Jenks got here he managed to enjoy himself and in particular the Saturday evening visits to Ascot Raceway, a popular Southern California dirt track that featured sprint cars. I last saw Jenks at Montreal in 1991; Long Beach was no longer on the Formula One calendar and Canada was as far as he got in North America that year.

It was a privilege to know and spend time with him. We could always count on plenty of laughs as we discussed the events of the day and excitedly awaited the next.

Another message from Jesse, this time a 'doctored' photograph of their two Porsche 356s on a ferry; a marker pen has them feigning sea-sickness.

220

"It was the most wonderful occasion..."

– Maurice Hamilton

A few minutes spent with Jenks would place life in perspective. The worries of the world seemed to pass him by and his enthusiasm never failed to provide graphic proof of how lucky we were to work in motor racing. It was fitting that his funeral should produce one final reminder.

During the course of his address, Canon Lionel Webber mentioned that thousands of people around the world, who had read the words of DSJ, would have given anything to have met the man and been there to pay their last respects. We were fortunate enough to be able to do both and, as such, we represented motor sport fans affected by the loss of this remarkable character.

Jenks' funeral was unorthodox, much in keeping with the man himself. I was amused, touched, humbled and invigorated. On the way home, I pondered Canon Webber's words. It had indeed been a privilege to be present on such a wonderful occasion and I immediately thought of my father, a year older than Jenks and living in happy retirement in Northern Ireland. He had met Jenks a few times. He would have loved it.

Maurice Hamilton couldn't resist taking this shot of Jenks waving to a passing local train in Austria in August 1982. They had stopped on a bridge over a river on their way from Nurburgring to the Grand Prix.

The convenience of telephone communication means that letter writing – in our family at least – has become a forgotten art. But this was one occasion when the written word would do more justice than a recitation down the 'phone line. The letter, written that evening, is reprinted below. Please forgive this personal deviation, but I can think of no better way of summarizing an extraordinary farewell to an extraordinary man.

221

Cranleigh
12 December 1996

Dear Dad
I thought you would like to see the enclosed copy of the Order of Service for Jenks' cremation, which took place this afternoon at Aldershot.

It was the most wonderful occasion, supposedly a private affair for his family and mates. Like you, I do not rate crematoriums highly on the list of social venues, but I quickly realized what sort of 'do' this would be as I drove towards the place, followed by two Fraser Nashes and a Lancia Aprilia running line astern!

The car park resembled a meeting of the VSCC; admiring glances, friendly chat, bonnets up, engines ticking over. Not surprisingly, perhaps, the small chapel was packed with more than 200 people, the majority standing along the sides and down the central aisle.

The gathering included folk from all walks of life; engineers, model-makers, a motorcycle policeman (in full gear!), businessmen in suits, lots of elderly boys in flat caps or leather driving helmets, motor bikers, former racers such as Bruce Halford and people like Patrick Head of Williams and Frank Dernie from Arrows. Not surprising, either, was the fact that the congregation was 95 per cent male, the women present being those to whom Jenks mattered and, more important perhaps, those who mattered to him.

But the key to it all was the service itself. Jenks had insisted on no religious trappings. This presented a major problem for Geoff Goddard and Doug Nye, old mates who had kindly undertaken the task of organizing the funeral. Canon Lionel Webber was the only clergyman whom Geoff and Doug could even think about asking to conduct proceedings.

How can I describe this man? He is a Chaplain to The Queen and to the British Racing Drivers' Club. That's the official bit. He's a London East-ender and a motor sport fanatic who, as he explained to us, read *Motor Sport* during his younger days as a monk by hiding it under his robes and studying DSJ's reports while seated at the back. He has a wonderful sense of humour and, while being a devoutly religious man, he fully appreciates that others may not feel the same way. In particular, his little bearded friend who shared a passion for cars.

"Just think of it like this," Canon Webber told the congregation. "When Jenks awoke on 29 November, he found himself up there with all his old mates – Ayrton, Gilles and Jimmy. And he will have met God and, for the past week, he will have been arguing with God, telling Him that he doesn't exist!"

Canon Webber spoke in place of Bill Boddy, Jenks' former editor being unable to make the long trip from Wales. Tony Brooks, whom Jenks respected enormously as a driver and a gentleman, made a wonderful address without the aid of notes. And, of course, there was Stirling Moss.

Stirling reminisced about the Mille Miglia in 1955. He wore his son's school tie in preference to his usual BRDC tie. "I chose this one," said Stirling, "because the colours (black with yellow stripes) have a significance for Jenks and I. He wore socks of this colour and pattern. I don't know how many pairs he had – I'd rather not go into that! – but he seemed to wear them all the time – such as 1954 and 1955!" Apparently there had been a scare of some sort over Colorado beetles invading Britain and people were watching out for the distinctive black and yellow colours. Jenks' socks were christened Colorado Beetles as a result, and those familiar with Jenks' cavalier personal habits knew what Stirling was getting at...

"Of course, I'll always remember the '55 Mille Miglia," said Stirling. "When we reached Florence, Jenks rubbed his hands. "Now we're really going to see something," he said, referring to the Futa and Raticosa which were about to follow. I thought: 'My God, I have been driving flat-out, ten-tenths all the way, and here he is expecting me to go even quicker on the mountain passes!' It was absolutely typical of Jenks and his enthusiasm."

As you can see from the Order of Service, there was no religious music, only Jenks' favourites which Geoff Goddard put together. I'm no more musical than you are, but I have to say there is a strong case for this sort of thing, particularly when the cheerful clarinet of Monty Sunshine piped the coffin into the chapel. I looked around and everyone wore a smile. When was the last time you saw such a thing at this difficult moment? I could almost hear the old boy chortling away up there.

Canon Webber said that, while he was only too happy to observe Jenks' wishes, the Committal itself would take place with due reverence. That's when they played a piece by Bach and everyone was left for a few minutes with their private thoughts and memories. When that was followed by Ella Fitzgerald gently singing '*Every Time We Say Goodbye*', many a bottom lip trembled...

Canon Webber finished by taking as his text passages from Jenks' report on the Mille Miglia, and from two of his books. Then he read out Jenks' self-penned obituary, written on 8 October 1991. It said:

Born in 1920, Denis Jenkinson died at xx years of age. He had planned to live to 100 years, a nice tidy number, but his luck ran out.

Anyone who did not know Jenks, or at least know of him, is of no importance or significance in the Motor Sporting world, which was his world for all but 10 years of his very active life with cars, motorcycles and aeroplanes. A product of the 20th century, he enjoyed and wondered at it all his life.'

It was so typical of his black and white attitude. Not only did he write his own obituary, he actually had the crust to say that if you didn't know of Jenks, then you weren't serious! The rest of us might think that, but Jenks would say it without batting an eyelid. He was quite right, of course. The chapel roared with laughter.

The assembled company then drove in colourful convoy to a hotel in Farnborough, where we reconvened for beer and sandwiches in the 'Biggles' room. By chance, the room was due to be redecorated, so the faded look was perfect for the occasion! Better than that, it was just across the road from the RAE where, appropriately, Jenks had served his apprenticeship in the aeronautical industry. It was a jolly gathering, full of reminiscences and smiles as friends studied the collection of photographs encapsulating Jenks' life.

Before leaving, I told Canon Webber that, while it may not be the thing to say, I really enjoyed the funeral. "Splendid!" he exclaimed. "That's exactly how Jenks would want us to remember him." Indeed it was.

On the way out, I passed a gentleman donning his leather helmet and climbing aboard an elderly sportscar. "Great, wasn't it?" he beamed. "Jenks will be bloody *furious* he missed it..."

You would have loved it, too.

Love

Maurice

This Geoffrey Goddard picture taken outside Jenks' cottage was his favourite of the many photographs taken of him over the years. Dressed characteristically, he is barely taller than the huge crankshaft of his Brooklands Duesenberg. When he first saw this picture, he commented 'Ah! Two cranks together.....' It illustrated the Order of Service at his funeral with the caption:

Denis Sargent Jenkinson
'D.S.J.'
'Jenks'
December 11, 1920 – November 29, 1996